D0458686

LOSING ISN'T EVERYTHING

DEY ST.

An Imprint of WILLIAM MORROW

LOSING ISN'T Everything

The **UNTOLD STORIES** and **HIDDEN LESSONS** Behind the
TOUGHEST LOSSES in **SPORTS HISTORY**

CURT MENEFEE

with Michael Arkush

DEY ST.

LOSING ISN'T EVERYTHING. Copyright © 2016 by Curt Menefee. All rights reserved. Printed in the United States of America. No part of this book may be used or reproduced in any manner whatsoever without written permission except in the case of brief quotations embodied in critical articles and reviews. For information address HarperCollins Publishers, 195 Broadway, New York, NY 10007.

HarperCollins books may be purchased for educational, business, or sales promotional use. For information please e-mail the Special Markets Department at SPsales@harpercollins.com.

FIRST EDITION

Designed by Paula Russell Szafranski

Library of Congress Cataloging-in-Publication Data has been applied for.

ISBN 978-0-06-244007-5

16 17 18 19 20   RRD   10 9 8 7 6 5 4 3 2 1

TO MY LATE MOTHER, SHIRLEY,
WHO BROUGHT ME INTO THIS WORLD,
AND THE LOVE OF MY LIFE, VIOLLETTE,
WITHOUT WHOM I COULDN'T GET THROUGH IT

Contents

LOSING ISN'T EVERYTHING

INTRODUCTION

What if your entire career—heck, your entire life—were to be forever defined by a single moment that went horribly wrong? How would you respond? Better yet, how would you *cope*, both in the immediate aftermath and in the long run? And what if that moment happened in front of tens of thousands of people, with millions more watching on television, and was replayed over and over for years and years to come, so that no matter what you did, or where you went, you could never truly escape?

If that weren't troubling enough, what if your "failure" became a prime example of exactly how *not* to perform when the pressure's on?

Fortunately for most of us, our imaginations are the only places we have to ponder such painful scenarios. That's because we don't know what it's like to be Calvin Schiraldi. Calvin, you see, doesn't imagine what it would feel like to come up short on a big stage. He knows all too well. He was the Boston Red Sox reliever who gave up 3 straight hits with 2 outs in the bottom of the tenth inning of Game 6 of the 1986 World Series, enabling the New York Mets to win the game, and eventually, the Series. Red Sox fans felt more tortured than ever, and that's saying something. Many of us, no doubt, remember the ground ball that went through the legs of first baseman Bill Buckner, but it was also Calvin's inability to secure that last out that cost his team a chance to win it all for the first time since 1918.

We would also have difficulty identifying with Craig Ehlo. Craig was guarding Michael Jordan when MJ hit that famous shot at the buzzer to beat the Cleveland Cavaliers in the opening round of the 1989 NBA playoffs. Even though the game took place more than a quarter century ago, people still approach Craig all the time. He played for fourteen years in the NBA, which is quite an accomplishment, but he is best known for what happened in those three seconds back in 1989.

Rodney Harrison also knows what it feels like to be on the wrong side of sports history. Rodney, one of the best defensive backs ever, is in the frame of every picture of what many refer to as the greatest catch of all time. His failure to keep wide receiver David Tyree from catching the ball against his helmet helped lead the New York Giants to a monumental upset in Super Bowl XLII. Gone, too, was the New England Patriots' quest for a perfect 19-0 season.

Those are just a few examples. There are many more. And, for every one of those athletes, the challenge has been the same:

How do they move on? How do they cope? How do they turn their "wounds into wisdom," as Oprah Winfrey would say? Because, except for a very fortunate few, these proud men and women were unable to make up for that one moment that didn't go their way.

Calvin, after also losing Game 7 in 1986, never pitched in a World Series again.

Craig never guarded Jordan again with a season on the line.

Rodney never made it to another Super Bowl.

Hoping to discover how they, and others, dealt with their fates is what inspired me to work on this book. I wanted to find out much more than just where they are now. You can find that anywhere. I wanted to find out *how* they are now, how they were affected in that pivotal moment and for the rest of their lives, and how they adjusted to our view of them as athletes who came up short at the worst possible time. What was it, in their makeup, or background, that allowed them to move on? If they ever did.

Both Craig and Everson Walls, the Dallas Cowboys defensive

back who couldn't stop "The Catch"—the iconic Joe Montana to Dwight Clark touchdown pass in the final minute of the 1981 NFC title game—interested me because they were victims of legends *before* they were legends.

Other athletes intrigued me for their historical significance, such as center Bill Curry and placekicker Lou Michaels, who were members of the mighty Baltimore Colts squad that lost Super Bowl III, 16–7, to the AFL's New York Jets in one of the most shocking upsets ever. And, in talking to star runner Mary Decker, tennis pro Aaron Krickstein, and champion snowboarder Lindsey Jacobellis, I wanted to see if the challenge of dealing with such a public defeat was any different for those who perform in individual sports and aren't able to share their loss with teammates.

When it comes to individual sports, nothing was more excruciating than watching the French golfer Jean Van de Velde throw away the British Open in 1999. I play golf, so I have plenty of experience with messing up, but to see a professional go through the kind of meltdown he did when he was in a position to change his life was brutal. Jean, to his credit, opened up about what took place that day in Scotland, and you might be surprised by what he had to say.

I've long believed sports teaches us everything we need to know about how to be a good winner, stressing such timeless values as teamwork, leadership, sacrifice, and discipline. No lesson, though, is more essential to learn than how to handle adversity. Adversity, after all, is the one obstacle that each of us must face at some point, no matter how privileged our background may be or how much we achieve. Which is why it's necessary to discover a way to "move on"—or, at the very least, make peace with it, so it doesn't hold us back in our careers and lives. How we manage that task will go a long way toward whether we enjoy a rewarding life or a future filled with sadness and regret.

Those of us who cover sports on a network level tend to focus on the winner, and there's nothing wrong with that. Sports history, like any kind of history, is written by the victors. Yet as soon as an event is in the books, we make sure to get a quick postgame interview with the losing coach or star. We thank them for being "gracious at this most difficult time," and feel confident we did our duty.

Did we? Or did we merely pay lip service?

Working for FOX Sports, I've done my share of those interviews. My former boss, Ed Goren, called it the toughest interview to do in sports. He wasn't kidding. I remember standing outside the Red Sox clubhouse in 2003 with Boston manager Grady Little. His team had just dropped a heartbreaking Game 7 to their bitter rivals, the New York Yankees, on a walk-off home run in the eleventh inning by Aaron Boone.

Before I spoke to Grady, and, literally, seconds after he had crossed home plate, I interviewed Aaron. I don't have to tell you which conversation was easier. But, to me, Grady was infinitely more fascinating. There was so much I was eager to know, but it was way too early for him to process everything. That kind of in-depth self-examination takes weeks, months, or sometimes years.

I wondered if Grady would second-guess himself for the whole winter for leaving his future Hall of Fame pitcher, Pedro Martinez, in the game in the eighth inning after it was pretty clear he didn't have his best stuff anymore. Would he second-guess himself for the rest of his *life*?

These types of questions have always intrigued me. In fact, after many of the major sporting events I covered or watched on television, I couldn't wait to find out how the "loser" would cope—not merely in the near future but in the years and decades ahead.

Take Everson Walls, who was just a rookie on the Cowboys when Montana hit Clark. Try dealing with that for the rest of your days. While living in Dallas, no less!

Take Aaron Krickstein, who was beaten by Jimmy Connors in an epic U.S. Open match in 1991. Aaron, as good a junior player as we've seen in the United States, was supposed to be a star. That didn't happen. Instead, he'll always be known as the guy who lost that match to Connors.

Take the two basketball players from the University of Kentucky, Deron Feldhaus and John Pelphrey, who couldn't prevent Duke's Christian Laettner from making a jump shot at the buzzer to beat the Wildcats in the 1992 NCAA tournament. Basketball is a religion in Kentucky. I wondered how Deron and John got over that loss. *If* they got over it.

Finally, I wanted to find out if, deep down, when he's alone with his thoughts, Seattle Seahawks coach Pete Carroll ever regrets calling for a pass on the play that was intercepted by the New England Patriots' Malcolm Butler in Super Bowl XLIX. You don't receive many opportunities to win back-to-back Super Bowls. Would the Seahawks be haunted going into the next season? Or even beyond that?

The players and coaches I spoke with shared their greatest disappointments, confessing there were times they weren't sure how they would go forward. A few still battle with those feelings from time to time. All of them, as you might well understand, suffered quite a bit during the days and weeks after their losses, long after our attention shifted to other winners and other victims. Some sought therapy. Some relied on family and friends. Some shut out the world. Whatever their stories were, and remain, I felt an obligation to tell them—better yet, to have them do it.

None of the individuals I interviewed came to me. They weren't looking for sympathy or an opportunity to rewrite history. To their benefit, they recognized right away what I was trying to accomplish, to examine not just the losses themselves but also how we, as a society, handle loss on the biggest stage—on any stage, really. No doubt the wisdom they gained over the years will inspire a lot of people, and not just those who play sports for a living. The interviews also made me reflect on how much emphasis we place on who wins and who loses. Bottom line: It's too much, and I'm as guilty as anyone.

I know that to many even expressing that viewpoint is blasphemous. And, no, I'm not suggesting that winning isn't important—it is. It's certainly a heck of a lot better than losing. Any athlete will tell you that. Besides, if winning weren't as big a deal as we make it, the athletes we look up to wouldn't make the sacrifices they do, year after year, to provide us with the glorious moments we cherish. All I'm suggesting is that winning shouldn't be the most important reason for competition. And because we put too much emphasis on the outcome, we label those who lose a Super Bowl or a World Series, or come apart down the stretch of a major golf tournament or—God forbid—fail to win a gold medal in the Olympics, as "a loser." Nothing could be further from the truth.

I was struck as well by how wrong we are about those in the spotlight. We assume the athletes in these moments will be haunted forever. They're not. Not even close. Dealing with the players I've gotten to know during my career, I had sensed this was a common misconception. Now, after spending time with Craig Ehlo, Everson Walls, Lindsey Jacobellis, and others, I'm more convinced than ever. The fans are affected by the losses much more than the players are.

The people who agreed to participate couldn't have been more gracious. Such as the speed skater Dan Jansen, who, only three days after his father's death, took time from writing his eulogy to share his story. I had heard Dan was a decent guy. Boy is he ever. So is Rodney Harrison, who started to tear up as we chatted about the David Tyree catch. Rodney wasn't emotional because his team lost the Super Bowl to the Giants. It was because, from the time he fell in love with the game at the age of six, he'd prided himself on making the key play at the key moment. This was one occasion when he hadn't.

I was equally moved by the honesty of Ron Washington, the former Texas Rangers manager, who didn't run away from the problems he had with cocaine and in his marriage. I understood right away why his players have had so much trust in him.

One of the fiercest debates we had about this book was over the title. For a while, we considered possibilities that would include the word "losers." That would definitely get the point across. Easy to remember, it would be very marketable. It would also be very unfair. These athletes, after all, found a way to bounce back, to make the best out of a difficult situation.

Vince Lombardi, the great coach of the Green Bay Packers in the sixties, once said, "Winning isn't everything; it's the only thing." He was later quoted as saying he regretted making that statement.

Either way, for those we interviewed, winning *was* the only thing to them at one point. But the more they lived, the more lessons they learned, about life and themselves, the more it occurred to them that winning isn't the only thing.

And that losing isn't everything.

1

THE CURSE

OCTOBER 25, 1986

Bye-bye, Curse of the Bambino. And of all places for it to be lifted, in New York City.

The curse, as Boston fans knew all too well, was the one put on their beloved Red Sox after they traded Babe Ruth to the New York Yankees in 1919. Sold, to be more exact, by Harry Frazee, the team's owner, who also produced plays on Broadway. Mr. Frazee needed the dough.

Over the next sixty-seven years, while the Bronx Bombers won one World Series after another, twenty-two in all, the Sox didn't win one. Nada. Zilch. But finally, on this late October evening in 1986, the curse would come to a glorious end.

The scene was Game 6 of the World Series between the Red Sox and the New York Mets at Shea Stadium. Boston had begun the night up three games to two, and were just 3 outs away from winning the whole thing. A tight contest the entire way, it went to extra innings tied at 3–3. The Sox scored 2 runs in the top of the tenth to take a 5–3 lead. Now it was up to their six-foot-five, 215-pound hard-throwing closer, Calvin Schiraldi, to put it away.

Calvin was the perfect guy for the job. The Mets were the team that had drafted him, but they had given up on him after he threw just 43 innings in the big leagues, trading Calvin to the Sox during the previous off-season. Who better to finish off his former teammates? Plus, since being called up from the minors in July, he had come through in key moments over and over. He would also be able to make up for the run he gave up in the eighth, which had tied the game.

Calvin threw his eight warm-up pitches to the veteran catcher Rich Gedman, waited for the ball to be tossed around the infield, and got down to work. Once he secured the 3 outs, the Red Sox' long-suffering fans could celebrate. For as long as they'd waited, the party might last forever.

The first batter was second baseman Wally Backman, a .320 hitter during the regular season. The idea was to pitch him away. Calvin got him in a quick hole, 0 balls and 2 strikes. On the next pitch, Backman sent a weak fly ball to shallow left that was easily snagged by Jim Rice. One out.

Next up was first baseman Keith Hernandez. If anybody on the Mets was likely to ignite a rally, it was Hernandez. He hit close to .300 every year, and many of the hits came when his team needed him the most. If he could get on base, the Mets would bring the tying run to the plate. The fans would begin to believe. They didn't need much.

Calvin got ahead with a strike but followed with 2 balls. For the Mets, a walk was as good as a hit, something coaches preach from Little League on. Calvin brought his usual good stuff on a 2-1 delivery but left the ball too close to the middle of the zone, and Hernandez crushed it. That's what good hitters do. The only problem was *where* he crushed it, toward the deepest part of Shea, where the wall in center was 410 feet away. Dave Henderson, the center fielder, ran it down just in front of the warning track. Two outs.

"Keith's ball, in any other ballpark, on any other night, would probably have been a home run," Calvin said, "except for the fact it was chilly and it was Shea."

Even NBC, doing the national broadcast, figured the game was over.

"Tonight's NBC Miller Lite Player of the Game," Vin Scully, the Hall of Fame announcer, told viewers, "is Marty Barrett [the Red Sox' second baseman]. Miller Lite [is] happy to present a check for one thousand dollars in the name of Marty Barrett to the National Multiple Sclerosis Society."

The choice made sense. Barrett finished with 3 singles and 2 walks, including a big hit in the tenth. He was one of the many heroes Red Sox fans would honor forever. Calvin, only twenty-four years old, was on his way to being another.

Calvin never expected to be on the major league roster this late in the year, let alone make an impact. When he was called up to fill in for injured reliever Steve Crawford, he figured he would be back in Pawtucket, the Sox' top minor league club, within a few weeks. There was no reason to think otherwise.

A starter everywhere—in college (where he helped the University of Texas Longhorns win the 1983 College World Series), in the minors, and during seven of his first fifteen appearances in the majors—Calvin was still getting adjusted to coming out of the pen. The Sox felt that's where he belonged. He wasn't in a position to argue.

He'd pitched very well in Pawtucket, with 12 saves, but, let's face it, Pawtucket was not Boston. Besides, the Red Sox didn't call him up to close games. They needed him for middle relief, to eat up innings to spare the other relievers.

Something then happened to change what they had in store for him.

Calvin began to throw strikes, tons of them, and they could not have come at a better time. He saved a game in August against the Kansas City Royals and two more games a week later against the Detroit Tigers.

Good-bye, Pawtucket. Hello, Fenway Park. The job of closer was essentially his, and he made the most of it.

"I was [surprised]," Calvin remembered, "but at the time the Red Sox were looking for a spark and I was the spark. You ride the hot hand, and I stayed hot pretty much the entire time I was there after the All-Star break."

He sure did. Even on the occasions he blew the save, he won the game regardless. His only two defeats came after he'd entered a tie game. More than possessing the right pitches to be a top closer, Calvin appeared to possess the right persona, and that was just as critical.

"I went out there and threw as hard as I could as long as I could," he said, "and I put things behind me the next day."

Want some proof? Just look at what occurred in back-to-back games in Anaheim against the California Angels in early October. At stake was the American League pennant, the winner moving on to the World Series.

On the night of Game 4 of the Championship Series, Calvin had come in with 1 out in the ninth. The Sox were ahead 3–1, but the Angels had men on first and second. After Gary Pettis hit a double to make it a 1-run contest, Calvin issued an intentional walk to load the bases. Allow 1 more hit, and the game would, in all likelihood, be over.

No worries. Calvin promptly struck out Bobby Grich and threw his heater to get a 1-2 count on Brian Downing. He was now only a strike away from pulling the Sox even in the best-of-seven series, at two games apiece. Meaning that no matter what happened in Game 5, the teams would head back to Boston for Game 6 and, if necessary, Game 7.

Gedman called for another heater. The fastball was Calvin's best pitch. No one threw the ball harder, except perhaps for his college, and current, teammate and close friend Roger Clemens. Downing, while an accomplished hitter, would have a tough time making good contact.

We'll never know. Calvin waved Gedman off and threw the curve, which hit Downing to force in the tying run. The Angels went on to win the game in the eleventh inning and assumed a 3–1 lead in the series. Calvin took the loss.

"It was something I hadn't felt before," he said.

He also took the blame. As he sat in the dugout and shed some tears, the other players tried to prevent the cameras from showing his emotions. A few even suggested he go to the trainer's room to avoid reporters. That wasn't Calvin.

"I always believed in facing the music," he said. "And I wasn't going to have someone write something that wasn't true."

As memorable as the loss was, it was what took place *after* the game that stands out. While he rested in his hotel room that night, he opened his favorite book, the Bible. Calvin routinely read the

Bible before going to sleep, one chapter at a time. It so happened that where he'd left off the night before was Romans 5:3, a passage dealing with life's tribulations and how they teach us about patience and perseverance:

> We rejoice in our sufferings, knowing that suffering produces endurance, and endurance produces character, and character produces hope, and hope does not put us to shame, because God's love has been poured into our hearts through the Holy Spirit who has been given to us.

"I read that, and I went, 'You got to be kidding me,'" Calvin said.

That was the first sign. The second was when the phone rang several minutes later. Calvin was so naive he didn't know enough to have the hotel receptionist intercept any incoming calls. Thank goodness he didn't. A fireman based in Pebble Beach, California, a complete stranger, was calling to let him know that everyone at his station had been praying for him. Calvin thanked the fireman and went to sleep. He felt a sense of peace he hadn't felt in a long time.

The following day, he came into the game in the eleventh inning, Boston up 7–6. The Sox should have been in the clubhouse by then, packing their bags for the winter. But thanks to a 2-run home run with 2 outs in the top of the ninth by Henderson, they were still alive, and now, after scoring another run in the eleventh, were handing their closer an opportunity to atone for his blown save the night before and extend the series.

"We were in the bullpen going absolutely bananas," he remembered about the Henderson homer. "There were cops on horses and cops on the ground." Before Henderson hit it, "the fans had been screaming at us. [Afterward,] it got so quiet, and we're giving it back to them like it was nobody's business."

Calvin got 2 quick outs. Who then comes to the plate to represent the tying run?

Brian Downing, naturally.

Calvin was as calm as one can be in that spot. The peace he found from reading the verse in the Bible and speaking to the fireman had a lot to do with it. Patience, perseverance.

"It made it seem like a game again," he said, "for just that moment, instead of a business."

Nor did it hurt that he went with the fastball this time, getting Downing to pop up to first base for the final out.

There was no stopping the Red Sox now. They won the two games in Boston easily to capture their first pennant in eleven years. Calvin was on the mound to finish Game 7, striking out five in two innings.

"We knew there was no way they were going to beat us at home," he recalled.

What curse?

With 2 outs at Shea, the crowd stunned, Gary Carter, the Mets' future Hall of Fame catcher, walked up to the plate.

Calvin was feeling pretty good about things, especially for somebody who had needed to refocus because he'd assumed he was done for the night. In the top of the tenth, with the game tied 3–3, he was told the Sox would pinch-hit for him. The move was the right one. He had pitched two innings already. Calvin threw as much as three innings only a few times the whole season.

"So now I'm relaxed on the bench, chilling out," he said.

Next thing he knew, Henderson led off the tenth with a home run to left. So much for chilling out. A pinch hitter wouldn't be necessary. Calvin, set to bat third in the inning, would stay in the game. The challenge for him to come through in the bottom of the tenth would be mental as well as physical.

An athlete, you see, digs deep to get into what is called "the zone" and tries to remain in the zone for as long as he has to perform. Once he leaves, even briefly—"You breathe," Calvin said—finding his way back into it isn't always easy. It might take time, and that was a luxury he didn't have.

Yet, after the Sox were retired, he went back to the mound and had no difficulty with Backman and Hernandez. With Carter representing the final out, there was no point in being precise.

"I'll just throw it down the middle and see what happens," he figured.

Even if Carter were to knock it out of the park, the Sox, who tacked on an insurance run after Henderson's homer, would still be leading 5–4. The one thing Calvin didn't want to do was walk Carter to bring the tying run to the plate.

There was little danger of that happening. On a 2-1 delivery, Calvin threw it right down the middle, as he had planned. Carter took advantage, stroking a single to left. The Mets weren't dead yet.

Next up would be pinch hitter Kevin Mitchell, who had to be summoned from the clubhouse. He, like many others, had figured the game was over.

Calvin and Mitchell knew each other, having been roommates on the Mets' top farm club, the Tidewater Tides, in Portsmouth, Virginia. The two used to talk about a day they might face each other. Now that day was here. Back in Portsmouth, Calvin had told Mitchell exactly what he would do: he'd throw a slider because it was a pitch that usually gave him a lot of trouble. He hadn't forgotten.

"He knows what's coming," Calvin said, "but if I throw a good one, he's not going to hit it."

Just one problem: Calvin didn't throw a good one. He threw a terrible one. He hung it. Mitchell, most likely remembering their conversation as well, was ready for it and lined a single to center to put the tying run on base. One of the most important pitch selections of the Series had come not from a manager or a catcher but from the fact Calvin and Mitchell had been teammates in the minors. Shea began to stir.

The next batter was third baseman Ray Knight, a .298 hitter in 1986. The first pitch was a fastball at the knees. Strike one. On the next pitch, Knight hit a slow roller along the third base line that went foul. The Mets were down to their last strike.

Now, with an 0-2 count, Calvin could afford to waste one outside the strike zone. Perhaps Knight would even help him by chasing a pitch in the dirt and striking out. At the very worst, the 1-2 count would still be in Calvin's favor.

That seemed quite logical, but that's not what Calvin did. He had no intention of wasting anything. All he thought about was rearing back and throwing the ball as hard as he could.

"I didn't know where it was going," he conceded.

Maybe not, but he, and everyone else, saw where the ball ended up: on the grass in center field. Knight didn't hit it particularly hard, but it was hard enough to allow Carter to score, and suddenly, the lead was down to just 1, the Mets still threatening with runners on the corners.

Calvin was angry with himself. He knew better. He picked the worst time to give up his first hit of the whole year on an 0-2 count. He was anxious to make up for his blunder right away.

"I was a little tired," he recalled, "but I wanted to finish. This was my doing."

He wouldn't get that chance. John McNamara, the Red Sox manager, had seen enough. With Mookie Wilson, a .289 hitter, due up, he handed the ball to another relief pitcher, Bob Stanley, known as "Steamer." Calvin understood the reasoning.

"Steamer had good success against Mookie," he admitted. "I had never faced him."

If Calvin, as fate would have it, wasn't the man to lead the Red Sox to their first World Series title since 1918, perhaps Stanley was. He saved 16 games that season, the most on the team.

Perhaps not. The baseball gods had teased the Sox and their fans long enough. It was time to torture them. After four pitches, Stanley was even with Wilson: 2 balls and 2 strikes. The Sox again were one pitch away.

But after Wilson fouled off the next two pitches, Stanley threw a wild one. Wilson had to jump out of the way as it went all the way to the backstop, allowing Mitchell to score and tie the game at 5–5. Knight moved on to second. Suddenly, amazingly, the Mets were a base hit away from winning the game and taking the Series to a deciding Game 7.

Wilson fouled off two more pitches before . . . well, you know the rest. The most famous ground ball in baseball history went off Wilson's bat and through first baseman Bill Buckner's legs. Buckner, with his ailing ankles, shouldn't have even been in the game at this point. His backup, Dave Stapleton, who was better defensively, had replaced him in the late innings of the Sox' victories in Games 1, 2, and 5.

Game over. Curse alive and well.

Calvin, who took the loss, watched the ending on TV in the clubhouse. He dressed in a hurry, and then faced the music again before going back to his hotel. The only consolation was that the Red Sox, and perhaps Calvin, would get one more chance. Game 7 was less than twenty-four hours away.

At the hotel, he opened his Bible. For a change, he didn't pick up at the section where he had left off. He went back to the passage that had moved him so deeply after he blew the save in Anaheim, dealing with life's trials and tribulations. Calvin needed to take in the comforting words now more than ever.

Heavy rain fell the next day in the Big Apple, postponing Game 7 for a day. Calvin doesn't remember much about the day off. He would prefer to forget the day after as well.

With everything on the line for the Sox, he came in a bit earlier than normal, starting off the seventh in relief of Bruce Hurst, the game knotted at 3–3. Leading off for the Mets was Knight. Perhaps Calvin could get him out the second time around, just as he got Brian Downing out the second time in the ALCS.

No such luck. Knight didn't hit a soft liner to center as he did in Game 6. On a 2-1 pitch, he hit a homer to left. The Mets went on top, 4-3.

Lenny Dykstra, pinch-hitting for Mitchell, followed with a single to right and advanced to second on a wild pitch. He then scored on a base hit by Rafael Santana. Facing only four batters, Calvin gave up 3 runs on 3 hits and a wild pitch, and recorded just 1 out. New York won the game 8–5. Calvin took the loss once more.

Mets: world champions. Red Sox: cursed again.

Now in his midfifties, Calvin spends a lot of his time these days either baking in the Texas sun or hanging out in his "office," a messy trailer that is attached to a shed and surrounded by dirt. When he's at work, Calvin is at peace. He doesn't cling to the past, that's for sure.

You can tell by the pictures on the wood-paneled walls across from the old air conditioner. Only one photo has to do with his time in the bigs, and that's of him at Fenway Park in Game 7 of the 1986 ALCS against the Angels. The only reason that's even up there is that somebody gave it to him at a reunion. All the other dozen or so photos are of high school kids. These are the memories that mean the most to him.

"Kind of hard to beat what I've got down here," he said.

Down here is St. Michael's Catholic Academy in Austin, only a few miles from where he grew up. Calvin came to St. Michael's five years after he threw his last pitch in the majors, in 1991 with the Texas Rangers. He was only twenty-nine. He'd lost that tremendous fastball of his and couldn't get it back. He wasn't the first.

"I crumbled down and had a conversation with God," he recalled. "I said, 'What am I supposed to do?'"

What he was supposed to do, he realized, was pass on his knowledge of the game to others by becoming a coach. He went back to the University of Texas and earned his teaching degree.

St. Michael's isn't very big, with about 350 students in grades nine to twelve. In 2014, only seventeen boys went out for baseball, including freshmen. That wasn't enough to field a full practice game. No matter. Calvin is more fulfilled here than when he was pitching in front of thirty-five thousand screaming fans at Fenway. He's able to make a living in the only world he has ever known and, better yet, make a difference.

"I like the younger guys," he said. "I can teach them more about the game. Kids in high school are very naive."

He doesn't care how many go on to play college ball; he counts ten in twenty years, with just three making it as far as the minor leagues, including his son, Lukas, who plays in the Seattle Mariners' organization. But Calvin cares tremendously about the values they adopt and the men they become. He expects them to be on time, have their shirts tucked in, and do their schoolwork.

"Take care of your stuff up there," he warns the teens, referring to the school's main building, about two hundred yards from the baseball field, "before you come down here. If I get an e-mail from a teacher that says you are messing up in class, it's your ass in practice."

Most of his players have been aware of who Coach Schiraldi was back in his day, although, with a handful of exceptions, they choose not to ask him about the past, or they don't care. He won't bring it up, either, except when it can be instructive.

"With the kids," he said, "it's all about St. Michael's and how far we can go in the playoffs."

Which is why it's no surprise his favorite moment in baseball wasn't when the Sox won the American League pennant in 1986 or when the Longhorns won the College World Series in 1983. His favorite moment was when his kids, the Crusaders, took their first of two straight state championships in 1997. They won three games on the final day. No small feat, for sure.

"It was awesome," Calvin recalled. "I just sat there and watched them celebrate and dog-pile the mound. They'd never had a chance to do that."

As for his best chance at a moment like that, on the game's ultimate stage, he decided soon after the 1986 Series he couldn't let himself feel bad about what he had missed. He felt he had no choice, really, if he hoped to be ready for the 1987 season, and any seasons after that.

"In order to perform," he said, "you got to put walls up. You fail one day, you could succeed the next fifteen. But if you linger on what happened the one day you failed, you're not going to be successful on the next fifteen. You shove it to the back of your brain and forget about it and move on."

Spoken like a true reliever, and if you're talking about one game during the long grind of the regular season, that's exactly the approach you would want your closer to have. Except we're not talking about 1 of 162 games. We're talking about *the* game, Game 6 of the World Series, the game the fans in Boston, and all over New England, would never forget, so close their Sox had been to finally ending the curse.

To be fair, he had put up walls before, when he learned that baseball in the major leagues was a lot different from baseball in college, a business more than a game. Which first became clear fifteen months after the College World Series, when he made his big-league debut with the Mets on September 1, 1984. He started the second game of a doubleheader at Shea against the San Diego Padres. It was hardly the kind of opening start Calvin was hoping for—he gave up 8 hits and allowed 4 earned runs in only 3⅓ innings—but that didn't mean he was prepared for the reaction he got when he left the mound. The fans booed.

"I was pitching behind Dwight [Gooden] that day, and I sucked; I'm not going to deny that," he said, then added, "[But] you screw up one time and there are freakin' boos."

He also learned how easy it was for false information to make it into the newspapers. Two of his teammates, Keith Hernandez and Ron Darling, a pitcher, decided to spread a rumor one day that a player on the Mets was about to be traded, just to see what would happen. Within twenty-four hours, the "rumor," as Calvin recalled, was in the *New York Post*.

The message couldn't have been any clearer: *I have to be careful in everything I do and say. We're not in Austin anymore.*

Building those walls wasn't so hard to do back then, and by the time 1986 rolled around, he was an expert. It wasn't so much the criticism he received for the Sox' loss that caused him to build higher walls than before; it was how disappointed he was in himself.

"I'm harder on myself than I am on anybody else," he said.

Though the fans did react horribly at times, on the road especially.

"'Eighty-six! You suck!" they yelled. "You lost the World Series."

After 1986, those walls weren't going to come down, not as long as he was in the majors and had to be on his guard. The problem is he's still putting walls up, from time to time, and he hasn't thrown a pitch in twenty-five years.

"You learn how to do it, and it becomes a natural thing to do in any situation," he explained. "It doesn't have to be baseball. It could be your kids, your friends, anything. Something happens and you automatically put up a wall."

The price Calvin is paying at this stage of his life is massive, and he knows it's because he never dealt with what took place in Game 6. He sees the price in his relationship with his wife, Debbie, who wants to have back the man she knew when they began dating in the minor leagues before it's too late.

"I don't remember that guy," he said.

He sees it, too, in other relationships, the kind many of us take for granted.

"I miss being able to have a regular conversation with a stranger," he said.

And he sees it in those moments when he reacts to something in a manner he doesn't quite understand, asking himself later, "Why the hell did I do *that*?"

In some respects, the walls Calvin put up aren't much different from the walls his father, Joe, put up between himself and the people closest to him, walls that never came down.

"I never saw the softer side of my dad," Calvin explained. "One time, at the state championship, he shook my hand and said, 'You did a good job.' It was the first time he had ever done that."

In 2005, while battling bile duct and prostate cancer, his father decided he didn't want to suffer any longer, nor did he want those near him suffering on his behalf. So, one day, he pulled over to the side of the road and shot himself to death. Calvin understood. He said he would probably have done the same thing if he'd been in that position.

"We watched his mom, who was ninety-seven, wilt away in a bed," Calvin said, "and he wasn't going to be the kind to do that."

Dealing with his father's suicide added another complication to what he's had to go through, which, as you can tell, is a lot.

The good news, though, is that he's receiving help from a therapist he sees every week or two. He's making progress. A few of the walls are starting to come down.

"My wife and I haven't been very close lately, and the walls are the reason why," he said. "I needed to break down and show that I'm trying to figure out things, to get inside myself. She's been fantastic about it. You can't do it alone."

Some of the truths he has learned about himself haven't been very pretty, but he vows to keep digging, no matter what else might turn up.

"It sucks," he said. "I'm just waiting for the end of it. I want to be like I was before, when I was twenty-two or twenty-three."

A topic that will no doubt come up is 1986. "We're getting there," Calvin said. "We still haven't gotten there yet." He knows 1986 might very well be the key to knocking the walls down for good.

"That's what I'm hoping," he said.

One thing that isn't a mystery is why he has been able to relate so easily to the kids he coaches. It's because being around them and helping them grow brings him back to his own past in the game that he still loves. Before he was booed, before he let a city, and himself, down.

"It's still a game to them," he explained. "I don't make it life or death to them. I get pissed when they screw up, they know that, but it's because I either haven't taught them what I want them to know or they haven't learned what I told them."

His goal is to make sure his players learn from his mistakes.

"Mine were on a big stage," he said. "I'm trying to make theirs as little [as possible] on a little stage."

One can't help but wonder, though, how different his life would have been if he'd gotten just one more out, instead of allowing those 3 straight hits in Game 6. Not only would the Red Sox have won it all, but perhaps he wouldn't have built any more walls. Perhaps, a hero forever in Boston, he would have even torn down the ones he built before.

Calvin doesn't see it that way. Of course, he would never have wished for his team to lose a World Series, especially in the manner the Sox lost, but he came to appreciate how it shaped him, in spite of the walls, and that could be a lesson for us all. Lose a lover, a job—lose anything of value—and as awful as it might feel at the time, you can't imagine the person you'd be today if you hadn't gone through the experience, if you hadn't grown. In Calvin's case, he wouldn't change a thing about Game 6.

"That's what made me who I am," he explained.

Think about it: if he had gotten any of those three hitters out, he probably would not have spent the past twenty years at St. Michael's, and that he can't fathom.

"I think I've affected a lot more people this way," he said, "than if we had won the World Series. I could have been a complete jackass."

As tough as Calvin had it, though, two of his teammates had it worse: Stanley and, of course, Buckner. Nobody has suffered more ridicule for one specific play than Bill Buckner, in baseball or any other sport.

"He has taken a lot of shit that is not deserved," Calvin said. "People make errors."

He's just as upset at how Stanley was mistreated.

"That was brutal," he said.

Does Calvin feel any guilt for what Buckner and Stanley have gone through? No, not really, although he quickly added: "If I had done my job, that would have never happened."

He's right, and when you think about it, he's gotten off pretty easy compared with what Buckner has had to experience. Giving up those three hits had a lot more to do with the Red Sox losing than one botched play by the first baseman.

Yet the Buckner blunder, a single, more dramatic moment of ineptitude, is what people recall about Game 6 of the 1986 World Series. That's how cruel history can be: those who lived it always at the mercy of those who remember it.

As for how Calvin feels about the city of Boston and Red Sox fans, he has nothing but good things to say. When he flew up there for a reunion several years ago, people couldn't have been nicer. Finally winning the World Series in 2004, 2007, and 2013 has certainly made it much easier for them to forgive.

Now if only he could forgive himself. The walls were supposed to protect him, but in the end, all they did was imprison him. It's taken Calvin a long time, but he now realizes they must come down if he is to ever truly cope with that horrible night at Shea.

And again be the man his wife fell in love with.

2

THE SHOT

Craig Ehlo took a seat on the bench and paid attention to his coach's instructions. Nothing new there. Respecting authority was something he'd been taught long ago, long before learning how to shoot a jumper or take a charge. Only on this occasion, his mind began to drift, ever so slightly. With good reason.

Craig had just made the play of his life, a layup past Michael Jordan to give his team, the Cleveland Cavaliers, a 100–99 lead with three seconds to go in the fifth, and deciding, game of their opening-round playoff series against the Chicago Bulls.

Those fortunate enough to be in Richfield Coliseum during that spring day in 1989 couldn't have been more pumped. The fans in Cleveland had suffered more than fans in any city should ever have to suffer, particularly on Sunday afternoons the past two years.

First there was The Drive, when John Elway, Denver's sensational quarterback, took his Broncos 98 yards in 15 plays to tie the Browns with only thirty-seven seconds left in the AFC title game in January 1987. Denver went on to win in overtime. Then a year later, when the same teams met again for a berth in the Super Bowl, there was The Fumble. With Cleveland trailing by 7 with just over a minute to go, running back Earnest Byner coughed it up near the goal line. The Broncos hung on for the victory.

Bottom line: No team in Cleveland had won a title in any sport since the Browns in 1964. The sporting gods owed the city big-time, and now, at long last, it looked as if they would deliver.

Okay, so this wouldn't be for a championship. Not yet. The Cavs would still have to get by three other quality teams, and while that would not be easy, that wasn't on anybody's mind at the moment. What mattered was that their heroes were about to knock off the mighty Jordan and the Bulls. It would feel almost as good as winning a title.

"I was thinking cover of *Sports Illustrated*," Craig admitted. "I just saw everything in the future being gold."

The future he saw would include one NBA championship after another, and he was far from alone in his optimism. No less an authority than Earvin "Magic" Johnson, still in his prime, predicted the Cavaliers would be the "team of the nineties."

They certainly had the talent.

Their center, twenty-three-year-old Brad Daugherty, the no. 1 overall pick in the 1986 NBA Draft, was a force offensively.

Their point guard, twenty-five-year-old Mark Price, was one of the most dependable passers and long-range shooters in the league. Other valuable contributors included off guard Ron Harper and power forward Larry Nance, an excellent shot blocker. Then there was Craig, who could do a bit of everything and hadn't missed a game the entire season.

The Cavs had sure come a long way in a short time. Just two years earlier, they went 31-51.

As a matter of fact, they were so inept that during Craig's first three NBA seasons as a member of the Houston Rockets, his coach, Bill Fitch, used to threaten players who screwed up with the joke that they'd better get it right, or he would "trade your ass to Cleveland." Going to Cleveland was like being banished to Siberia. End up there, and you might never be heard from again.

The Cleveland unit Fitch poked fun at was long gone by 1989. These new and vastly improved Cavs, besides being extremely gifted, had a lot of guts.

Take the possession when Craig made the layup past Jordan. There were just six seconds to go when the Cavs, trailing by 1 point, called timeout, the game and season on the line. Everyone assumed the ball would go to Price, but Lenny Wilkens, Cleveland's coach, had something else in mind.

Price would be a decoy, with Harper and Daugherty setting screens to clear an opening near the top of the key. They had to make the Bulls believe that was where the ball would be going. Meanwhile, the play designed by Wilkens was for Craig to throw the ball to the six-foot-ten Nance and cut to the hoop, a textbook give-and-go.

In the huddle, Wilkens, who always trusted Craig to make the inbounds pass, told him exactly what to do.

"Make your pass when the guy [guarding the throw] jumps, so he will be out of position," he said.

After the huddle broke up, Wilkens grabbed Craig and reminded him: "Make him jump!"

Craig did just that, hitting Nance in the perfect spot, and darted immediately to the basket. Nance threw it back to him. The plan worked. The Bulls were fooled.

"When I got the ball," Craig recalled, "it was like the Red Sea parted, and I saw nothing but rim."

In that split second, Craig considered his two options: lay the ball in or go for the dunk. He chose to lay it in. In his peripheral vision he spotted Jordan, like Pharaoh and the Egyptians, closing in quickly. Had he tried to dunk it, he has little doubt that MJ would have made the block. He ducked under him and laid the ball in to put his team up by 1 point. Chicago called timeout.

The noise in the Coliseum was the loudest Craig could ever recall. The basket gave Craig 24 points for the game, a career playoff high, and it was quite a turnaround for a guy dealing with an ankle he injured—get this—playing the part of Michael Jordan while running the Bulls' offense in practice against the Cleveland starters.

"If I had just run their plays and not tried to be like Mike," he said, "I probably wouldn't have rolled my ankle."

The ankle hurt him so much that, two days earlier, in Game 4, he could stay on the court for only seventeen minutes, missing all six of his field goal attempts. He wasn't sure he would even be able to suit up for the decisive Game 5.

Now the Bulls were the ones in dire need of some heroics.

The ball, everyone assumed, would go to Jordan, and he wouldn't be a decoy like Mark Price was. You don't use Michael Jordan as a decoy. You can live with him missing the shot. Players miss shots all the time. You *cannot* live with him not taking it, given what was at stake.

The Cavaliers set up their defense, with Nance assigned to guard the guy tossing the ball in bounds, but didn't commit to a strategy, not yet. By having a timeout remaining of their own, they would first see how Chicago lined up and then call it to make any adjustments. Jordan stood a few feet from the top of the key, while Scottie Pippen, their other star, was in the right corner. Everyone was close to the baseline except Jordan. The Cavs called their timeout.

Wilkens decided again to mix things up. He would try something the Cavaliers hadn't attempted the whole season while guarding Jordan: they would double-team him with Craig and Nance.

The plan was to force anyone other than Jordan to beat them. MJ had scored 42 points, hitting 16 of 31 shots from the field. The rest of the Bulls had *combined* for 57. Except there was a problem with the plan. During the timeout, Wilkens told Nance to stand in front of Jordan and told Craig to stand in back of him, close to the free throw line. Nance, though, as he left the huddle, was still uncertain about how much room he should give MJ. He asked Craig what he thought. There couldn't have been a more inopportune time for the slightest indecision.

"Larry wanted to know if it would be better to be closer to Michael," Craig recalled. "He was probably about two feet off him and I was standing a couple of feet behind him. Larry thought it would be better not to body up."

Craig suggested Nance attempt to force Jordan toward the sideline, where it might be easier to trap him. The help would then come from John "Hot Rod" Williams. At six-foot-eleven, Hot Rod had the wingspan of a player a good four or five inches taller.

That wasn't the only problem. Craig's ankle was hurting again. He'd landed on it hard after making the layup.

"It had been taped, and I'd had two days of recovery time," he said, "but it was still swollen and tender."

Now there was no chance Craig was going to say a word and ask to be taken out of the game, not after all the work he had put in to get himself in this position. He prided himself on his mental toughness, his ability to play through pain. Yet, during both timeouts, and for a short period afterward, the ankle was on his mind, and he had enough to think about already.

"I wasn't big on excuses, but when I was standing there," he admitted, "I was thinking, 'I hope I don't have to plant my right foot in a defensive situation,' when I should have been concentrating on, 'Okay, Larry, let's not let him out of this double-team,' or denying him the basketball."

Still, bad ankle or not, Craig and the Cavaliers would not have to contain Jordan for long. No one could do that anyway. They'd just have to contain him long enough.

Assistant Coach Dick Helm put it best:

"All right, three seconds, boys, that's all we have to play defense for," Helm reminded the players. "Three seconds and we're moving on."

Just before play was about to resume, Craig stopped thinking about his ankle.

"I was fully focused," he said. "The athlete in me kicked in."

So did the talker in him. Craig did something he never did. He tried talking trash to Michael Jordan—"tried" being the key word, because what Craig came up with was about as lame as trash talk could possibly be.

"Mr. Jordan," he began, "I can't let you score."

That was it. MJ didn't respond—not with words, anyway. This wasn't the time.

"Michael had his hands on his shorts," Craig said, "and just looked at me with that grin he always had. He was so focused."

Craig knew the moment he spoke to Jordan that he had made a huge error. He was trying to get inside the head of one of the most fiercely competitive athletes of his era. Good luck with that. Worse yet, Craig was going outside his comfort zone, never a smart idea when the pressure is on. You need to do what you're familiar with, now more than ever, and for Craig Ehlo, that wasn't talking trash.

"What the hell was I doing?" he wondered.

Trash-talking was what Jordan used to do to others, and the

reason he could was that he backed it up, as Craig can attest only too well.

Like the one game where MJ couldn't miss.

"You seriously think I am not going to get fifty?" he asked Craig. Which he did, of course.

In another game, Jordan asked Craig, "Is your mom watching? I'm sorry I'm embarrassing you."

Early on, Craig went to his father for advice on how to guard him.

"Dad, have you seen this guy?" Craig asked.

"Oh, yeah, he's good," his father said.

"What can you do? Think I should physically play him, or use my quickness?"

"Take him out."

Craig's father was kidding . . . wasn't he?

The fact Craig was even on the same court with Michael Jordan was quite an achievement, considering the journey he took to get there.

In the late seventies, when he was coming out of high school in Lubbock, Texas, not a single Division I school offered him a scholarship. Craig settled for nearby Odessa College, the home of the Wranglers. Yet having to go to a junior college didn't get him down. He worked on his craft, day after day. This kind of single-minded approach was something he was used to.

"Even from high school on, I never dated any girls," he said. "I hung out with the guys on the team. A week before senior prom, I didn't have a date. My mom found me one. She knew a bunch of girls at my school."

Hard work was common in the Ehlo family. His father was a plumber who switched to the air-conditioning business.

In Craig's case, the extra effort paid off. After two years at Odessa, he transferred to Washington State, a Division I school. He was a key contributor for the Cougars, averaging 12 points per game his senior year. Of course, those aren't the kind of numbers to impress the scouts, so Craig had no expectations on the night of the 1983 NBA Draft.

"I was coaching a bunch of second graders at a camp," he said. "One of my assistants came over and said, 'Hey, you got drafted in the third round by Houston.'"

His hard work was just beginning. First, Craig needed to make the roster, and that was no guarantee. Then, once he did, he had to battle to get playing time.

For a change, all of his efforts didn't pay off. He appeared in just 88 games in his three full seasons in Houston, scoring a *total* of 208 points. Still, Craig was taken aback when the Rockets, who had just lost the NBA Finals to the Boston Celtics in six games, let him go after the 1985–86 season. The timing couldn't have been much worse. Craig and his wife, Jani, had been married for only a year and hadn't saved a lot of money. He had no clue how to break the news to her.

"I didn't go straight home," he recalled. "I went to the driving range, which I'd never done my whole life. I just pounded balls for an hour. It felt good to whack them."

When he finally did make it home, his wife was very supportive. So was his agent, who assured Craig that once teams made their final roster cuts, someone was certain to give him a call in November.

Well, November came and went, as did December, and the phone didn't ring. Maybe those three years in Houston would be it. Sometimes, though, hard work pays off indirectly. You just have to give it time.

With Craig unemployed approaching the New Year, Rockets assistant coach Rudy Tomjanovich made a call on his behalf to the Jacksonville Jets of the Continental Basketball Association. The CBA was a far cry from the NBA, but it gave Craig an opportunity to play again, and an opportunity was all he needed.

Craig didn't waste it. After he played only a few games for the Jets, the Cavaliers took notice, signing him to a ten-day contract. He would stick around for seven years.

The twenty thousand fans in the Coliseum shouted, "Deeee-fense, deeee-fense." They couldn't wait to celebrate. Like Red Sox fans in 1986, they'd already waited a long time.

An official handed the ball to the Bulls' Brad Sellers at midcourt. He would have five seconds to throw it in bounds or the ball would go back to the Cavs.

The whistle blew.

Five . . . four . . .

Jordan headed back toward midcourt, Nance backpedaling in front of him. Jordan made a quick fake step to his right before redirecting back left toward the sideline. The move got him away from Nance and created the opening Sellers needed to get him the ball.

"Oh, shit," Craig thought, "this isn't good." So much for the double-team.

"All of a sudden, the part of denying him the basketball on the high side was over," he said.

Craig looked to see if any help might be coming. It wasn't. He would have to stop the best player in the game by himself.

"If I could have forced him to the baseline, I had help," he said.

Jordan took two dribbles toward the center of the court, a few feet behind the free throw line. Craig closed in on him, except he was running instead of sliding his feet, and that was a mistake he would long regret.

"My close-out was bad," he said. "I knew he was going to change directions, but I was still going in the opposite direction when he caught the ball."

By the time Craig realized what was going on, it was too late. Jordan, about 18 feet from the basket, jumped straight up. Since Craig was out of position, he couldn't jump straight up. His momentum took him by Jordan, who hung in the air for a lifetime, it seemed. As a result, MJ got, as Craig recalled, a "bird's-eye view of the rim" and let the ball go.

At that point, it was out of Craig's control. All he could do was hope. The ball still had to fall in the net, and from Craig's vantage point, when it left Jordan's hand, the shot appeared to be flat.

"Usually, a flat shot either hits the front of the rim or the back of the rim," he said.

Flat or not, the ball hit the back of the rim but still fell through. It was over: Chicago 101, Cleveland 100.

Jordan punched the air three times in triumph. Craig fell to the floor in despair.

Craig held on to one last, desperate possibility. Perhaps MJ didn't get the shot off in time. He didn't cling to that possibility for long. He glanced at an official, who indicated the shot was good, and in those days, there were no replays.

He was crushed. He would not be on the cover of *Sports Illustrated*. He would not be the hero. Jordan would be, as he would be so many times in the years to come.

"We were all stunned," Craig recalled. "We were supposed to go all the way."

He and his teammates then had to walk through a tunnel and into an area that looked like a garage, before reaching their locker room. The Bulls took the same route. The seconds couldn't go by fast enough.

"We had to watch them celebrate," he said.

In the locker room, there was no cussing or throwing chairs. The Cavs were a relatively sedate group, much like Wilkens.

"He was always in control," Craig said. "I played like six hundred games with him and I remember him getting thrown out just once."

Wilkens praised his team's effort.

"Remember what it feels like," he told the guys, "because that's what's going to drive us to the next one."

The coach didn't have anything to worry about. His players wouldn't forget what it felt like. Ever. Craig normally lingered in the locker room for a bit after a difficult loss, as did a few others, but this loss was different. He could have lingered for days and he wouldn't have felt any better.

"Everyone wanted to get out of there really quick and deal with it on their own," Craig said.

Some of the players got together later that day at one of their usual spots for a bite. No matter what took place on the court in the grueling eighty-two-game season, meeting as a group for a postgame meal was a chance to leave behind any bad feelings and to be grateful for their good fortune and for one another.

There was nothing to be grateful for this time.

"We all just ate and stared," he recalled.

Craig needed support from his teammates after that game unlike ever before. He didn't get much. A tap on the leg in the locker room from Price. A few encouraging words from veteran forward Phil Hubbard.

"Hey, you played great," Hubbard told him.

But nobody said then, or has said to this day, what he perhaps most wanted to hear: "It's okay, Craig. He's the greatest player in the history of the game."

His family wouldn't go there, either, starting with Jani. On the twenty-five-minute drive to their home in Akron, she said a lot of things, but not a word about the game. She brought up the vacation they always took after the season was over.

"We can drop by Spokane on the way to Hawaii," Jani suggested.

Craig knew what she was doing, and he loved her for it. If she had brought up the game, he said, it would have been "like a bomb exploding." Instead, the bomb kept ticking inside him.

His parents were also upbeat. Since they didn't go to the game—they were planning to attend the next round of the playoffs—they left a message on his answering machine. Craig played it when he arrived home: *"Wow, what a game!"*

His mother, who paid close attention to his individual stats, couldn't contain the pride she felt: *"You had 24 points coming off the bench!"*

Craig's parents were always upbeat. Back in high school, he played poorly in the final game of his senior season, costing his team a chance to advance to the state's final four. Yet on the 160-mile ride from Abilene to Lubbock, his father wouldn't allow him to feel sorry for himself. He had already moved on, and so should Craig.

"We got to figure out where you're going to school," he told his son.

Moving on wouldn't be as easy this time. As much as he appreciated the support, he couldn't take his mind away from the game—and away from The Shot.

"If I would have had a phone number for a psychiatrist," Craig said, "I would have been like, 'I need to talk about this.'"

He couldn't stop thinking about how differently those three seconds could have turned out.

If only he had been sliding instead of running when Jordan made his move.

If only he and Nance had sandwiched him so he wouldn't have gotten such a good look.

If only his ankle hadn't been hurting so much.

If, if, if. Craig drove himself crazy with ifs.

Yet, of all the what-ifs that played out in his head, here's another he might not have considered: What if someone close to him—a teammate, a friend, a family member, anyone—had given him a chance to express his grief? Or what if he had initiated the conversation himself? He would, most likely, have been able to start coming to terms with The Shot sooner than he did. He didn't. He felt the need to appear to those close to him that he had, indeed, moved on, when he hadn't. That's what they did, and that's what they expected of him.

"I guess you got to move on to the next play," said Craig, sounding a lot like Calvin Schiraldi. "When I got to the pros, I learned that if you don't develop a thick skin, it can affect your performance in the next game."

Except there wouldn't be a next game, not for months. He could have allowed himself to feel the extent of his pain and been none the worse for it. Or, at the very least, talked about the loss with his teammates. The problem was his teammates weren't in the mood to talk about the loss, either. Not at the meal after the game or the next day. Maybe not ever.

"You come [to the arena], clean out your locker, maybe have your meeting with the coach, and then we all go our separate ways. Everyone was quiet, and I guess we just hadn't processed it yet that we were done."

Craig doesn't blame them one bit. Nor does he blame his wife for avoiding the subject.

"She was probably too worried about damaging my confidence," he supposed. "I think everybody was just afraid to bring it up."

So the summer came and went, including that vacation in Hawaii, and soon Craig and his teammates were back at camp, ready to be what Magic Johnson said they would be, "the team of the nineties."

Besides working on his shooting and conditioning, Craig spent a lot of time on improving his close-outs. He and Mark Price played one-on-one day after day. Not once did Craig have the ball.

"I took it upon myself after The Shot to become a better defender," he explained.

Ironically, the game against the Bulls gave him confidence. Sure, he wasn't successful during the most important possession, but he'd played extremely well until that point. Nothing, and no one—not even the immortal Jordan—could take that away from him.

"I felt like I belonged," he said.

Which makes you wonder why feeling better about his future in the NBA didn't make it easier for Craig to come to terms with The Shot. His explanation tells you why he was such a valuable player.

"In basketball, and with all team sports," Craig said, "the individual performance is not the top dog on the list. The winning is."

The best way he could redeem himself would be by stopping Jordan when it mattered, in the playoffs. No such luck. The Cavaliers, as a matter of fact, didn't get another crack at the Bulls in the postseason until 1992. Chicago won in six games and proceeded to sweep the Cavs in 1993 and 1994.

Magic had it wrong. The team of the nineties was the Chicago Bulls, with six titles in eight seasons, not the Cleveland Cavaliers. Heck, the Cavs never made it to the finals! Craig blames The Shot and the damage it caused.

"The Shot took the heart out of our team," he claims. "I don't think anyone, like Brad or Ron or Coach Wilkens or Wayne Embry, our general manager, would say that," but because of the way the Cavs lost, "it seems like we questioned ourselves. It seems like there was a curse or bad karma."

Through much of the nineties, while Craig was still playing, he didn't truly grasp what a huge deal The Shot would be in the years and decades to come. No one did. Only later did those three seconds take on the special meaning they have to this day, shown over and over on television, especially during the playoffs.

The reason is clear: Michael Jeffrey Jordan. Say, for example, Craig Hodges, the other starting guard on Chicago, had scored the game-winning bucket. Nothing against Hodges, but no way would it occupy such a rarified spot, but with MJ as the leading man, each moment he was involved with came to be perceived then, and in looking back, as being bigger and better.

We knew how great Michael Jordan was before The Shot. He'd led the league in scoring for three consecutive seasons. He did things with the basketball no one had done before, not even Dr. J or Pistol Pete Maravich. But Jordan had yet to win an NBA championship, and The Shot, the ultimate example of coming through under pressure, was when he started his climb to an even higher plateau, from great to legendary, which is how we think of him today. You don't get to such a status without a moment like that—many great scoring champions have been forgotten; legendary is forever.

So forever would be the attention Craig received for being on the other side of such a memorable moment.

At first, the attention bothered him. Craig was one of the best in the world in his profession for fourteen years, and all anybody wanted to talk about was what took place in the matter of three lousy seconds. Why didn't they ask him about any of the other hundreds of games he played in?

Come to think of it, how many of those people were aware that it was Craig who made the shot just before *The* Shot? That shot, *his* shot, spectacular in its own way, would become lost in history.

Some of those who asked questions assumed he had to be haunted by The Shot, such as the radio host in Chicago who, Craig recalled, interviewed him in May 1999, on the tenth anniversary.

"I can't believe I'm talking to you right now," the interviewer said. "I thought maybe you would have committed suicide."

Now you'd like to believe a radio host would never say anything so insensitive. We all know better. Obviously, this guy was going for a cheap laugh, except he didn't get one from Craig. The comment made him angry, something that's actually pretty hard to do.

"Why would you say that?" he responded. "It's a game."

What made Craig angry was that he was very familiar with the story of Donnie Moore, the former major league pitcher who did kill himself. He'd given up the home run to the Red Sox' Dave Henderson in 1986, which played a big part in the California Angels' losing the pennant. Craig and Moore had gone to the same high school in Lubbock.

By the time Craig spoke to the interviewer in Chicago, he had decided he wouldn't "drag that ball and chain" any longer. He'd own what he did—or didn't do—that day at the Richfield Coliseum. Craig told him, as he'd tell many others, how privileged he was to play a game for a living. He meant every word.

"Wouldn't you have wanted to be in my shoes?" he asked the guy.

Ask Craig where such a mature approach comes from, and there's no single reason. His attitude can be traced back, as these things often are, to how he was raised.

"My dad never said, 'Hey, you could have made a few more baskets,' or 'How come you didn't stop that guy on defense?' It was always 'It was fun watching you play.'" If there was criticism, it was always constructive.

Craig also learned a lot by watching the way his father cheered for his beloved Dallas Cowboys.

"When they lost their first Super Bowl [Super Bowl V, in 1971]," Craig recalled, "he was just happy that they were there."

He benefitted as well from being around coaches, in high school, college, and the pros, who urged their players to give everything they had but kept things in perspective.

"If I ever played for a coach who couldn't take a loss, I might have seen the way he handled it and handled it the same way," he admitted, "but I never had anyone like that in my life."

The biggest reason of all, no doubt, is the support Craig has received from his wife. Jani knew little about basketball when they met. She fell in love with who Craig was, not what he did. But ever since, she has guarded her husband's reputation as fiercely as Dennis Rodman guarded Larry Bird. Whenever a stranger hassles Craig about The Shot, she's right in his face.

"Do you even know what the score was?" she will say. "Do you know he played on a hurt ankle and they had to shoot him up with cortisone?"

Last year, in San Diego, a man tapped Craig on the shoulder: "Aren't you that guy who . . ."

Jani didn't wait for him to finish the sentence.

"Get over it!" she said.

These encounters, on occasion, can get a little dicey, as you might expect. Such as the time a man, who appeared to be drunk, approached Craig and his family when they were on vacation in Disneyland. Craig grabbed his kids and briskly walked away.

"I don't give that [kind of] person the time of day," he said.

Even so, as the years went on, Craig began to see his unique role in the history of the game as an opportunity.

"I used it in a positive way to help other people who may have had some failures in their lives and say, 'Hey, it's not that bad,'" he said.

No, it definitely is not. Being linked to Jordan has actually paid off financially—he received checks from Nike and Gatorade for commercials that aired the clip—and in other ways.

The first time he spoke with MJ about The Shot was during a charity golf tournament a year or two afterward. Craig was walking down one fairway, Jordan another.

"He had a big cigar and was in his group," Craig recalled. "He said, 'Hey, look, guys, that's him.'"

Craig didn't offer much of a response.

"I should have gone over and punched him," he joked.

Jordan has appeared in many photos with Craig and his family over the years. On those occasions, he never uttered a word about those fateful three seconds, except for one time.

Craig's teenage son, Austin, was attending MJ's basketball camp in Santa Barbara, California. On the last day, like the others in attendance, Austin waited patiently in line for a signed picture. The meeting would have lasted a matter of seconds—that is, until Jordan was informed of the youngster's last name.

"Are you Craig's son?" he asked.

For five minutes, as the other kids waited, Jordan told Austin about the game in Cleveland and about what a hard-nosed competitor his father was. No compliment Craig received could ever mean as much.

He cherished his connection to Jordan so much that he even felt a little slighted when MJ placed the jump shot he hit against Byron Russell of the Utah Jazz in the closing seconds of Game 6 of the 1998 NBA Finals as the most pivotal basket of his career.

"I was getting all [this attention]," Craig told Jordan. "Why did you move [The Shot] down below?"

"It was the last shot I made," he said, referring to his years with the Bulls.

After his own retirement in 1997, Craig settled down in Spokane, Washington, where his in-laws resided. He remained in the game he loved, working as a TV analyst on Gonzaga University's games, and, later, as an assistant coach at Eastern Washington.

The Shot, naturally, was never far away. Prior to every home game, two Gonzaga players—Jeremy Pargo, who was from the Chicago area, and Andrew Sorenson—reenacted the play during warm-ups. The first time he saw the two in action, let's just say Craig wasn't very thrilled. Once Pargo insisted that he wasn't poking fun at him, he came around, and the reenactment became a ritual.

Everything in his post-NBA life was going quite well. Until it wasn't.

His troubles began in 2010 when he underwent back surgery for the third time; the other operations were in 2003 and 2007. He couldn't move around for months. To deal with the pain, he started to take hydrocodone, an extremely powerful drug.

Before long, he was addicted, taking as many as fifteen pills a day, and he'd do whatever was necessary to get them. That included buying them off the streets, even from a woman he ran into at a convenience store whom he had met at an NA (Narcotics Anonymous) meeting. Craig, ironically, had gone there to speak out against drug abuse. Talk about being in denial.

"These people were addicted, not me," he assured himself. "I've got my nice home, I've got my nice truck, my kids have gone to college."

The pills weren't cheap, some costing him as much as $50 apiece.

He was soon spending at least $500 a day. *A day.* Every so often, he'd quit for two, maybe three days, but never for good.

The pills numbed a lot more than the pain in his back. They numbed another pain that had always been there, hidden from the ones he loved and from himself. The pain had to do with The Shot and the title he never won. Because Craig never discussed the damage The Shot inflicted, because he never truly grieved, the hurt stayed under the surface.

"Like a blister, it festered and festered," he said.

Oh, there were occasions the pain would emerge, before going under the surface again—mostly when Craig was reminded of what he had lost, or never had.

Such as when his former Cleveland teammate Steve Kerr, then with the Bulls, made the winning basket on a pass from Jordan in Game 6 of the 1997 NBA Finals against the Utah Jazz to secure another title. Craig used to hang around after practice to do some extra shooting with Kerr, who wasn't receiving much playing time. From his three years on the bench in Houston, Craig knew exactly what his friend was going through.

"Just hang in there," he told Kerr, "and be ready when your time comes."

Craig felt excitement for Kerr when he made the bucket in Game 6, but that wasn't the only thing he felt.

"I was angry," he said. "I was angry that it wasn't me."

If Jordan had missed The Shot, he went on, "I might have the three rings" instead of Kerr, who won his other two with the Bulls in 1996 and 1998. "I've played that scenario out a lot."

Taking those pills allowed Craig to check out. There's no other way to put it.

He didn't speak to his daughter, Erica, about any problems in her personal life, or speak to Austin, a guard at Whitworth University, about his problems on the court. The only problems that mattered were his own. He was aware of the pain he was causing his wife and children, but he wouldn't, or couldn't, kick the habit.

Jani knew about the pills. She found out from her brother, who managed the family's finances. Like most addicts, as smart as Craig was in finding places to hide the drugs, he was just as naive in thinking she would never discover the truth. Checks in the amounts he was writing couldn't be so easily covered up. Every time Jani confronted him, he changed the subject. He was good at that.

Except he couldn't run forever. On July 31, 2013, as the family was packing for a trip to Las Vegas, where they would be attending a black-tie affair for Jani's employer, they told Craig he would have to leave the pills at home or he couldn't go with them. To show how little they trusted him, his son took away the backpack Craig carried where he stashed the stuff.

He was outraged. High on hydrocodone and Ambien, another potent drug often used to treat the insomnia brought out by the hydrocodone, he collected his nicest suits and burned them in his driveway. The message he was sending was clear: *I have to wear a suit to the event in Las Vegas, but now I don't have a suit, so guess what? I'm not going!*

As the clothes burned, Austin grabbed Craig and wouldn't let go of him. He was afraid the next object his father would throw into the flames was himself.

The police arrived, and Craig was charged with domestic violence. When people heard that, they assumed he hit his wife, which wasn't true.

Jani and the kids went to Vegas. Craig went to jail. When he was let out the next day, he moved in with Jani's mother because of a restraining order that was in place until authorities could resolve the matter.

Starting the fire was the best thing that Craig could have done. By hitting rock bottom, he finally got the treatment he should have received long before. He enrolled at Gosnold, a rehab facility in the Cape Cod area. Here, at last, he could be a man seeking help instead of the man who let Michael Jordan score that basket.

Or so he assumed. He wasn't on the grounds more than a few minutes before he was recognized by the attendant who was escorting him around. The kid, eighteen or nineteen, wore a Boston Celtics jersey and had one topic on his mind.

"I'm here to get better," he told the attendant the next day. "I don't need to talk basketball."

He got better, eventually, and received a second chance with Jani and the kids, and, as far as second chances go, this one meant a lot more than the one he never got at guarding Jordan in a big game.

Don't get him wrong, Craig is still disappointed he let MJ score and that he didn't win a championship, and that disappointment will never go away, even if he's finally grieved the way he should have grieved long ago.

In 2015, when Kerr won another ring in his first year coaching the Golden State Warriors, who defeated Craig's former team, the Cavs, in the finals, he sorted through those same complicated emotions again.

"I rooted for Steve," he said, "but it hurt."

A part of Craig will always wonder what would have happened if MJ had missed. Maybe the Cavs would have won one championship after another, even beginning that season, and maybe Craig would have been a hero in Cleveland forever. And maybe, like Kerr, he would have gone on to be a coach or general manager in the league, or gotten a job with one of the networks.

The future he missed out on, when it comes down to it, is what has upset him the most, not any lingering sense that he may see himself as a loser. He doesn't.

Even his battle with the pills might have turned out differently.

"Maybe because I would have gotten a better broadcasting job," Craig said, "I wouldn't have taken a chance of ruining that through addiction."

Yet, despite The Shot, if he'd just dealt with his feelings at the time, or shortly afterward, there may have been no battle with the pills in the first place. He came to realize, many years later, that even if others believe you should move on quickly after experiencing a difficult loss, you are the only one who truly knows how much time you need to come to terms with it. Trying to rush the grieving process, or avoid it entirely, will do a lot more harm than good.

In any case, because Craig almost lost something far more important than that game or *any* game, he found the courage to face the truth. Luckily, before it was too late. And as ugly as it has been, he continues to face it.

One day at a time.

3

THE UPSET

Jimmy Orr was open. You couldn't believe how open he was.

All Earl Morrall, the NFL's Most Valuable Player that season, had to do was throw the ball anywhere close to Orr, who was around the 10-yard line, and the game would soon be tied, 7–7.

Not just any game, mind you. *The* game. Super Bowl III between the Baltimore Colts and New York Jets at the Orange Bowl in Miami. With just seconds remaining in the first half, the touchdown would be exactly what the Colts needed.

Up to that point, they hadn't looked anything like the team that had gone 15-1 to get here, the team many experts claimed was one of the best in pro football history, if not the best.

A missed field goal. An interception. Another missed field goal. Another interception. All those mistakes would be forgotten now. Once Orr caught the ball, the Colts would finally be on the board and have the momentum to begin the second half. From there, they would go on to show why they deserved to be such a heavy favorite.

Bill Curry, the Colts' center, remembers the play as if it took place last week, Orr wildly waving his arms to get Morrall's attention. Bill blocked his man, defensive tackle John Elliott, on the first part of the play, a handoff to running back Tom Matte, and then quickly went to protect Morrall from the Jets' pass rush after Matte tossed it back to him.

"It was a sweep to the right, a flea-flicker," Bill explained, "and every time we called that play—we probably called it three times that year—it was an easy touchdown. I glanced down the field and saw Jimmy near the end zone, no Jets within twenty-five yards. So I thought, 'Okay, touchdown.'"

Bill and the rest of the offensive line had done their job. The rush was not going to get to Morrall. He let the ball go. He didn't have a great arm, but he didn't need a great arm. Not on this play. Not as open as Orr was.

While all this was going on, Lou Michaels, the Colts' placekicker, watched intently from the sidelines. He couldn't believe how poorly his team was playing, and with him missing two field goals, from 27 and 46 yards, Lou was one of the reasons. Now, though, with Orr about to score, Lou would come in to kick the extra point, and, assuming he made it, he'd at least have something to feel good about going into the locker room.

The ball would land softly in Orr's sure hands, and the teams would be even again.

Lou, like so many others, couldn't believe what happened next.

"Sometimes, I wish I didn't play in that game," he said.

One thing the best athletes have in common is that they hate to lose. At anything. At any age.

Bill Curry was no different. In Little League, Bill cried every time his team didn't win. His dad tried to console him, just as his wife would years later, and assure him there were more important things than who wins or loses. Learning to be gracious in defeat, for example.

"You go shake those boys' hands," Willie Alexander Curry used to tell his son after a loss.

"I would not do it," Bill said. "I couldn't."

Baseball was his favorite sport growing up in College Park, Georgia, just outside Atlanta, his dream to pitch for the New York Yankees. But as a teenager, he drifted toward football. A full decade before playing in one of the two most seminal games in NFL history, Super Bowl III, Bill sat with his father to watch the other, the 1958

NFL title game between the Colts and New York Giants at Yankee Stadium.

Like so many others around the country, he was hooked by what came to be known as "The Greatest Game Ever Played," the Colts winning in overtime 23–17. Little could this boy of sixteen imagine that one day he would be snapping the ball to the hero of the game, Johnny Unitas.

"That would be like telling me that I was going to climb Mount Olympus and hang out with Zeus," Bill said.

In college, Bill played for Georgia Tech and the outstanding Coach Bobby Dodd. He learned a great deal from Coach Dodd about the game of football and about life. Dodd didn't have many rules, but the rules he did have were pretty straightforward. One was not to miss class.

So what did Bill do his second week on campus? You guessed it. His penalty for skipping chemistry was to run up and down the steps at Grant Field, the football stadium, for what seemed like a thousand times.

"It almost killed me," he said. "[After that], I decided chemistry at eight o'clock in the morning was okay."

The punishment served its purpose. Over four and a half years, Bill didn't skip another class, and by putting more energy into his academics, he became a better student than he believed was possible.

"If you sit in the front row and take notes," he said, "and read the notes before the quiz, remarkable things can happen."

As for remarkable things, nothing beats what happened to Bill after he graduated from Georgia Tech. He became a Green Bay Packer. The story is one he's told over and over, and one can see why.

In the twentieth, and final, round of the 1964 NFL Draft—keep in mind there were only fourteen teams in those days—Vince Lombardi, the Packers' legendary coach and general manager, was so burned out that he told Pat Peppler, the director of player personnel, to make the last selection on his own.

Lombardi was going to sleep. Safe to say that would never happen in today's NFL.

"Do something humorous," he suggested.

Peppler chose an unknown 212-pound center from Georgia Tech. If Bill, who was the second-to-last pick of the entire draft, made the squad, fine. If he was cut, no one would ever notice.

Bill made the squad, all right, and though he got a championship ring in each of his two years in Green Bay, he, like a lot of players, had some issues with Lombardi.

"He coached through fear," Bill told reporters a few days before the 1969 Super Bowl. "Most of the Packers were afraid of him, of his scoldings and his sarcasm . . . I got so bad I couldn't sleep, thinking about what kind of a mistake I'd make the next day. My wife, Caroline [sic], had to nurse me through the season and I mean that. At the end I was close to being a mental case."

The headline the next day in the New York Times said it all: "Lombardi Is Not Curry's Dish."

Uh-oh.

"I didn't know they would do that," he said, in looking back.

Yet, at the time, Bill meant every word. He was still furious with Lombardi for not protecting him in the 1967 NFL Expansion Draft; he was taken by the New Orleans Saints, who, in turn, traded him, before he ever took a snap for them, to the Colts.

"All I heard was You're not good enough to play for me anymore," Bill said. "He [Lombardi] didn't say anything like that, but I took it that way, which was a sign of gross immaturity."

In 1970, as Lombardi was dying of cancer, Bill visited him in the hospital. He realized how wrong he'd been about him.

Lou Michaels went through his share of losing long before his Colts took on the Jets. One brother died in World War II at Guadalcanal, another of black lung disease from working in the coal mines. Black lung disease also took his dad's life; he was in his fifties and had spent thirty-five years underground.

Then there was the day, his sister, who was twenty-one, complained of a headache. She had fallen off a horse, banging her head on a rock, but had neglected to tell anyone, even her mother.

"The whole week she was sick, and she laid on a couch," said

Lou, who was twelve at the time. "She thought it was just going to be a cold. She finally went to the doctor. He gave her some pills and said she'd be okay in the morning."

The next thing he knew, Lou saw two members of his family carrying chairs into the living room, where the funeral would be. His sister was dead from a brain hemorrhage.

Growing up in the small town of Swoyersville, Pennsylvania, next to Wilkes-Barre, Lou wasn't sure what he would do after he was finished with high school. He knew one thing he didn't want to do, and that was work in the mines.

Lou's only way out was football. He realized that the day his mother showed him the NFL contract his older brother Walt—Lou was one of eight kids—signed with the Cleveland Browns.

"Mom, he gets *paid* to play football?" Lou asked. "That's what I want to do."

Fortunately, he was very talented, just like Walt. He made varsity in high school as a freshman and was offered a scholarship by the University of Kentucky. An All-American two years in a row, he was an offensive and defensive lineman with the Wildcats, finishing fourth in the 1957 Heisman Trophy balloting his senior season. Lou was also the team's placekicker. The Los Angeles Rams made him the fourth overall pick in the NFL Draft.

Lou spent three years in Los Angeles and three with the Pittsburgh Steelers before he was traded to Baltimore. More like deported, the way he tells the story. He was hanging out in a bar on the last day of training camp when the girlfriend of one of his teammates walked over to his table. The woman was in tears, having found out the player she'd been dating was married and had been lying to her the whole time. She asked Lou to take her home.

"I can't give you a ride home," he told her.

The other player saw him and the woman talking, and according to Lou, lost control.

"He grabbed me by the neck and he was going to choke me," Lou claimed. "I had to fall on the floor to get away from him."

Lou got up and fought back, and, just like that, he was on his way to Baltimore. See ya. He was upset about how the trade went down, but he didn't remain upset for long, especially once he arrived at the Colts' practice facility. The first person he ran into was Unitas, who treated him as if they were old buddies.

"Say, Lou, park the car and have lunch with us," Unitas said. "Welcome aboard."

Bill and Lou were first teammates with the Colts in the 1967 season, and what a season it had the potential to be. The Colts had been an impressive team the past few years but couldn't come up with the big victory when they needed it most. Their problem was they weren't as impressive as Lombardi and the Packers. No one was. Sure enough, in 1967, the Packers captured the NFL title once again, beating the Cowboys, 21–17, in the famous "Ice Bowl" game in Green Bay. The Colts went 11-1-2, but, because of a worse point differential in their two head-to-head matchups with the Los Angeles Rams, finished second in their division and didn't make the playoffs.

But in 1968, there would be no Lombardi to get past. He'd quit his coaching job, and not a moment too soon. The Packers were getting old. The Colts, meanwhile, still had future Hall of Famers Unitas and tight end John Mackey, All-Pro flanker Willie Richardson on the opposite side of Jimmy Orr, and a hard-nosed running back in Tom Matte. This year, at last, would be their year.

Then it happened, the one thing the team couldn't afford. Unitas tore a muscle in his throwing arm in the final preseason game and would, as it turned out, be done, essentially, for the season. The Colts were done as well . . . at least they were supposed to be. You just don't replace a Johnny Unitas, who had won the league MVP award the previous year.

As Bill put it, in describing Unitas, "It's as if the Almighty sat down one day and said, 'You know what? I think I'll make a football player here.'"

Trying to *fill in* for Unitas would be Earl Morrall. Although Morrall had been a pretty decent starter on several different teams since the mid-fifties, he wasn't Johnny U. Morrall appeared a bit lost out there at first. In fact, in the opener against the San Francisco 49ers, he tried to call a play in the huddle but couldn't get the wording right. He took so long, Bill recalled, the Colts were penalized for delay of game.

Matte, who had played some at quarterback, most notably during a playoff game in 1965 when Unitas was injured, chimed in.

"Out left flank, right split," Matte barked.

"That's it," Morrall said. "Out left flank, right split."

Before too long, Morrall found the right words and the right rhythm. Baltimore won its first five games of the year, lost to the Cleveland Browns 30–20, and then won its final eight to finish a league-best 13-1. The key, besides Morrall, was the defense. During one seven-game stretch, the Colts allowed only 32 points!

In the first round of the playoffs, they got past the Vikings, 24–14, to set up a rematch with the Browns. Revenge was sweet indeed, the Colts destroying the Browns 34–0 in Cleveland to win their first NFL title since 1959. But there was still one more game to play, and, as the champions of the NFL, that would be against the champions of the American Football League, the New York Jets. They called it the Super Bowl.

The Packers represented the NFL in each of the first two years that the game was played and coasted to easy victories—35–10 over the Kansas City Chiefs in Super Bowl I and 33–14 over the Oakland Raiders in Super Bowl II. There was no reason to expect this year's matchup would be any closer. The NFL had been around since the twenties, the AFL since only 1960.

The oddsmakers listed the Colts as 18-point favorites. Some thought they might win by a lot more. That's how little respect there was for the AFL in those days, and for the Jets.

Yet, as game day approached, the Colts didn't take anything for granted. That's because Don Shula, their coach, wouldn't let them.

"We knew they wouldn't be there unless they were good enough to beat us," Bill said.

Shula made certain his team practiced as hard as ever. His practices were longer than Lombardi's, and they usually paid off.

"Shula could get more out of us than anyone I ever played for," Bill said.

The Colts were as sure of themselves as a group of professional athletes could possibly be. That included Lou, who had come to an agreement a few months earlier with Father Ed Sokolowski, the priest from his parish back home.

"Father, if you do me a favor, I'll do you a favor," Lou proposed. "If we go to the Super Bowl and win it, I will give you $5,000."

A victory, Lou knew, would be worth $15,000 to each player on the winning team. In return, the father would have to say a prayer for the Colts. He had himself a deal, Father Sokolowski told Lou.

The Jets were just as sure of themselves, especially one in particular, who didn't keep his opinion, or anything in his life, a secret. That was their popular quarterback, Joe Namath, and the guarantee he made that his Jets would pull off the huge upset is as memorable as the game itself. Players weren't very bold in 1969, unlike today. Now, good luck finding a big game in any sport in which there *isn't* someone who guarantees victory.

What isn't as well known is another comment Broadway Joe apparently made that week. As Lou recalled, he was in a Miami Beach bar having a drink with a teammate, offensive lineman Dan Sullivan, when Namath walked in.

Namath spotted Lou. Lou figured he was going to swing by just to say hello. The way Lou tells it, he said a lot more than that.

"We're going to kick the shit out of you," he boasted, according to Lou, "and I'm going to do it."

"But we got John Unitas," Lou said.

"He's over the hill," Namath responded.

Lou didn't back down. Lou Michaels never backed down.

"I would like to go outside," he told Namath.

"I ain't crazy," Namath said. "I'm not going outside with you for one minute."

Everybody simmered down after a while. Namath even paid for the drinks and drove Lou and Sullivan back to their hotel. Yet Lou could never get over how Namath behaved.

"He wasn't a nice guy at all," he said.

Finally, on the afternoon of January 12, it was time to stop talking and take the field for Super Bowl III.

Early on, the game went pretty much as everyone thought it would. Baltimore moved the ball. New York did not. The Colts were in position to strike first when Lou trotted onto the field. No gimme for sure, from 27 yards, but no sweat, either. Lou had been making kicks that long forever.

He didn't make this one. At least, that was the ruling on the field. Lou made his own ruling and always stuck to it.

"It went over the top of the right upright," he insisted. "It was good. I don't care what they say."

Good or not, it was the one kick, out of more than three hundred he attempted in his thirteen-year NFL career, that Lou agonized over more than any other. He blamed himself for the miss, not just the officials. He should never have left the slightest doubt.

"If we had gotten on top first," Lou said, "I don't know what would have happened. I kicked a field goal first in the Cleveland game, and we won 34–0."

Lou wasn't as hard on himself on the kick he missed later in the first half of the Super Bowl; 46 yards was a long way in 1969. Kickers have gotten a lot better since then.

"I just didn't hit it good," he said.

Nonetheless, with twenty-five seconds to go in the half, the Colts were still very much in the game, down just 7–0, and on the Jets' 41-yard line. That's when, instead of trying to get in position to try a field goal, they went for it all, calling the flea-flicker, and the Jets fell for it.

"*All alone is Jimmy Orr!*" NBC play-by-play announcer Curt Gowdy said, raising his voice in anticipation of the almost certain touchdown.

Everyone saw how open Orr was. And no one was surprised.

"He was not a big guy," Bill said. "He was not a fast guy. He just had such instincts and he had those phenomenal hands."

Everyone saw Orr . . . except the person who mattered most, Morrall. Instead, he threw the ball underneath, intended for running back Jerry Hill in the middle of the field. But defensive back Jim Hudson came up with the pick, securing the Jets' 7–0 lead going into halftime.

No one could understand how Morrall didn't see Orr. That

includes Orr, though, strangely enough, he didn't ask his quarterback about it for twenty years.

"Jimmy, I just didn't see you," Morrall supposedly told him.

Morrall didn't see Orr, as the story goes, because, with it being just before the intermission, the Colts' marching band had come onto the field and were gathering behind the end zone, its blue uniforms blending in with the blue worn by the Baltimore players.

The chance to tie the game was gone, and there wouldn't be another this good.

The Jets mixed passes from Namath with a running attack led by Matt Snell and Emerson Boozer to keep the Colts at bay in the third quarter. The Colts hadn't helped themselves by turning it over, yet again, on the very first play of the quarter, when Matte fumbled on his own 33. Jim Turner kicked a 32-yard field goal shortly afterward to make it 10–0.

"You can't play a good football team and turn the ball over a bunch of times and miss scoring opportunities again and again and again," Bill explained. "You are going to get beat. If you study NFL statistics over the last hundred years, you would find that set of variables would hold up almost 100 percent of the time."

Nonetheless, Bill never stopped believing.

"Other people had us down in the fourth quarter," he said, "but they couldn't beat us. We always came back. I just expected we would find some crazy way that we would get the ball and win. That was part of our magic because we all felt that way."

To a point. Late in the game, the Jets leading 16–7, it was becoming obvious the magic had run out.

Even bringing in Unitas for Morrall late in the third quarter didn't make a difference. Some said Shula should have brought him in sooner. He's Johnny Unitas, for goodness' sake. Others said Unitas was still not close to 100 percent and that Morrall had earned the right to see this thing through to the end.

Lou wasn't thinking about any of that as the final minutes ticked off.

"What am I going to tell the people of Swoyersville?" he asked Unitas.

"Tell them that if I'd had three more minutes, I would have won the game for us," said Unitas, who led the Colts to their only score.

Soon it was official. The New York Jets were the Super Bowl champs, in one of the biggest upsets in sports history. Joe Namath did exactly what he told Lou he would do. He kicked the you-know-what out of the Baltimore Colts.

Bill didn't fully recognize what the defeat meant at the time. He was too busy trying to get over the shock.

"Like a death in the family," he put it. Besides, he elaborated, "we wouldn't have been interested in [the game's] historical significance. We just knew we cost ourselves a chance to be remembered as one of the greatest teams of all time. We were 26-2-2 [in 1967 and 1968] going into Super Bowl III. What is remembered about us? One thing: *They're losers.* That's all."

But if history wasn't on his mind that day, history certainly made it tougher on Bill, and his teammates, as the years went on. Because of what the game came to signify—a team representing the upstart AFL stunning a team from the dominant NFL—it was guaranteed to become a Super Bowl no one would ever forget.

"It's thrown in our face over and over and over again," Bill pointed out. "Instead of Unitas throwing to [wide receiver] Raymond Berry in the 1958 game, you have Joe Willie [Namath] running off the field with his number one signal up above him. We're reminded we failed, and that's not a good feeling. There are historians who suggest that was the key game for the NFL to evolve the way it did. I don't know if that's true or not. It's been so difficult for me to think about that game, for obvious reasons."

After the game, Bill and other players went to a party hosted by the team's owner, Carroll Rosenbloom, at a home he owned in the Miami area. Some party.

"It was like a wake," Bill said. "Mr. Rosenbloom was standing out there with Burt Lancaster, the actor. So I waited respectfully. I waited till that broke up and I asked Mr. Rosenbloom if I could speak to him. I don't know what possessed me to do that, but I said, 'I want to tell you one thing. We will come back here and it won't be long and we will win, I promise you.'"

Lou didn't go to the party. He caught the first flight he could back to Baltimore.

"I didn't feel like seeing anyone," he said.

No chance, not in a place like Swoyersville, where he soon ran into Father Sokolowski. The father might have been as upset about the Super Bowl loss as Lou was. Word was, according to Lou, the father canceled vespers the Sunday evening after the game.

"Father, I tried," Lou assured him. "We just couldn't do it. I wanted to give you that money so bad."

Lou felt so horrible about letting his parish down he gave the priest a thousand dollars. Better than nothing.

Bill couldn't escape, either. He attended a banquet several months after the game, at which he and defensive end Willie Davis, his teammate in Green Bay, were the co-speakers. After they wrapped up their remarks, Davis turned to Bill, seated next to him on the dais, and, loudly enough for everyone to hear, blurted out: "I'd just like to ask Bill Curry what happened."

Davis was speaking for a lot of NFL players who couldn't believe the invincible Colts had lost to a team from the AFL. The AFL! Bill was taken aback. He had such tremendous respect for Davis. Somehow he quickly regrouped.

"I'd like you to explain to everyone," Bill countered, "what happened when we came to Green Bay this year and kicked your ass." The Colts had won 16–3.

Davis and the others got over the shame of Super Bowl III; in 1970, the AFL merged with the NFL. The same can't be said for the Colts players. Whenever they got together, they undoubtedly talked about their families, their health, and the state of the game that has given them more than they could have ever imagined. Miami didn't come up.

"I think it's too sore to this day, I really do," Bill said.

A perfect example was when the subject was mentioned at a cocktail party in Baltimore sometime after the loss. A fan, Bill recalled, said something to the effect of: How much did you guys get for throwing that game?

"Matte was going to throw him out the window," Bill said. "I had to restrain him."

Besides, the ex-Colts don't have a chance to get together very often. You see, the Colts not only lost the game, they have since lost their identity. A year after the Super Bowl, Shula left to become head coach of the Miami Dolphins. In 1972, Rosenbloom traded—yes, traded—the Colts to Robert Irsay in return for the Los Angeles Rams. A decade later, Irsay moved the team in the middle of the night to Indianapolis.

The 1968 Baltimore Colts became prodigal sons without a home. Indianapolis doesn't honor them, nor does the city of Baltimore, which today embraces the Ravens. Having no place of their own has made it tougher for the Colts of the late sixties to get over their darkest moment.

"It's as if we never played," Bill pointed out. "I played only two years for the Green Bay Packers, but we get invited back all the time. I will have gone to three Packers games this year. Not only are we not invited back to Baltimore Colts games, there are no Baltimore Colts. It's like [the film] *Brigadoon*. We disappeared."

You could tell how much that hurt them when players showed up for Unitas's funeral in 2002 and Mackey's in 2011.

"We grieved, and not just the loss of our teammates," Bill said, "but also the loss of all that stuff that old performers love to do, which is to celebrate those great accomplishments."

Bill, as it turned out, knew what he was talking about when he made that promise to Carroll Rosenbloom. Two years after losing to the Jets, the Colts defeated the Dallas Cowboys in Super Bowl V, 16–13, on a last-second 32-yard field goal by rookie kicker Jim O'Brien. One might assume that redemption, coming so soon and in dramatic fashion against a marquee team such as the Cowboys, would go a long way toward making up for the loss in 1969.

That wasn't the case. To Bill, Super Bowl V was about much more than winning a football game; it was about playing the *kind* of football game he believed the Colts should have played against the Jets, but they again failed to perform well, at least on offense, against the Cowboys. Baltimore turned the ball over seven times. Unlike Super Bowl III, Super Bowl V is one few people remember.

"All of it seems like a bad dream," he said, "to have had the most significant loss in the history of the world, in the minds of the so-called experts, and then go back down there with a great chance to put on an outstanding performance and fall on our face again. I've never read histories of the Bolshoi, but I'd think Nureyev or Baryshnikov, if the troupe doesn't have a good performance, they'd remember that."

For Bill Curry, there were many other losses after the one to the Jets. That's what happens when you become a coach, which he was for twenty years on the college level. He did all his coaching in the South—at Georgia Tech, Alabama, Kentucky, and Georgia State. In only seven of those twenty years did he win more games than he lost.

Every defeat affected him, some more than others. He wasn't much different from the boy who cried after every loss in Little League.

"I think there's a mental illness and I have it," Bill explained. "If you have this affliction, as you mourn a loss, you change the mood for the people around you."

In his situation, those most affected were his wife, Carolyn, and their two children. Carolyn kept assuring him he would win the next one. Perhaps. But he couldn't stop thinking about the *last* one and what could have been done to prevent it. Or what others should have done.

"I'd sit there, moping, thinking it's not my fault," he said, "that it was the fault of our defensive back who fell down on the deep ball or the fault of the punter."

Whoever was at fault, Carolyn got so frustrated with the way he dealt with losing that she left the house at times to go on errands just to get away from him. His son, William Jr., didn't tell his father how it felt to be around him after losses until a few years ago.

"Dad, we knew it was okay to be happy [only] if your team won the previous week," he said.

Bill had no idea what his son was going through. That's how much he was focused on winning. He said he would make it up to him.

"The last three years have been a real awakening," he said. "I'm just thrilled that we were not so alienated that I didn't have a chance."

About twenty-five years ago, Bill went to see the minister at his church, who was also a psychologist, and not one to use profanity. The minister gave him some simple advice: "Hell, Bill, it's just a game," he told him. "Don't you get it?"

Boy, did he try to believe that. He just couldn't. Bill told his players that if they competed as hard as they could, the final score didn't matter. Only the final score did matter. It mattered a great deal.

In 1987, Bill accepted an offer to coach at the University of Alabama, the home of the legendary Paul "Bear" Bryant. Alabama, you would think, would be the *last* place on Earth someone like Bill Curry should coach. A place where no loss was accepted—by the students, the alumni, the whole state, for heaven's sake. Moral victories? Somewhere else, maybe. Not in Tuscaloosa.

"Those of us who have the addiction," he explained, "are drawn to the most competitive circumstances."

His record, 26-10, would have been good enough at most schools. It wasn't close to being good enough at Alabama. After his quarterback failed to complete a single pass in a 1988 loss to the University of Mississippi, someone threw a brick through Bill's office window. At least he hadn't lost his sense of humor.

"If we had thrown the ball as well as the guy with the brick, we would have won the game," he joked.

What was no laughing matter was that he received death threats his whole time on campus. There was, however, one Alabama man who was on his side from the start. Before he came to the Jets, Joe Namath had been a star at 'Bama in the early sixties. How ironic that the person who played such a prominent role in the most painful loss in Bill's NFL career became one of his key supporters.

"He came to our house for dinner and stayed for about four hours," he recalled. "Carolyn said, 'That's the biggest mistake I ever made.' She had thought he was a playboy."

Yet even Namath couldn't save him, as Bill resigned to take over at the University of Kentucky. His crime: failing to beat the Crimson Tide's most hated rival, Auburn, even once in his three seasons as head coach. Alabama's best chance came in 1989, his final year. The Tide was 10-0 heading into the game and ranked no. 2 in the country. Auburn won 30–20. Suddenly, the first 10 wins meant nothing compared to the 1 loss.

"You know what the deal is if you go to Alabama," he said, "and you lose to Auburn three years in a row."

Being around such a rabid fan base made Bill see, more vividly than ever, his own obsession to win. You know how powerful that obsession can be when somebody as self-aware as he is felt there was nothing he could do to stop it.

But as the years went on, what his father told him finally started to sink in: there really are things more important in sports than winning. Almost every day, one of his former players calls, often thanking him for the values he taught, and how they are trying to pass on the same values to their children. The calls mean a lot to Bill. They remind him of the impact he has had on many lives and still does.

Yet, as rewarding as the calls may be, they still can never make up entirely for the victories that didn't come, especially the victory that didn't come on a Sunday afternoon in January 1969. Seeing any moment from that game brings it all back.

"The same chilling feeling comes over me and it's not something I've chosen," he said. "It's just the way I'm built."

Lou derived even less satisfaction than Bill did from the Colts' Super Bowl title in 1971. Cut by the team before the 1970 season, he watched the game in his basement with friends. He later reflected on how different his life would have been if he, not O'Brien, had made the winning field goal.

"Everyone would know I won a Super Bowl," he said.

There is more to reflect on, such as how Lou would have coped with the loss over the years if he hadn't stayed in Swoyersville, if he'd lived in a place where people didn't remind him constantly of what he *failed* to accomplish instead of all the impressive things—he played in the National Football League, for heaven's sake—he did achieve.

The fact that his hometown was even on his mind in the last few minutes of the Super Bowl proved how daunting the challenge in front of him would be. No wonder he made the mistake of allowing others to see how deeply any references to the loss got to him. Once they saw how vulnerable he was, he didn't stand a chance.

Super Bowl week every year was the worst. He would be having coffee at a gas station with several friends when one of them, trying to be a wise guy, would joke, "Hey, Lou, I watched Super Bowl III again . . . and you lost again." Another would say, "Lou, I believe they're going to show Super Bowl III tomorrow. Will you tell me what time it's coming on and call me?"

The one person who didn't give him any grief, and had every right to, was his brother Walt. By the time Lou made it to the Super Bowl, Walt was an assistant coach for, of all teams, the Jets. Meaning that not only was he on the opposite sideline during Super Bowl III, but he would forever be on the opposite side of history.

Wait, there was that one time Walt gave Lou a little dig. Lou was wearing the ring he received for being a member of the College Football Hall of Fame. A stranger approached.

"Lou, is that your Super Bowl ring?" the person asked.

Walt, who was standing a few feet away, couldn't resist. He showed the fan the ring on his hand.

"No, this one is!" Walt said.

Shouldn't it be satisfying enough, Lou was asked, that he played in a Super Bowl? Most players never get that chance.

Not really. You get that far, Lou said, you gotta win it.

"What does everybody say to get ready for the season?" he said. "Win the big one. Win the Super Bowl. If you don't win it, what are you? You're a loser."

And shouldn't Lou, after the losses he experienced growing up, recognize how meaningless it was, by comparison, to lose a game, even a game as big as the Super Bowl?

Sure he did. He never suggested that losing to the Jets was worse than losing a brother or a sister, and he would have happily traded seven Super Bowls for more time with the loved ones who left him so soon. Only there was nothing he could have done about black lung disease or the Japanese at Guadalcanal or a sister falling off a horse.

There was plenty, on the other hand, that he could have done in the Super Bowl. He could have made the field goal from 27 yards and not left it up to the officials. Lou was right. Who knows how differently the game may have unfolded if the Colts had scored first?

Lou, unfortunately, never got a chance to redeem himself. Unlike Calvin Schiraldi and Craig Ehlo, who, if long delayed, eventually realized how they'd failed to come to terms with their losses, he didn't reach that point. There was no larger lesson he learned about losing. But try not to judge him too harshly. Lou worked hard for many years to become the best football player he could possibly be, and in doing so, he avoided a future he dreaded, a future in the mines. That makes him a winner, no matter what happened in Super Bowl III.

On January 19, 2016, Lou Michaels passed away from cancer at his home in Swoyersville. He was remembered for being a wonderful man. Lou wouldn't be surprised one bit if he knew that the game that haunted him for years would follow him to his grave: "Lou Michaels, All-Purpose Player, Dies at 80; Missed Kicks in '69 Super Bowl," read the headline in the *New York Times* obituary.

Some losses you can never escape.

4

RISKY BUSINESS

FEBRUARY 17, 2006

Every four years, whenever the Winter Olympics came around and people paid more attention to snowboard cross, something went wrong for Lindsey Jacobellis. Terribly wrong.

Start with the first—and worst—experience, the 2006 Games in the city of Turin, in northern Italy. It was the first time the Games included her sport, which requires great skill and daring. Not only do you have to go fast on your board and pull off high, precise jumps, but you also must avoid the obstacles spread out all over the course.

At the time, Lindsey was, without question, the top woman on the planet in snowboard cross, and because she'd won every other big event—X Games, World Cups, and so on—the previous year or two, it was a foregone conclusion, to the experts, she would win the biggest event of all. That was the problem. The press, you see, didn't say she might win the gold. The press said she *would* win. Having to live up to such billing, she grew so anxious in the days before the competition she started to have another thought in mind. She would leave the sport for good after she got her medal.

"I'll move out to California and make a bunch of money," she told herself. "I'm not going to have to deal with the media."

Imagine that, retiring. At the ripe old age of twenty! If that doesn't tell you how much the pressure was getting to her, nothing will.

"It was built up so much in my mind," Lindsey recalled. If not for those expectations, "I would have been there as a young athlete, seeing how amazing this is and what a wonderful opportunity, instead of going there and being like, 'I have to perform. The world is looking to me.'"

Even so, when the race finally got under way, Lindsey did what she did best. She performed. Like no one else in her sport. So well, as a matter of fact, that she found herself 50 or so meters in front of her closest pursuer, Tanja Frieden of Switzerland, with about 100 meters to go. The experts had known what they were talking about after all. The gold *was* a foregone conclusion. She'd gotten herself all worked up for nothing.

With such a huge lead, the last stretch was, obviously, not the time to do anything fancy. Just finish. Just finish, Lindsey, and walk to the podium to receive your medal and soak it all in during the national anthem. Even shed a few tears, if you must. Makes for great television. Then go speak to the media and thank your parents and coaches and anyone else along the way who helped make your dreams come true.

Neither Frieden nor the other two women in the event, to be honest, had a prayer of catching her.

"I remember starting to come down to the finish," Lindsey said. "'Oh my God, I'm in the lead. I'm going to do this.'"

So then what did Lindsey do? She did something fancy, that's what. She tried what in snowboarding is called a "method grab."

"You can grab your snowboard in a couple of different places," she explained, "and they all have names." For the method grab, you "grab with your lead hand close to the nose of your board. It's a more difficult grab, so it can throw you off balance more easily."

As she knows better than anyone. Lindsey landed on the heel edge of her board and fell. There went any chance for the gold. She got up to finish the race and somehow took home the silver, although that wasn't what anyone would remember then or for years to come. They would remember her as the woman who threw away the gold.

To no one's surprise, Lindsey received a lot of criticism for what she pulled. The word often used to describe her most unexpected maneuver in the air was "showboat," and there was no denying the fact that she took a chance she didn't need to take. She would be the first to admit it.

For what precisely, if one might inquire?

For fun, that's what. That's what she said shortly after the race was over. Up to that stage of the proceedings, she hadn't been having enough fun, simple as that.

"How stupid could she be?" people asked. Still, remember, she was just twenty years old, and the very essence of snowboarding is to entertain, to do things in the air and on the snow you don't see in other sports. So maybe there's a right time and a wrong time to take risks, but if you take no risks, you don't have much of a sport.

"You've got people just tearing you apart," Lindsey said. "'You were showing off. What were you doing?' I'm like, 'I don't know. I was having fun.'"

Even more hurtful to her was being told she had let her country down, which was outrageous, no doubt, but Lindsey, in the state she was, believed it.

"What would you think in hearing that if you were twenty years old?" she said. "Would you take that a little bit more to heart?"

She felt so bad that the silver medal didn't mean anything to her.

"I never even looked at it for probably five years," she admitted. "I had no clue where it was."

Lindsey's parents, it turned out, knew exactly where the medal was, in their house in Vermont, and they were so proud of her that they framed it.

"So many people never even go to the Olympics, never even have a dream like that," they told her. Their encouragement did little good.

"I hear what you're saying," Lindsey responded. "I don't like hearing it. Let's move on."

Lindsey was so eager to get past Turin that, similar to Craig Ehlo, she not only didn't truly grieve in those early weeks afterward, but she allowed the people around her, except for her parents, to believe she had moved on. She wouldn't really grieve for years, as Craig didn't.

"I put off this persona that I was fine, that [the method grab] was just a mistake, and that it wasn't affecting me poorly. And it was," she said. "I fooled a lot of people for a really long time."

That wasn't all. One of the companies that was sponsoring her, get this, told Lindsey it was so ashamed of how she performed in Turin that it wouldn't pay her the Olympic bonus she was expecting to receive, and, what's more, it no longer wanted her to represent its products. The move cost her about $50,000. And you won't believe how she received the news: in an e-mail. How classy.

"That's like getting a breakup message through a text message," she said. Lindsey and her family looked into taking legal action against the company but felt it would take more time and money than it was probably worth.

As the months dragged on, she found it was nearly impossible not to think about Turin, though thinking wasn't the same as grieving. Trying to have fun, she came to realize, wasn't the only explanation for why she went with the method grab.

"I just had that moment where I kind of checked out," she admitted, "and I'm very present and aware in everything that I'm doing, whether it is racing or in my daily life."

Checked out? Whatever for?

"I'm not sure," Lindsey answered. "I was so young that maybe that was how I was handling all of the stress that was being put on me."

She had at least one thing going for her. Being so young, she knew there would be more opportunities to win the gold, a lot more. Over the next two years, Lindsey won a ton of races, just as she had won a ton of races before the Games. She was still the best female snowboarder out there.

Yet she could never win, even when she did.

Any time she won, someone in the media would tell her, "Oh, but you still don't have your Olympic [gold medal]."

"I was like, 'I just won. When is it ever going to be good enough for you?'" Lindsey said, adding, "I expected myself to win every time and maybe that would make me feel better, but it still never did. So I didn't race a lot when I was younger because it was too much of a build every time."

And that was when she won. When she lost, she felt even worse.

"I would be so hard on myself," she recalled. "I'd be so drained that I failed that it would take so much out of me that I'd be susceptible to getting sick."

Not until February 2010, at the Winter Games in Vancouver, did Lindsey get her chance to redeem herself for the blunder in Turin. Which explains why she was so motivated—if, perhaps, for the wrong reasons.

"I wanted to win to be able to stuff it in everyone's faces that said negative things about me," she said.

That's Lindsey for you—honest almost to a fault.

Too bad the day of the snowboard cross semifinals—only the top four racers advanced to the final—wasn't her kind of day. It was rainy and foggy.

Worse yet, the rain and fog meant a delay of a few hours. Athletes hate delays. They pace themselves for the moment they have to be at their best. Lindsey was no exception.

"You get lethargic and lose fire," she explained, "like the horse that is waiting to go in the starting gate and they're all freaking out, and then the gate opens and they go mad after the dash. If they stay in there for a while, it's really agitating to them."

Once the conditions improved, the race finally got under way. She was ready to take another step toward earning the medal she should have earned four years earlier.

She took another step, all right. A step backward.

On her first jump during one of the heats, Lindsey collided in the air with another racer, which knocked her off balance. Unprepared for the next turn, she hit a race gate and was automatically disqualified.

"I just wasn't able to hold the turn," she said.

What happened this time was significantly different than in 2006.

"That [the collision] was out of my control," Lindsey said. "That was not something I did wrong, and it was just the luck of racing."

Whoever was to blame, the truth was an easy one for the reporters to tell and a hard one for her to accept: Lindsey Jacobellis, the biggest star in the sport, had failed yet again on the stage that mattered the most, and she would now have to wait another four years—four years that must have felt like forty.

"They were guaranteeing themselves a story again: 'She wins in her redemption' or 'She doesn't win, oh God, again,'" Lindsey said.

While she waited for 2014, there was little to do except try to win every race she could. She won her share, as usual. Only, as was the case before, she didn't enjoy the victories as much as she thought she should.

"I won almost as a relief," she explained, "and then, it was 'Oh God, my next race is next week, I got to win that one.' There was never any satisfaction."

Then came the 2012 Winter X Games in Aspen, Colorado. She was going for her eighth X Games championship. During a practice session, she tore her ACL and meniscus in her left knee. Lindsey knew how bad the injury was right away.

"I went too high and far, and landed way too far down the landing," she said. "I heard the knee snap on impact."

Her season was over. She hoped her career wasn't as well.

Losing wasn't an option for Lindsey from the beginning. When she was eight or nine years old, her mom took away the Monopoly board. She and her brother, Ben, five years older, had taken their attempts to bankrupt the other a little too far.

"It's so unfair," she complained after landing on Park Place, the second most lucrative property on the board, which Ben owned. "You always get it."

Growing up in Roxbury, Connecticut, the two lived a long way from their friends.

"We had to play with each other," Lindsey said, "and he made me do all sorts of athletics."

Whatever the sport was, Lindsey wanted so much to beat Ben and to be, she said, "cool in his eyes." But Ben won most of the time, which irritated Lindsey to no end. Until, many years later, while they were surfing, it finally hit her: she didn't have to try as hard any longer. Their age difference and the fact that he was stronger would always give him an edge.

"Living was kind of easier after that," she said.

When Lindsey was ten, her brother introduced her to snowboarding. She has been in love with the sport ever since. At first, her parents drove her and Ben to Stratton Mountain in Vermont each weekend. Three years later, they moved the whole family there for good. Ben was a freshman at the University of Vermont while Lindsey went to a private school. Before long, she won a slew of titles, and at age fifteen, she was invited to compete in the X Games, the biggest stage at the time for her growing sport.

Her parents saw no limit to what she could achieve in snowboarding.

"You can be done after high school," they said, "but what if it's made an Olympic sport? We always figured you were going to go to the Olympics for something. This could be it. Wouldn't it be amazing?"

Sure would. Lindsey was an enthusiastic supporter of the Olympics from the start, one of her favorite athletes being Picabo Street, the skier who won a gold medal at the 1998 Games in Japan.

"You could go to the Olympics and be just like her," her mother said.

From the moment she hurt her knee, Lindsey approached her rehab, in Park City, Utah, the same way she approached her racing. Losing wasn't an option. Only her will to succeed wouldn't be enough. The graft, where a ligament from her hamstring was taken to replace the ACL, didn't work. It was a tough blow. She had been in rehab for ten months and was about to start preparing for the 2013 season.

"You're in the three percent in which we don't understand why the graft failed," the doctor told her. "There was no reason. You didn't injure it. You didn't do anything."

Lindsey had a choice: live with the knee at 90 percent or go under the knife once more. Some choice.

"Are you kidding me?" she said. "I have to do this again?"

She had the surgery the following day. Trying to beat the best in the world with a knee that was 100 percent was tough enough. One thing was certain: she wouldn't give up.

"It's not like me to quit something," Lindsey said. "I will exhaust all options before. I wanted to see if I could get to where I was again, to see it to the end."

At least she wouldn't have to be on crutches as long the second time. She was worried, though.

"Oh my God," she wondered, "is it going to feel the same way when I race? Am I going to be scared? Is my knee going to fail on me? I don't know if I'll feel like me racing again."

There was only one way to find out. She had to get back on the snow. In June 2013, Lindsey chose Mount Hood in Oregon for the crucial test.

"I got out to camp probably a week earlier [than most of her teammates] to see where I was at," she recalled. "I was riding with a brace and just kind of taking my time, taking a few runs, and then the next week, I started to get that peppy liveliness back on the course and the coaches noticed it."

If anything, the injury, and eighteen months off the snow, might have been the best thing for her. Soon after getting back on the slopes, she felt something she hadn't felt in a long time.

"I started noticing that I was having fun doing what I was doing in making a living," she explained. "I always think back. Was it fun and I didn't realize it when I was younger? Why was it feeling like such a job when I was seventeen to twenty-five, and it's not a job now?"

Perhaps that's because Lindsey didn't know how fortunate she was until her career was almost taken away from her. While in rehab, she met with a therapist. She had postponed her grief about 2006 long enough. The therapist gave her excellent advice: every day, remind yourself of three things you're grateful for and make sure your goals are attainable. For Lindsey, that meant she could no longer expect to win every race. That was new for her.

"I *want* to win every time," she explained, "but it's okay if it doesn't happen. Because you make a mistake and you fall, and it just wasn't your day. And then the days I would win, I would really stay in that moment."

This realization was all well and good, but the true test came in 2014 at the Winter Games in Sochi, Russia. Because that's when the reporters, as one would expect, asked her over and over about

2006, and about 2010 as well. She could let their questions get to her or not.

Not. This time, as Lindsey prepared for her race, she wasn't thinking about redemption and stuffing it in everyone's faces. She wanted to win for the right reasons.

"Going up in the chair lift, I was with my coach," she said, "and I was like, 'You know, I can win today. But it could also not happen, and I'm okay with that.' It does not define me as an athlete."

She'd have to be okay with it. Lindsey didn't "check out" like she did in 2006 or collide with another racer like in 2010. Still, the script was too familiar. She fell in the semifinal heat, on one of her last turns. No gold yet again.

"It was a timing issue," Lindsey said. "My timing was off and things did not align. I felt like I was totally present in the moment, but I wasn't used to racing in mashed-potato-y snow. I was wearing a sports bra and my jersey and a bib. Normally we are bundled and I'm not having to race in that kind of heat. The snow was changing and I just got thrown really funky. I couldn't hold how I landed."

The time away from the sport because of the knee injury also had a negative effect.

"I realized that maybe I need to change my equipment up a little bit," Lindsey said. "I need to have a different length, so I can handle this kind of maneuverability on the snow if I land funny. I have always been racing on these shorter boards, [but] the courses have changed."

In any case, Lindsey took the setback much better than she did her two prior Olympic disappointments. She'd become, one might suggest, a tad philosophical about her pursuit.

"With the Olympics, the stars have to be aligned for you," she said. "The weather, the board, all your equipment has to be working. You have to be feeling good, other people have to be off. There are so many variables you can't control."

Another factor out of her control is Father Time. If she qualifies for the U.S. team, and that's never a guarantee, Lindsey will be thirty-two during the 2018 Games in PyeongChang, South Korea. That might not seem especially old, but she's been racing for well over a decade now and will have to beat women who are younger and just as motivated. Lindsey won't be able to win on speed alone anymore.

"It used to be I went out on the start and girls couldn't pass me, but now I'm definitely not winning the starts at all, and I'm relying on my skill and experience to help me make decisions down the course," she said. "I rarely have big leads anymore unless someone crashes and creates a big pileup and only one person makes it through."

Maybe, but make no mistake about it: that skill and experience can still pay off big time.

Take the X Games in January 2016, when she won her tenth gold medal with a time of 1:00.957, edging Eva Samková of the Czech Republic, who had won the gold in Sochi.

"That was pretty amazing and had some good poetry to it," she said. "I won, basically, by the same margin I won my first X Games medal in 2003."

And don't think she won't take a chance if she spots an opening. Okay, perhaps she won't go for another method grab if she has a sizable lead, but the lesson of 2006 wasn't that she needed to be more cautious on the slopes.

"I will always try to go for the pass," she said. "I'd rather try and fail, knowing that I went for it," than ride behind another racer "when I didn't see a great opportunity or sure thing to pass so I got second or third. That's always how I've raced, and I've noticed that's how I go through life. That's how I engage with people. A lot of people tell me I'm intense, but it's who I am."

Intense, no doubt, but also supportive of her fellow competitors. She loves how her sport has grown over the years, and the role she has played pleases her as much as anything she's accomplished on her own.

"All the women have raised their level of competition, and I know I was the reason for that," she said. "We've got ten girls who are capable of winning, and it just comes down to the day, the conditions."

Not having the gold, as a matter of fact, doesn't bother her as it did before.

"In a very small place," she said, in describing where, in her mind, any thoughts about past Olympic failures reside.

Whenever Lindsey sees women in her sport agonize over a loss, she wants them to understand it's not the end of the world. She knows as well as anyone. She used to feel the same way, yet life went on.

"I have been seeing a lot of girls on tour getting upset with certain races," she said. "I look back, and I'm like, 'Am I being too hard on them, saying they shouldn't get upset?' Because I was upset." She tells them, "It's not a big deal; it's just a race. You got through the season without any major injuries. Look at the positive."

If she's fortunate to have another go at it, in South Korea, Lindsey is determined to approach the experience in a whole different way.

"You know what, I'm just going to try to enjoy this," Lindsey said. "Because every other Olympics I've never enjoyed. And it's not going to be about winning. I'll have qualified for another Olympics. How many people get to do that? Revel in that moment."

Get her going on the subject for a while, and she'll tell you her dream scenario, and it's not what you imagined it would be. Oh, she wins the gold; that part of the dream is predictable. It's what she does *after* she wins the gold.

"If I could orchestrate a moment in the Olympics," Lindsey said, "if they're going to put on the gold—'No, no, no, actually, just hold that in your pocket—I am going to put on my silver instead.' I persevered through all of that. It shaped me as an individual. I didn't quit. I still loved what I was doing, and I was still pushing myself to achieve."

Lindsey might have never reached this level of understanding if not for the knee she tore in Colorado. Unable to race, she had time to reflect, to discover what she'd lost for all those years, and it was a lot more than a gold medal. She had lost the capacity to savor what she'd achieved and to have fun.

Now thirty years old and without the expectations of others, or her own, weighing heavily on her in every event, she can compete with a certain peace of mind she didn't enjoy before. Not only is Lindsey not expecting to win, she's also not afraid to lose. From here on, she'll accept whatever awaits her. She gets more out of the wins than she used to and isn't devastated anymore by the losses.

Lindsey is fortunate. Many athletes—Craig Ehlo and Calvin

Schiraldi are prime examples—don't begin to confront their losses until long after their playing days are over. If only they could have learned those lessons a lot sooner, they could have avoided so much pain later on. But unlike those others, her story is still being written. The fact that she's learned her lessons puts her in a better spot to deal with the challenges ahead.

Of course, she's not there yet. You'd like to believe that, as she claims, she's moved on from those earlier setbacks to see her career, and herself, in a different light. Perhaps she has. She certainly handled the loss in Sochi like somebody who had learned from the past. But we won't know for sure until we see what happens in 2018, when she hopes to go for the gold, quite possibly for the last time.

Until we see how she copes if, again, something goes terribly wrong.

5

NO GOOD

Mike Lantry was a lucky man.

He was about to be granted a second chance in a sport where second chances don't come too often. And if he were able to take advantage, and there seemed no reason he wouldn't, all would be forgotten.

You see, in late November 1973, Mike, a twenty-five-year-old walk-on kicker for the University of Michigan football team, missed a field goal from 44 yards in the closing seconds that, barring a miracle, would have given the unbeaten Wolverines a 13–10 victory over no. 1–ranked Ohio State and sent them to the Rose Bowl in Pasadena. Instead, the game ended in a 10–10 tie.

No rivalry in all of college football—heck, in all of sports, period—was more intense than Michigan vs. Ohio State.

Mike was devastated. Anyone in his position would be. When his family and friends gathered at his house that evening in Ann Arbor, he refused to leave his bedroom. His wife, Linda, couldn't persuade him to make even a brief appearance.

He spent the time feeling sorry for himself. He couldn't stop thinking about the teammates and coaches and fans he let down.

In front of a crowd of 105,223, the largest in NCAA history, in the place now known as the Big House, and a national television audience on ABC, Mike had failed. There was no other way to put it. Not only on the 44-yarder but also on another almost sure game winner—albeit from 58 yards—the possession before.

"It started to hit me more and more that night," he said.

Fast-forward almost exactly one year later: Same two teams. Same chance to be a hero, this time in Columbus, Ohio.

Mike trotted onto the field. The kick wouldn't be long, 33 yards. With that strong left leg of his, he'd converted kicks a lot longer than that. In one game, against Stanford in 1973, he made two from more than 50 yards. No Michigan kicker had ever done that.

The no. 3 Wolverines, who were 10-0, trailed the no. 4 Buckeyes 12–10 with only eighteen seconds to go. The Rose Bowl was at stake again. So was an undefeated season and a chance for the national championship.

"You've done this a million times," Mike told himself as the ball was about to be snapped.

The wind was behind him. The snap was clean. The kick looked good.

Before he ever enrolled at the University of Michigan, Mike Lantry faced a lot more pressure than trying to win a football game. A Rose Bowl wasn't on the line back then. A life was. His.

In 1969, the United States sent nearly a half million men to Vietnam. Mike was one of them. He arrived in January and was assigned to a battalion as part of the Eighty-Second Airborne. His job was to supply artillery to three separate units.

"I was afraid," he admitted. "I was in God's hands. There was nothing I could do other than what I was told and try to survive."

Mike will never forget the first day he saw this strange, new land. He was flying in from Tokyo, after boarding a commercial flight from Fort Lewis in Washington State.

"It was just like those pictures I had seen in *Life* magazine," he said. "People were out in the rice paddies with those lampshade hats on."

A few days later, he got a sense of the enormous challenges he would be dealing with the next twelve months. An alert was sounded and everybody was told to quickly go into the bunkers.

Not too long afterward, as the men stood in formation, a soldier no more than 15 yards away from Mike was shot by a sniper. Many of the same troops later made it to an outpost in the Mekong Delta, close to the Cambodian border.

Mike never saw actual combat during his tour, but that didn't make him feel the least bit more secure. Each day that went by was a day closer to the day he could go home. Home was Oxford, Michigan, roughly forty miles from Detroit, where he would be able to sleep on a mattress instead of a cot and not be concerned with rats, as he was during the monsoon season in Vietnam. Ah, the simple things we take for granted.

"You're part of a fighting team to complete a mission," Mike said, although, "looking back, I don't know what that mission was."

Some days were better than others, especially those days that made him think of home, if for just a few fleeting moments. Such as the day Mike was on guard duty and a fellow soldier climbed to the top of the bunker to whisper to him that the University of Michigan and its first-year coach, Bo Schembechler, had shocked Woody Hayes's no. 1–ranked Buckeyes in Ann Arbor, 24–12, and were going to the Rose Bowl. Mike was elated, but he had to be careful about showing his emotions.

"It's hard to jump up and down," he said, "while you have people out there lurking, and you've got loaded machine guns. I could have shot fifteen or twenty rounds and been court-martialed."

Mike had enlisted in early 1968, when the war wasn't yet the lost cause it would become. Though Mike seemed to be.

"I was a C-minus student in high school," he said, "so I really didn't have too many other options other than going to the army."

Perhaps not, but that hadn't always been the case. Early on, there was a chance he'd be offered a college scholarship in track and field. The high hurdles, the low hurdles, the shot put, the 100-yard dash—name the event, and Mike was good at it, setting records at his school. The letters poured in from dozens of universities.

If only he'd been even a B student. If only he hadn't left his books in his locker before he got on the bus every afternoon and lied to his mother about doing his homework assignments, a lie he knew he couldn't possibly keep up.

"The grades would come out," he said, "and tell a different story."

So, with those grades, or perhaps because of them, he ended up in Vietnam.

Finally, though, in January 1970, his one-year tour came to an end. Mike was in such a hurry to leave the country behind—not only physically but also in his mind—that as soon as he landed at Travis Air Force Base near San Francisco, he threw away all the military clothing in his duffel bag, except for a fatigue jacket with his name on it.

Only he wasn't done serving his country just yet. He spent one more year in the army, at a desk job in Washington. By this stage of the conflict, a number of Vietnam vets were against U.S. involvement and weren't afraid to say so in public. Mike was not one of them. He kept quiet, biding his time in D.C., just as he had in Vietnam, until he could try to build the life for himself he failed to build the first time he had the chance.

By early 1971, his obligation to the service was over, and thanks to the GI Bill and Jack Harvey, the university's track coach, Mike enrolled at Michigan. Five years late, perhaps, but better late than . . . you know.

He was so excited his first day on campus. Then he arrived at South Quad, the dorm where many of the athletes stayed. Mike heard loud music coming down the hallway, and the closer he got to his room, the louder the music became. He knocked on the door. A young man with rather long, messy hair answered.

"I'm your new roommate," Mike told him.

The two spoke, but just for a few minutes. Mike put his duffel bag on one of the bunk beds.

"I'll be right back," he said.

He immediately went to a resident advisor.

"You have to move me to another room," he told the advisor. "I'm not going to survive this. I have one chance, and one chance only, to compete at the University of Michigan, from an academic standpoint."

The plea worked. He was moved to a larger room with regular beds. The music would never be too loud, and his new roommate had short hair.

Now if he could only find the same level of comfort in the classroom. The transition from high school to college is challenging enough, and it was not as if Mike was a great student in the first place. No one knew this better than he did. He studied day and night. That was all he could do. He was at his parents' home in Oxford when the grades from his first semester came in the mail.

"I had one of those panic attacks," Mike remembered. "Oh God, what happens if I didn't make the grade?"

There was no reason to be alarmed. His grade point average was a more than respectable 3.1. He was going to make it.

Mike began to work out with members of the track team, and with the encouragement of some of the football players, decided to give that sport a try as well. In high school, he had been a defensive back and running back and was the team's kicker. There was nothing to lose. He'd have track to fall back on if football didn't pan out.

He got along well with the players from the start. As much as these men saw themselves as warriors, here, they knew, was someone who had been in an actual war. They wanted to know what it was like. He told them.

Yet, in going out for the football team, there was one minor detail Mike forgot. One afternoon, he received a not-so-gentle reminder.

"Come here a minute," a man told him while Mike was working out. The man motioned for Mike to follow him so they could enjoy some privacy. "Don't you think that if you want to go out for football at the University of Michigan, you'd want to talk to the head coach first?"

"The point was well taken," Mike said, "and I apologized."

That was how Mike Lantry met Glenn "Bo" Schembechler. They met again the next day. Mike told him about high school and Vietnam and how determined he was to prove he belonged on the team. Schembechler understood; he'd been in the army himself, in the early fifties. Mike would get his chance.

He tried running back at first but broke three ribs in practice, and besides, Michigan was loaded at running back. Schembechler suggested he focus more on the defensive backfield and kicking. Michigan had a pretty solid kicker in Dana Coin, but he was a senior, which meant there'd soon be an opening.

Mike did what Schembechler told him, kicking for the freshman team, and in the spring game of 1972, he won the job.

"After what I had been through, it was an unbelievable feeling," he recalled. "I didn't know how long it would last, but I couldn't wait to tell my parents and family. I started to work my ass off."

Not that it would matter much. In that first season, the team was so dominant, it really didn't need a kicker, except for extra points. Michigan finished 10-1, losing only to the Buckeyes 14–11 in Columbus in the final game. Mike made five field goals *the whole year*. One of them, at least, was a 30-yarder with a minute to go to beat Purdue 9–6.

The next season was more of the same. Until, to no one's surprise, the last game, in Ann Arbor against—who else?—the Buckeyes.

With the score tied 10–10, and just over a minute left, Michigan faced a fourth-and-2 on the Ohio State 41-yard line. The field goal, if Schembechler were to attempt it, would be from 58 yards. That's a long way for any kicker, not to mention what was at stake: a Big Ten title, the Rose Bowl, a chance to win the national championship. Mike had one thing going for him: a strong wind at his back.

"Can you make it?" Schembechler asked him.

"Absolutely," he said.

Mike wasn't merely saying what he knew his coach wanted to hear. He believed it.

"I knew I had the leg to do it," he said.

He sure did. The moment the ball left his foot, there was little doubt the kick would be long enough.

And, for the longest time, it appeared the kick would also be straight enough, just inside the left upright. The one-hundred-thousand-plus fans in Michigan Stadium were about to go bonkers. Until . . .

"There was a small gust of wind," Mike recalled.

Small? The gust might as well have been a tornado for the damage it caused. The ball tailed to the left. The kick was no good. The game was still tied, and the Buckeyes would have the ball with an opportunity to win it themselves.

Mike was disappointed but not dejected. The kick was 58 yards, for heaven's sake, and he had come extremely close to making the damn thing. No one could fault him one bit.

"It didn't shank off the side of my foot," he said proudly, "or bounce off some guy's ass and go backward. I've seen pictures of the kick, and it almost grazed the upright, but it was no good."

Besides, Mike wouldn't have time to be dejected. Before he knew it, he was back on the field, thanks to an interception by defensive back Tom Drake on the first play after the missed kick, which gave the Wolverines the ball on the Ohio State 33. Woody Hayes hated to throw the ball. He was the coach who said, famously, that when you throw the ball, "three things can happen and two of them [an incompletion and an interception] are bad." This one was as bad as it gets.

Michigan picked up a few more yards before Mike would get his chance. The kick would be significantly shorter than the first one, at 44 yards. Now there were just twenty-eight seconds to go.

Mike had a plan.

"I just missed that one this way," he told himself. "Let's make an adjustment."

The adjustment was to aim more toward the right goal post, taking into account the direction of the wind, which would, presumably, steer the ball to the left, as it did with the earlier attempt.

"I was in the moment," Mike said. "I wasn't thinking of being carried off the field. I just wanted to focus on making that kick."

Once again, the kick had plenty of distance, though the ball started to the right of where Mike wanted it. He waited for the wind to do its job. He waited and waited and . . .

"It went to the right and stayed to the right," Mike said.

This time, he *was* dejected.

"The first one, it was a long shot," Mike said, "and I felt I did my best effort. The second one was on me."

Yet all was not lost.

The Wolverines didn't win the game, but they didn't lose, either, and were still unbeaten at 10-0-1, and sharing the conference lead with the Buckeyes, they appeared a good bet to go to the Rose Bowl. They had rallied from 10 points behind to tie the no. 1 team in the country. Besides, Ohio State had gone the year before, and the Big Ten athletic directors wouldn't want to send the same team two seasons in a row. As a matter of fact, up until just two years before, there had been a rule forbidding back-to-back appearances.

The ten ADs would hold an official vote the next day. Few doubted how it would go.

Including Bo Schembechler, who offered some positive words to Mike in the locker room after the Ohio State game. Schembechler couldn't afford for his kicker to lose confidence. He'd need him for the game in Pasadena a little more than a month away.

Only there would be no game in Pasadena. Not for the Wolverines.

The athletic directors voted 6–4 to send Ohio State instead, as they were concerned about the status of Dennis Franklin, the Michigan QB who had broken his collarbone in the fourth quarter. No one could be sure if Franklin would recover by New Year's Day.

Mike learned about the vote while he was home watching an NFL game on Sunday afternoon. A news bulletin flashed across the bottom of the screen. He was stunned.

"I thought it would be 9–1 [in our favor]," he said. "There seemed to be no chance in hell that we weren't going to get the nod."

If you think Mike felt horrible the day before, now he knew the true cost of missing the two kicks.

"I could have solved the whole problem by making one of those," he said.

Mike's teammates were just as upset. Their season was over. For the seniors, so was their college career. Back then, the Rose Bowl was the only bowl game for teams in the Big Ten, no matter how good you were. Sitting in on the team meeting several hours later, Mike said, "felt like going to a funeral."

He got over it, in time, and practiced hard that summer. The first game, at home against the Iowa Hawkeyes, would be here before he knew it.

In 1974, Michigan was as dominant as it had been in 1972 and 1973.

For the third straight year, the Wolverines entered the season finale against Ohio State without a loss. On the way to a 10-0 record and the no. 3 ranking, they had allowed an average of less than a touchdown per game, giving up just 63 total points. Only two opponents, Wisconsin and Stanford, reached double figures. Four teams didn't score at all!

The problem, as usual, was that Ohio State was also dominant, losing just once, on the road to Michigan State, and that was on a disputed call at the end. The Buckeyes were as deep as ever on both sides of the ball. They loved to run it, and had the premier running back in college football, Archie Griffin, who'd win the Heisman Trophy that year and the next.

The hype leading up to the game was as huge as ever. Neither school would have wanted it any other way.

Michigan wasted no time, seizing the lead on its first pass of the game, a 42-yard strike from Franklin to wideout Gil Chapman. Ohio State fumbled on the next possession, leading to Mike's 37-yard field goal. The game was barely ten minutes old, and the Wolverines were up 10–0. As stingy as Michigan's defense was, a 10-point advantage was enormous.

"This is our time," an excited Mike shouted on the sidelines.

Too excited, perhaps.

"Settle down, Lantry," offensive line coach Jerry Hanlon told him in a phone call from the press box. "It's a long game."

Man, was he ever right.

In the second and third quarters, the Buckeyes got four field goals from Tom Klaban to assume the lead. Each kick had come in the north end of Ohio Stadium, with the wind at his back. Every point so far, in fact, had been scored with the wind behind the offense.

Needless to say, when Michigan, down 12–10, took over with fifty-seven seconds to go on its own 47 and with the wind in its favor, its chances were pretty good. Even better after Franklin, on the opening play of the drive, connected with wideout Jim Smith at the Ohio State 32. The Wolverines were already in Mike's range.

Then, after an incomplete pass, Franklin handed the ball to running back Rob Lytle, who took it to the Buckeyes' 22. Lytle rushed for 6 more yards on the next play. They were now in position to win the game and could play it conservatively. Schembechler called time. There were eighteen seconds left.

Mike couldn't have asked for anything more. Here was his chance, from 33 yards, to make up for the kicks he missed in '73. Anyone fated to wind up on the losing side of history dreams of a second chance like this.

He made the sign of the cross on the sidelines. Schembechler grabbed him by the shoulder pads.

"Go out there and win the game," he told him.

Mike planned to do just that. The week before, against Purdue, he made three field goals, the longest from 43 yards, and had outstanding practices the whole week.

"I felt really good about myself," he said.

And, just like those two misses in '73, Mike, kicking from the right hash mark, felt really good about the kick as soon as the ball left his foot, as did his holder, Tom Drake, who raised his hands in celebration.

"I thought it had the angle," Mike said.

So, for a split second, did Bob Ufer, the excitable Michigan play-by-play man who told his listeners: "It's snapped, it's spotted, it's kicked, it's end over end. And it is . . . it is . . . it is . . . good."

No, Ufer quickly corrected himself, it was *no* good. That was what the officials ruled, and their opinion was the only one that would matter, then and for eternity. The score stayed the way it was: Ohio State 12, Michigan 10.

The fans stormed the field and ripped down the goal posts, although there were still sixteen seconds remaining. Mike walked slowly to the sidelines and took a seat on the bench. No one came near him.

Once the field was cleared, the Buckeyes took a knee, and the game was over. Ohio State was going to the Rose Bowl for the third year in a row. Michigan was going nowhere, also for the third year in a row.

As for Mike, he couldn't believe it had happened again. He felt worse than he had the year before, and he never thought that could be possible. In 1973, at least, he knew he would have another chance, as a senior, and on a team that would be as good, if not better. That wouldn't be true this time.

Mike's only thought was to get to the locker room, get dressed, get on the bus, and get the hell out of Ohio Stadium, and Columbus, as quickly as humanly possible. He wouldn't talk to Jim Lampley, the sideline reporter for ABC who grabbed him by the shoulder pads. He wouldn't talk to his mom, who had been diagnosed the year before with bone cancer. He wouldn't talk to anyone.

Mike doesn't recall much about what was said in the locker room, except for what Schembechler said. *That* he'll never forget.

"I don't want anyone to pin the blame on Mike Lantry," Schembechler told his players. His point: Michigan wins as a team and Michigan loses as a team.

But pin it on him they would, and Mike knew it. Such is the price an athlete must pay whenever he or she fails. The bigger the stage, the bigger the price. Mike had failed again, there was no question about that, and on a stage as big as they come.

"I wanted to be in that position," he said. "I can't then ask 'give me a break' if it doesn't work out."

A break, absolutely not, but sympathy—that he'd receive, and plenty. Letters soon poured in from fans throughout the United States, even Ohio—"literally, thousands of them," he recalled. Such as this one from Dick Vitale, the basketball coach at the University of Detroit, who would later become a well-known TV broadcaster:

> I'm sure you'll prove to everyone you are a real CHAMP by holding your head high! You have not a damn thing to be ashamed of—I've seen the greatest miss 10 yd f.g.s! Be T-O-U-G-H.

Or this one from the top major league baseball analyst for NBC, Joe Garagiola:

> I think the Mike Lantrys of this world are the winners.

One couple sent a telegram that said more than he ever expected:

> Yesterday My Best Friends Son Drowned In A Boating Accident Keep Your Chin Up High.

Mike saved the letters, but for reasons he can't explain, he did not open all of them. Maybe there was a limit to how much he could take. He stuck them in a closet. Years later, once he had moved on with his life, he saw no point in revisiting something so painful. In the closet they stayed. The letters didn't make his pain go away, but they reminded Mike that there were more serious things in life than a football game.

Not that he didn't know it already; Vietnam made sure of that.

Which makes you wonder: Shouldn't experiencing losses in a war zone have helped him realize the insignificance, by comparison, of losses on a football field?

Not necessarily. Don't get him wrong, he doesn't minimize the lives of those who came home in a body bag. He knows he could have easily been one of them. As much as he has kept his distance from Vietnam—he hasn't stayed in touch with anyone he served with—the war will always be a part of who he is, like it or not.

But the fact is he worked so hard for a second chance to go to college and be an athlete that when he got there, at age twenty-two, it was almost as if nothing that took place in his life before counted. So when he missed those kicks, letting down his teammates and his university, they were the only losses he could think about. There was no broader context to place them in. Not yet, anyway.

Perhaps it's inherent in the mentality of kickers, but there are certainly echoes in Mike's attitude of Lou Michaels after the Colts lost to the Jets in Super Bowl III. You get there, you finish the job.

"When you are on that level," Mike explained, "and you play in that environment, nothing can compare to that."

The first few months after the 1974 Ohio State game were as tough as one could imagine. Yet there was real life to deal with, and it couldn't wait, forcing Mike to put the errant kicks, if not behind him, at least not front and center. His wife, a nurse at the local VA hospital, had been the breadwinner while he earned his degree, but once Mike graduated in the spring of 1975, it was his turn to earn a living and help take care of their two-year-old son. He went into the auto business, with assistance from Michigan's athletic director, Don Canham, and his father-in-law, a former Ford executive.

Mike also had his mother to worry about. She was the one he always relied on. Walking right past her in Columbus said more about his mind-set that day than anything else. He didn't stop to consider how hard it was to fight her way through the crowd to comfort him. He felt awful about it.

Yet as real life went on, he couldn't stop thinking about his football life and how it had ended. One lost opportunity against Ohio State was painful enough. Now there were two. There would always be two. He could separate 1973 from 1974, the circumstances being quite different, but to fans, the years would be grouped forever as one, him as the villain. How he would cope, he didn't have a clue. He'd been given the chance to make up for what happened in 1973, but again he'd fallen short. If it had been only one game, perhaps that would be surmountable, but *two*? That's hard to live with, and for Mike, redemption was now out of reach.

"I wondered if this would permanently affect my ability to move forward in my life," he said. "After a substantial period of time—I can't tell you if it was a year or two years or what—I knew I had to move on."

What helped enormously was Michigan's 22–0 win over Ohio State in Columbus in November 1976. Though Mike wasn't on the field that day, a number of his former teammates were, and they hadn't forgotten him. Several days after the victory, he ran into close friend Rob Lytle, the senior running back, in Ann Arbor. Lytle had been on the line of scrimmage when Mike missed the 33-yarder two years earlier.

"Mike," Lytle told him, "this one was for you."

Mike was deeply moved.

"The [message he got] was *Lantry, in our hearts, you've always been vindicated, but you're really vindicated now,*" he said.

That didn't mean his pain would go away forever, because it didn't. To this day, he never knows when somebody, out of nowhere, will bring up the kicks. Only that somebody will.

Take the time he went with several businessmen to a political event in Detroit. One of them seemed to know more details about Mike's career at Michigan than he did, and he was so excited to be in Mike's company he introduced him to everyone he met. Except he couldn't stop at giving his name and that he played for the Wolverines. He kept adding, ". . . the guy who missed those field goals against Ohio State."

Not wanting to cause any tension, Mike let it go the first few times, but after a while, he gently asked the man, "Can you tone it down a bit? I'm a little bit more than that."

It wasn't so much that Mike was trying to rewrite history; it was that he wasn't willing to let someone else define him. Only he could do that.

As the years went by, Mike had no interest in watching a tape of the two Ohio State games. Not that, on occasion, he didn't see a brief clip of his misfortunes. You couldn't escape that if you lived in the state of Michigan, especially in late November during the week of the big game, when the TV stations in Detroit showed highlights from the past.

Then one night, in the late nineties, while he was flipping channels at home, there it was, the 1974 game in its entirety. Mike had never seen the game from start to finish. He wasn't sure what to do: change the channel or take the risk.

"It could bring up wounds that had healed, opening them up again and not being able to close them," he thought. "Why go through that again?"

In the end, he took the risk, and he's glad he did.

"I didn't go back into shock," he said.

Watching the game, as it turned out, was a very pleasant experience. He was reminded of how gifted and evenly matched the two schools were, and how they played a brand of football—"three yards and a cloud of dust," as Woody Hayes put it—many sorely miss, Mike included.

"Just hard-hitting, going-at-it-type football that you don't see that much anymore," he said.

Going back in time was a bit surreal, as one might expect. Though he knew what was going to happen, that didn't make the events less dramatic.

"I felt like I was looking at some other young man at some other place in time," he said.

Looking at "some other young man" didn't change his opinion of what took place. The kick was as good in the nineties as he remembered it being in the seventies.

"I thought it got through the plane of the upright," Mike said, "well before it started to tail off to the left. Right down the middle would have been better, but it was good."

He wasn't the only one who thought so at the time. So did Penn State coach Joe Paterno, who was doing the analysis for ABC. What made the call even tougher was that the ball went from the sunshine into the shadows.

Good or not, Mike doesn't dwell on the 1974 game or the 1973 game. Does he wish he'd made the kicks? Of course he does. Michigan would have gone to the Rose Bowl and perhaps won a national championship. And, for the rest of his life, he wouldn't have to wait for someone, at any moment, to bring up who he is and how he messed up.

Yet when it comes to his four years in Ann Arbor, he doesn't think about what he missed. He thinks, rather, about what he gained in going to the University of Michigan and, more to the point, what he learned about himself precisely because he had to endure the kind of heartbreak few college athletes experience. Not just once but twice. The education he got, and the friendships he made, he didn't take for granted. As a matter of fact, he might never have reached the same level of appreciation if he'd made any of those kicks.

"I wasn't recruited," he said. "No one gave me anything. They just gave me an opportunity."

In October 2015, another University of Michigan football player, Blake O'Neill, went through his own heartbreak. O'Neill is the punter who muffed the snap on the last play of the game against Michigan's hated rival Michigan State, which the Spartans scooped up and ran in for a miracle touchdown, as the Wolverines lost 27–23. The play—the play of the year in college football, you could argue—was shown over and over on TV for days.

Mike was at the Big House that night. He flashed back immediately to what happened to him all those years ago. He knew the exact emotions the kid was going through: that you didn't do your job and let down your teammates and the fans. He would have welcomed the chance to speak to O'Neill. Mike's message would have been simple and heartfelt:

"Keep your focus on all the positive things. Being able to play for the University of Michigan, you should cherish everything you've done for your team."

6

UNFORCED ERROR

The kid, at last, was about to beat the old man, and what a time to do it. Flushing Meadows. The U.S. Open. Round 4. It didn't get much better than that.

The kid was Aaron Krickstein. To be fair, maybe he wasn't such a kid anymore. He was twenty-four years old and had been a professional tennis player for almost a decade.

Anyway, the first time he took on the old man, Jimmy Connors, seven years before in Boca Raton, Florida, he didn't do very well, and that's being more than generous. In tennis, whenever a player wins a set 6–0, they refer to the shutout as a "bagel." Connors won back-to-back bagels. You couldn't be more humiliated than Aaron was.

"We had a seven P.M. match, and it was a packed house," Aaron recalled. "Ten minutes before the match, Jimmy comes in a helicopter right next to the court. And that was it. I was frozen. I was completely shell-shocked. It was over forty-five minutes later. I thought it was the end of my career, believe me."

Hardly. Aaron's career was just beginning. He won his first tournament, in Tel Aviv, in 1983, only two months after he turned sixteen, and three more in 1984. Injuries set him back a bit between 1984 and 1988, but Aaron won three times in 1989, and at the U.S.

Open in '91, he was healthy and playing well. There was still time to become the player many thought he would be after a spectacular career in the juniors.

The player he thought he would be.

In the opening round, Aaron beat the no. 8 seed, Andre Agassi, in straight sets, 7–5, 7–6, 6–2. He then got by Peru's Jaime Yzaga, a former French Open junior champion, and Spain's Francisco Javier Clavet. Next up, on Labor Day, would be Connors, who was unseeded and hadn't won a tour event in two years. And who, on that very day, was turning thirty-nine years old.

On paper, Aaron was probably the favorite. Then again, the fact that he'd never beaten Connors was something he would have to deal with, perhaps as much as the man himself.

"He was the only guy I was in awe of," Aaron said.

Their most recent meeting had occurred just a few months earlier, during the second round at Wimbledon, Connors dominating once again 6–3, 6–2, 6–3.

"Beat me like a drum," Aaron said. "It wasn't even like a match. I played really bad. I was not hitting the ball or moving well. I just felt like once we got out there, I'm losing to Connors, I have no chance, and I'm never going to beat this guy. It was always an uphill battle. He's Jimmy Connors. I'm Aaron Krickstein."

He seemed a lot more confident at Flushing Meadows, at least early on, as he took the opening set 6–3. Knowing his opponent as well as he did, Aaron tried to mix up the pace and hit a lot of sliced backhands low to his forehand. The idea was to keep Connors from getting in a groove.

"It was very benign," Aaron said, referring to the first set. "The crowd was filling in. It was a nice day. There wasn't much going on."

Connors came back to win the second set in a tiebreaker. Aaron took the third. Then Connors rallied again to capture the fourth and square the match at two sets apiece. A lot was going on now.

You had to give Jimbo credit. To even be *competing* in a Grand Slam at the age of thirty-nine was quite an achievement. Many of those who came up around the same time he did—Vitas Gerulaitis, Roscoe Tanner, Guillermo Vilas, and so on—were gone from the tennis scene. And then to extend the match to a fifth set against one of the better players—don't pay any attention to the rankings, which put Aaron at no. 47—was downright heroic.

No way could Connors keep it up, and he didn't. Aaron gained a 5–2 advantage in the fifth playing his usual game, ripping one ground stroke after another from the baseline, forcing Connors to chase the ball from one end of the court to the other. Aaron didn't come to the net too often. He didn't have to.

The old man, on the other hand, looked exhausted. He had been a star in his day, perhaps the brightest star there was, but his day was long gone.

The kid had him.

Aaron took up the sport at the age of six. His three older sisters also got started early, which pushed him even further. He didn't want to be left behind.

He lost his first official match 6–0, 6–0, but beat the same kid in similar fashion about a year later, and kept on winning from there. When Aaron was eleven years old, his father, Herb, a pathologist in the Detroit area, brought him to meet some of the top instructors. Herb Krickstein knew his son was good. He wanted to know *how* good.

One of the instructors was Pancho Segura, a top player in the forties and fifties who later coached Connors. Segura saw something right away in the youngster.

"To Aaron," he wrote on the inside cover of a book he gave him, "in seven years' time, your game should be as good as Björn Borg's."

That was saying a lot. Borg had won eight Grand Slams by the late seventies.

At age twelve, Aaron was the no. 1 player in the country in his age group. He was on the court 30 to 35 hours a week. Tennis was his life.

"I didn't have any friends in high school," he said. "I never went to a party. I was completely sheltered."

Others who gave up that much of their childhood to the sport would later resent it (Agassi comes to mind). Some would rebel and never be the same player again. Not Aaron.

"People would have loved to do what I did and experience what I did," he said. "When you're good at something, it's easier to like it."

He was good, all right. If anything, Aaron may have been *too* good. No one could beat him. In search of stronger competition, his dad took him to the Hopman Tennis Academy in Largo, Florida. Harry Hopman, a premier player from Australia during the thirties and forties, had taught, among others, Vitas Gerulaitis and John McEnroe.

Fourteen-year-old Aaron didn't stay more than a few hours.

"I was on the court with about ten kids, and he didn't give me the time of day," he recalled.

That was enough for Herb Krickstein. There was not a moment to waste. He took his son off the court and drove that very day to the Nick Bollettieri Tennis Academy in Bradenton, roughly forty miles away. Bollettieri did more than give Aaron the time of day.

"He rolled out the red carpet," he said. "He had great players there, and I loved it."

Over the next two years, Aaron flew from his home in Michigan to Bollettieri's every other weekend. Testing himself against better players made him better, and he began to expect more of himself—perhaps too much.

"I couldn't forget about what had just happened in the last set or the last game," Aaron said. "If I blew a five-one lead, I'd be talking about it the next tournament or the next three tournaments. Everything was about winning and losing. That's all I cared about. If I won, everything was going to be okay, and if I lost, everything was the worst thing in the world."

His father was even tougher on him. After one especially ugly loss to a weaker opponent, Herb let his son have it.

"I just played like a dog and he was so disgusted," Aaron said. "Losing wasn't an option for him, especially when I played like that. He said, 'This is unacceptable. Your effort, your attitude, all this has got to change.'"

Several years earlier, Aaron's mother, Evelyn, had taken him to an event in Winston-Salem, North Carolina. His father couldn't go because of his work. Aaron made a ton of mistakes that day and lost. Afterward, his mother consoled him.

"You played a good match," she told him. "We just want you to be happy, to enjoy yourself."

When he found out what his wife said, Herb was furious. Whether Aaron was happy and enjoying himself wasn't the point. Winning was and always would be.

"She was fired and never saw another match," Aaron said, and laughed. "She was one and done."

Aaron didn't lose very often. When he did, at the junior national championships in Kalamazoo, he felt so awful he wrote a letter to his father:

> I know it won't be easy but I finally understand what you've been telling me for 4 years. Everytime I walk on the court I'm going to try to drive myself and give 110% effort every minute I'm out there . . . I will not wine [*sic*] and cry on the court again . . . I'm not a babie [*sic*] anymore!

How he ended the letter said everything you needed to know about how serious he was about his future:

> And next year the 1982 Kalamazoo champion is Game-set-match KRICKSTEIN.

He didn't forget. When he returned to Kalamazoo a year later, he did just that, beating Patrick McEnroe in the final.

In Tel Aviv, he beat Christoph Zipf, 7–6, 6–3, in the final to become the youngest ever to capture a singles title on the ATP Tour. Being Jewish—his grandfather and great-grandfather were rabbis—made his victory in Israel even sweeter.

Later that year, he defeated Stefan Edberg and Gerulaitis in the U.S. Open. He dropped the first two sets to Gerulaitis, the no. 15 seed, before winning the next three 6–4, 6–3, 6–4. In 1984, with his three titles, he rose to no. 9 in the world and was still only seventeen years old. There seemed no reason he couldn't go down as one of the all-time greats.

He may well have, if not for the injuries that kept getting in the way, one after another. Stress fractures in his feet. Trouble with his knees and wrists. Throw in a car accident in 1987, and you began to believe maybe the guy was cursed.

Which is why his run at the Open in 1991 was encouraging. He had overcome so much already for someone still relatively young in his sport. Perhaps he would finally show what Pancho Segura and others saw in him.

The big stage was nothing new for Aaron. He had performed well at other Grand Slam tournaments. In 1989, he made it to the fourth round at Wimbledon and the semis at the U.S. Open before falling to Boris Becker both times. Now here, in the Big Apple, the path was clear for another trip to the semis, and perhaps even further. The winner would take on Paul Haarhuis from the Netherlands in the quarters. Haarhuis was a solid player, but not elite by any stretch.

First things first: Aaron would have to get past Connors. His idol. His friend. Yes, his friend. Connors was quite the competitor, that much was obvious. You could make a strong case that no athlete in *any* sport during the seventies or eighties was more intense. At the same time, Connors could also be a lot of fun to be around. Ask Chris Evert, who was once engaged to him. Ask Aaron.

The two got to know each other when Connors, who was represented by ProServ, a top marketing firm, phoned Herb Krickstein to persuade his son to become a client, which he did, eventually. Herb was sure Aaron could benefit a lot from being around Connors.

"He thought Jimmy would be a good influence," Aaron said, "as far as learning from his vast training and work ethic."

Sounds reasonable enough, as long as tennis was where his influence on the kid would end. It wasn't.

"He didn't know [Connors] would get me into gambling and all of his bad habits," he said.

Aaron chuckled as he talked about the time he went to his father after a bet he made didn't work out.

"You've got to give me some money," he said.

"What are you talking about?" Herb replied.

"I think I lost a couple thousand."

"What the hell is going on?"

Quite a bit, and there was more than gambling.

"I shot my first gun [at Connors's ranch in Santa Barbara, California]," Aaron recalled. "He had some shotguns and Uzis. He had everything there. I went to shoot the gun, and I almost blew my head off. I was like, 'Jimmy, you didn't tell me there's a nine-foot kickback.'"

The two spent a lot of time together in the mid-eighties. Aaron loved every minute.

"I thought it was cool to hang out with Jimmy Connors," he recalled. "I was like the great sparring partner, a player he could spend some time with to help his game and use me whenever he wanted, and it wasn't like Connors had a lot of friends."

Ahead 5–2 in the fifth set, with Connors serving, Aaron could afford to conserve some energy. He'd been on the court for four hours, and though he was fifteen years younger than his opponent, four hours was still a long time.

Aaron was also bothered by a blister on his right hand. During a break, the trainer took a look, but there was little he could do.

"I would never make an excuse," he explained. "However, the thing I would say is that it distracted me more than anything, having to deal with something when, at that stage of the match, you want to be completely focused."

Connors won the game easily. No big deal, Aaron figured.

"I basically tossed the game to, hopefully, do it on my serve," he said. "I was saving everything for the 5–3 game."

The strategy appeared to be paying off when Aaron recorded an ace, his seventh of the match, on the first point. Only three more points, and he would be headed to the quarters.

"I'm looking really good," Aaron said. "Because usually when you're broken, you lose the first point of the game."

Connors, however, grabbed the next 2 points to put the pressure squarely on Aaron. The fans were as loud as they could be. This was New York City, and Connors was their guy.

Serving at 15–30, Aaron hit another errant approach, and now, suddenly, Connors was a point from the break he needed to get back in the match. Getting that point wouldn't be easy. Of his 20 break point chances, he'd converted only 4. Make that 4 of 21, as he missed on a forehand.

At 30–40, Aaron saved another break point with a low passing shot. Deuce. He was 2 points from winning the match.

That was as close as he would get. After another deuce, Connors took the next 2 points to secure the break: 5–4, Krickstein. The players were back on serve. The fans seemed even louder, if that were possible.

Connors, given new life, captured the next game, his third in a row, to even the set at 5–5. Aaron began to get a feeling, and it wasn't a feeling he recognized, or welcomed.

"I knew I was going to probably lose the match, and I never felt that way in a five-setter late in a match," said Aaron, who, more often than not, won matches that went the distance. "I always felt I was the one who was going to hit the great shots. Once I blew that lead, I was in a fog."

Fog or not, he was still very much in the match. He held serve in the next game to go up, 6–5, and then, with Connors serving at 30-all, Aaron was, again, just 2 points from victory. After a Connors stab volley near the net, Aaron had room in the open court to hit a winner, which would give him match point. The ball sailed about a foot over the baseline. 40–30, Connors.

"I don't want to say I choked," Aaron said, "but maybe the moment kind of got to me. I missed a shot I'd make in practice ten out of ten times. It was shocking to me. That was a huge mistake."

Connors finished off the game on the next point. The set, and match, went to a tiebreaker. Of course it did. Any other ending wouldn't have been right.

"This is what they paid for," the old man said, looking directly into the camera while he took a breather during the changeover. "This is what they want."

Aaron went up 1–0, but Connors took the next 3 points. The first player to 7 points, with at least a 2-point edge, would be the winner. Aaron got a point to make it 3–2, but Connors won the next 2 to go up 5–2.

At 6–4, and match point, Connors put Aaron away with a cross-court winner. The crowd went nuts. The comeback was complete. The kid didn't have the old man after all.

There wasn't much Herb Krickstein could say this time.

"The match shook him up, probably as much as me," Aaron said. "It killed him. I think he knew that I blew it."

The U.S. Open had the nerve to go on without him. Connors defeated Haarhuis in the quarters but finally looked his age in falling to the no. 4 seed, Jim Courier, in the semis. Not that anyone remembers, but Edberg beat Courier to win the title.

The three days after the loss were the most difficult. Aaron couldn't sleep or see anyone. He stayed at his house in Boca Raton and thought about what might have been. What should have been.

"It was really a gut-wrenching experience," he said. "I shut it down. I couldn't function. The ducks were in line for me to have a great run."

Tennis being an individual, and not a team, sport made the loss, in some respects, more challenging for him. There was no one to share the blame.

"The eyes are on you," he said. "You can't hide."

In addition to losing the match, Aaron lost his coach. For the prior four years, he and Tim Gullikson had worked side by side, day after day. After the U.S. Open, the two never worked together again. Gullikson quit and hooked up with Pete Sampras. He'd thought Aaron was ready to go to the next level, to win a Grand Slam, maybe several. Heck, Aaron thought so, too. But it hadn't happened.

"He was done with me," he said. "We worked on certain things, and I think he felt that I didn't do what he wanted me to do, to play aggressively. I kind of let Jimmy take everything. Part of it was mental, part of it was physical. Part was who I was as a player. Maybe I wasn't capable of doing what he wanted."

He certainly wasn't capable of behaving like Connors. Then again, with the exception of McEnroe, no one was.

"That wasn't my cup of tea," Aaron said. "I was the quiet, shy type, and not confrontational."

Sure didn't seem that way in the second set tiebreaker. At 7–7, Connors had smashed a forehand that was initially called good by the linesman closest to the ball.

Connors had smashed a forehand that was initially called good by the linesman closest to the ball. Aaron, for once, didn't let Connors take everything. He gestured that the ball was out, and the chair umpire, David Littlefield, who was on the other side of the court, agreed, overruling the linesman: 8–7, Krickstein.

The point, at this stage of the proceedings, was critical. Aaron would now have a set point to go up 2–0, instead of Connors being 1 point from squaring the match. A steamed Connors walked up to Littlefield and, in the most abusive manner, let him know what he thought of the overrule.

"Get your ass out of the chair, you're a bum," he told the umpire. "I'm out here playing my butt off at thirty-nine years old and you're doing that!"

Littlefield listened to the tirade but did nothing about it. He'd made his call, and this was many years before players could use challenges to ask for a shot to be reviewed. The overrule appeared to be the worst possible break for Connors at the worst possible time.

It wasn't. In reality, it got Connors more animated than before, and the more animated Connors was, the more the crowd was into it. That was the last thing Aaron needed. Connors saved set point and took the next 2 points to capture the tiebreaker, 10–8. He was still in the match. If he had fallen two sets behind, it would have been difficult to imagine the old man climbing out of that big a hole.

Looking back, Aaron wonders if he'd been better off not gesturing the ball was wide, even if it would have resulted in set point for Connors. These are the what-ifs you replay in your head after a defeat like this on a stage like this. His thinking is that perhaps Littlefield wouldn't have overruled the linesman. Connors wouldn't have had any reason to confront the umpire. And the fans wouldn't have rallied around him even more.

"That point incensed the crowd more than anything," Aaron said, "and Jimmy kind of got really motivated to kick butt."

Aaron knew a moment like this was probably going to come at some point during the match. His dad and coach had warned him over and over that Connors would be, well, Connors. He knew no other way, especially in an atmosphere as lively as Flushing Meadows.

"Jimmy was who he was and he was going to do whatever it took to win the match, as he always did," Aaron said.

Knowing an outburst was coming, however, didn't make Aaron feel any better when it did.

"I thought he went over the top," Aaron explained, "with his stalling, with his intimidating tactics. I tried not to let it bother me, to kind of walk off to the side," but it did.

The three days in Boca Raton came to an end. Mercifully.

Aaron played in an exhibition tournament in Florida and began to prepare for the 1992 season. The Australian Open was only four months away. Besides, he figured, people would soon forget about the match with Connors. So should he. There'd be, as long as he stayed healthy, plenty of other memorable matches in the years ahead.

"At the time of the match, and just after," Aaron said, "I didn't know the magnitude of how big it would become."

No one did.

As the years went by, people, however, couldn't forget about Aaron's match with Connors. CBS wouldn't let them. During rain delays at the U.S. Open, and there were quite a few, the network often showed highlights of the match to kill time.

Amazing, when you think about it. The match wasn't a final, or a semifinal, or even a quarterfinal. And yet there it was, with each passing year, becoming, if nothing else, the most watched tennis match in history, except perhaps for the Battle of the Sexes in 1973 between Billie Jean King and Bobby Riggs.

The appeal was understandable. James Scott Connors was the star, and the 1991 U.S. Open was his final starring role. He certainly didn't need the run he went on to establish his greatness and what he meant to tennis. Yet that's how many remember him, perhaps even more than from the Grand Slams he won. All of us like to imagine we can be young again, at least one last time.

"If he would have been twenty-six, the brash, still-hated Jimmy Connors, it would've been great," Aaron explained, "but because of his age, they loved him. Love him or hate him, he tried his ass off, and he got people in the seats, which a lot of people can't do today."

Only one person was annoyed the match received so much exposure.

"I didn't think I'd have to see it, or hear about it, year after year," Aaron said. Whenever it would come on, he'd think, "I can't believe they're showing this *again.*"

Not until a decade later did he begin to see the experience in a whole different light. Aaron was standing at a urinal during a Bruce Springsteen concert in Florida when a stranger approached.

"That was a great match yesterday," the man said. "I thought you had him."

Aaron wondered if the man had watched the match on TV for the first time and thought it had actually taken place the day before. Aaron's hair was still a bit on the long side, and though he was in his late thirties, he could easily pass for his twenties.

Either way, he realized that he'd be remembered, and isn't that what every athlete craves, really, more than the money, the titles . . . anything?

"Wow, that's kind of cool," he thought. "I've been off the tour for six years."

What wasn't cool was that Aaron lost more than a match, and a coach. He lost a friend. He lost Connors. The two didn't see or speak to each other for months.

"I was still not over the match," he said. "Wasn't like I hated him, but I was still kind of hurt by the whole thing and how it happened. I wanted to disassociate with everything surrounding it, and he, obviously, was a big part of it. I might have been that way with anybody, not just Jimmy Connors."

In any case, the fact that he lost to his good friend wasn't what made the defeat so difficult to take; it was the chance, at twenty-four, to break through on one of the game's biggest stages.

"That's kind of your peak time," Aaron said, "and, as a tennis player, the older you get, and the more opportunities slip away, they hurt more, especially at a Grand Slam. There are only so many."

The next time Aaron and Connors saw each other was in Memphis in February 1992. On the court. Not in the locker room, and not during practice sessions. Aaron wasn't ready.

"It was still painful and I just didn't want to hang out with him," he said. "I was more concerned with winning the match. It was just like another opponent."

As he did at the U.S. Open, Aaron got on top early. Then, once again, the match slipped away. The final: Connors, 3–6, 6-2, 6–3.

"I was up a set and [later] a break in the third," Aaron remembered. "Even in that match, it was like, 'Are you kidding me?' And when I didn't win, it was like, 'Oh, geez, I'm never going to beat this guy and I'm probably never going to play him again,' which I never did."

When they met at the net afterward, Aaron shook his opponent's hand and told him, "Good job, nice playing."

That was it. That was all they would say to each other for more than twenty years. Connors would soon be done. Even Jimmy Connors couldn't defy Father Time forever. That didn't mean that their friendship had to end, but it did. Connors himself was at a loss.

"Since [the U.S. Open match] I haven't seen Aaron once. Not once. Wait. Is he avoiding me?" he wrote in *The Outsider,* his 2013 memoir, neglecting to mention Memphis.

Perhaps he was, as he had avoided him in Memphis.

No, Aaron insisted. There were a number of occasions he thought he might bump into his old friend, and he looked forward to it. One year at the Open, he walked toward Connors in the locker room ready to catch up, but got distracted for a moment by Agassi. By the time Aaron turned around, Connors was gone.

"I wasn't holding a grudge because I lost a difficult match some years ago," he said. "And it wasn't like he called me. If he would have, I'm sure that would have broken the ice as well . . . I'm not sad about it. I'm glad we had our thing. It was what it was when I was younger."

Whoever is to blame—if anyone is—Connors and Aaron met again, at last, in early 2015 to play another match. Aaron by then was the tennis director at St. Andrews Country Club in Boca Raton. He phoned Connors to ask if he'd take part in an exhibition at the club. In calling Connors for the first time in decades, Aaron was as nervous as that day he saw him get out of the helicopter.

"I didn't know how to begin the conversation, what to say," he said.

He began with small talk, and much to his delight, Connors agreed to show up. Aaron believes Connors had another reason besides helping out the club.

"He didn't want to end it with me this way," he said.

About seven hundred fifty people showed up to watch the match. By now, Connors wasn't the only old man. Aaron was forty-seven. The two shared some laughs and entertained the fans. Aaron took it easy on him, winning the set 8–5. Connors, sixty-two, couldn't move around so well anymore.

"I just had to wait until he was sixty and I couldn't lose," Aaron joked.

At no point did they have enough time alone to talk about the 1991 match, or why they didn't see each other for so long. Maybe they will one day, maybe not. Either way, they will always be linked together.

In Florida, Connors mentioned that his run at Flushing Meadows was his proudest achievement as a player, and his victory over Aaron was a big part of that. "You have got to be kidding me," Aaron thought, given all the titles Connors won.

"I was a damn good player," Aaron said, "but I wasn't one of the best ever, by any means."

Perhaps not, but when healthy, he was one of the better players of his time, and his career certainly didn't end with the loss to Connors. In 1995, he reached the semifinals of the Australian Open, rallying from two sets down in the fourth round to knock off Edberg, the no. 6 seed. In the semifinal, he dropped the first two sets to Agassi 6–4, 6–4, before his usual problem, injuries—to his groin and hamstring—forced him to retire in the third.

"That was probably a better opportunity to win a Slam than the '91 Open," Aaron said. "That was really disappointing. I had a lot of good wins and was playing some of the best tennis I played."

Aaron left the game in 1996. He was only twenty-nine.

"If I had to do it all over again," he said, "I'd concentrate more on stretching, fitness, maybe eating habits. I didn't hit any more balls and play any more than [Ivan] Lendl or Courier, or the other baseline players."

The injuries weren't the only issue. He was also having trouble with his marriage, which would end in divorce. Aaron started losing to players who never beat him before.

"I was just playing the string out because I felt I was too young to stop," he said. "What else was I going to do? Even though mentally, I had checked out."

Ask him to judge his career, and the review is mixed, as it should be. He should have won a Grand Slam. Players with less talent did. He never became what Pancho Segura said he would be.

"I won't lie," he said. "I had higher aspirations. I was expected to be the next great American hope, after Connors and McEnroe. I won my last forty-five junior matches, my last five junior nationals."

So instead of his legacy being as one of America's greats, it's *losing* to one of America's greats. No wonder he was crushed for a long time. Later, though, he realized, when the stranger came up to him at the Springsteen concert, that it was better to be remembered, even for losing, than not be remembered at all. That brought him closure, which allowed him to cope with, if not embrace, his spot in history.

"I'm certainly at a good place," he said. "I was part of a famous match in history with a legend like Jimmy Connors. A lot of people know me from that, where they otherwise wouldn't. Just this week, I heard about it three times. Twice last week."

Still, one can't help but wonder: If Aaron had won the Connors match, would the rest of his career have gone any differently? Aaron doesn't believe so . . . Then again:

"You never know," he admitted. "The farther you get, the more you believe in yourself."

As the years wore on, the fact that his loss came in an individual sport made it easier for him to heal. Some Boston fans, after all, will never forgive Calvin Schiraldi, and the same for Cleveland fans and Craig Ehlo. Much more was expected from them because they were part of a team of highly paid professionals that let us, the fans, down. Try to think of one team that lost a World Series or Super Bowl that we think of as winners for how courageously they competed.

You can't. If they lost, they lost, and that's how they will always be remembered. As losers.

That's not, on the other hand, how we normally treat the athletes in individual sports. Even if they lose, we look back and admire the effort they gave under intense pressure. Because each of us is flawed, we empathized with Aaron when his flaws, along with Connors' incredible performance, kept him from winning the biggest match of his life. We know all too well how our own flaws have kept us back.

"People feel sorry for me," he said.

7

ONE STRIKE AWAY

OCTOBER 27, 2011

As soon as the batter made contact, Ron Washington, the manager of the Texas Rangers, thought the game—and season—might be over.

If it was, we would see the same scene we see every October when the final out of the final baseball game goes into the books:

- The manager and coaches gathering for a group hug.
- The whole team sprinting onto the field, teenagers once more.
- Everyone putting on the championship hats and T-shirts made in advance.

The scene, like the ceremonial pitch on opening day, is one in our national pastime that never gets old. To the winning team especially, and its fans.

The game appeared it might be over because the batter, David Freese, the St. Louis Cardinals' third baseman, had gotten good wood on the ball, but not good enough to hit it out of the ballpark. Ready to prevent any doubles that would tie the game—Texas was up 7–5, but the Cards had runners on first and second—right fielder Nelson Cruz would take just a couple steps back and make the catch to end the inning . . . the game . . . the season . . . and begin the celebration. Folks, presenting your 2011 World Series champions, the Texas Rangers.

For Ron Washington, or Wash, as everyone calls him, a baseball lifer if ever there were one, nothing could possibly surpass this moment. He had molded the ball club in his image from the day that he accepted the job five years earlier. *Aggression.* That's his word. Aggression on the base paths, in the field, at the plate—aggression everywhere. The man knew no other way to play the game.

"That means, when the bell rings," Wash said, "I'm going to take it to you from game one. I'm looking to steal. I'm looking to hit-and-run. I'm looking to bunt. I'm looking to take extra bases. Keep the pressure on, and with that, there's mistakes, but when you get a group that can handle that, man, it's beautiful to watch."

Wash had such a group in the 2011 season. The Rangers finished 96-66 to take the American League West by 10 games, and got by the Tampa Bay Rays and Detroit Tigers in the playoffs to reach the World Series. Now, with the ball floating harmlessly toward Cruz in right, the Rangers were about to close out the Cards in Game 6.

"We had every element that you need," Wash said, "pitching, speed, defense, power."

That was definitely true, but shortly after the ball left Freese's bat, the defense part was looking a little shaky. Cruz, you see, froze instead of drifting backward. The ball wasn't floating harmlessly any longer. The ball was floating . . . over his head.

Wash could do nothing but watch and hope that Cruz could track it down. He backed up toward the wall and stuck out his glove.

This game might not be over just yet.

Raised in New Orleans, one of ten kids—eight boys and two girls—Wash learned early on how to work hard and make the most of his abilities. Two older brothers, James and Alvin, were never easy on him, and he wouldn't have wanted it any other way.

"A guy might be bigger than you," he realized. "He might be stronger than you. But you can still compete at the same thing."

His big break came in 1970 when the Kansas City Royals invited him to join a new baseball academy they were setting up in Sarasota, Florida. All he did in his tryout was rifle two balls down to second base—he started out as a catcher—run the 60-yard dash, and take one swing. The coaches didn't need to see any more.

"I almost decapitated the pitcher," Wash recalled.

He was only eighteen years old. Kids that age can be a little full of themselves, and Wash was no exception. Before signing the contract, he asked for a bonus of thirty thousand dollars! Where did Wash ever come up with that amount? "It just came out of my head," he said.

Whatever he was asking for, his mom dragged him out of the room. She was ready to kill him.

"What are you doing?" she asked.

"My high school coach told me, 'Ask them for some money,'" he said.

"My mom told me, when she pulled me outside, 'You got an opportunity. Take your butt back in there. Go sign that contract,'" Wash said. "She didn't say 'butt.'"

He went back in, needless to say, and of the 156 youngsters who tried out in New Orleans, he was the only player the Royals signed. Wash spent two years in Florida. He learned a lot about baseball and about people. The players attended school together, ate together, traveled together.

"They taught us respect, work ethic, attitude, commitment," he said. "They taught us to be one."

Even though he struggled at the plate in the beginning, he never lost confidence.

"I just had to figure it out," he said. "I taught myself through failure. I failed, but I only failed in that moment. I'm not a failure. And when I started coaching, this is the way I preached to my players: 'You failed, but you're not a failure.'"

By the late seventies, Wash was as far from failure as you could get. Now an infielder—he was too skinny to catch—he was rising in the Dodgers organization, traded by the Royals in 1976. In September 1977, when teams were allowed to expand their rosters, Los

Angeles called him up. He took advantage of the opportunity, with 7 hits in 19 at bats, a .368 average.

Only the Dodgers were loaded in the infield—Ron Cey, Bill Russell, and Davey Lopes were still active—so, in 1978, Wash was with the club's top farm affiliate, the Albuquerque Dukes. Early in the season, the Dukes traveled to Salt Lake City. There was ice and snow all around.

"We shouldn't have been playing," Wash said.

But play they did, and in that game, he hit a ground ball to short. Man, could he fly in those days.

"I ran down the line," Wash remembered, "and I was thinking, 'He [the shortstop] is not going to get me.' Then my leg popped, and that was the end of that."

Wash tried to come back in July, but it turned out he had torn up his knee. He was operated on in September. The doctors put him in a half cast for six weeks, until the swelling went down. The prognosis wasn't encouraging.

"Hey, Wash," Dr. Frank Jobe, a noted orthopedic surgeon, told him in the operating room, "I think your career is over."

Most ballplayers might have been too shaken to say very much in a moment like that. Playing baseball is usually plan A *and* plan B. Not Wash. The man was hardly ever at a loss for words.

"Dr. Jobe, you don't know me," he said. "My name is Ron Washington and I'm from New Orleans. I'll be back."

Not for a second did he think he wouldn't be, even after his friends and members of his family suggested he give up what appeared to be a hopeless struggle.

"I couldn't give it up," he said. "I was born to be a baseball player. When I was in elementary school, the first time I filled out one of those cards, 'What do you want to be in life?' I put 'professional baseball player.' I knew I loved the game of baseball."

Nor did he ever feel sorry for himself, approaching rehab the same way that he approached every at bat: with aggression. He worked with a therapist seven days a week. For about six months, when he had a brace on, he could only do quad lifts to repair the damage. He did the lifts about an hour each day.

Wash made it back in 1981, although not with the Dodgers, who couldn't wait for him to recover and traded him to the Minnesota Twins. And, sadly, not as the player he was before. The injury robbed him of, essentially, three full years—years he could never get back.

"Before the injury, I could do everything," he said. "I still was able to run. I just wasn't able to run with the intensity that I ran with before."

He hung around Minnesota until the Twins let him go during spring training in 1987. Over six seasons with the ball club, he averaged about 200 at-bats a season, although his contribution was much greater than that. You might say he was a manager in training.

"Everybody on the team would come to me for advice," he said, and not just about how to play the game. Having trouble with girlfriends, kids, whatever, go see Wash, he'd tell you how to handle it. "I always dealt with it in right and wrong, and when you put it on a table and dealt with it [in those terms], you always make the right decision."

Yet even as his playing career was winding down, first in Baltimore, then Cleveland, and, finally, with the Houston Astros in 1989, he pictured himself as a future third-base coach, not a manager. "I was always an action kid," he explained, "and I saw the action in that third-base coaching box. My expertise in this game has been infield, so that's what I wanted to do."

The New York Mets noticed his potential to be a mentor as well.

"They told me whenever I decided to give it up, please give them the first call," he said.

He coached in the Mets' minor league organization for five seasons before the Oakland A's hired him in 1996 to be their first-base, and infield coach. One year later, he moved to third base.

Talk about being in the right place at the right time. The A's were filled with young, talented infielders, like third baseman Eric Chavez and shortstop Miguel Tejada. Wash made them better. He showed Chavez how to use his feet to field grounders. Chavez went on to win several Gold Gloves, and he gave one of the trophies to Wash. Tejada was the American League's MVP in 2002.

"The first time they asked me about Eric Chavez being a Gold Glove, my statement was 'It's up to Eric Chavez,'" he recalled. "He put in the time."

Just as important, the players, on many occasions, went to him with any issues instead of seeing the manager, Art Howe, and later, Ken Macha.

"You always have to have a go-between [for] the manager and the players," he said, "and I was that guy."

Wash knew which issues he could deal with and which ones he couldn't. On those he couldn't, he told the players, in no uncertain terms, what they needed to do for themselves and for the good of the team.

"The attitude you have is going to infest itself in the attitude we have throughout the clubhouse," he told them, "and we can't have that. The only way this is going to be settled, in your favor or not, is for you to go up there and see the man."

Typically, Wash would escort the player to the manager's office, the player assuming Wash would sit in on the conversation. He had no such intention. Shortly after bringing the parties together, he'd be gone. He could still fly. The players called him all sorts of names afterward but had to admit he'd been right. The matter was usually resolved.

No wonder his name would pop up when teams were looking for managers. Every time he went for an interview—in Florida, and twice with the Oakland A's—he was convinced he'd knocked it out of the park.

"There wasn't anything they could ask me about the game of baseball that I couldn't answer," he said.

Only he didn't receive a single offer. Some guys might become a bit resentful and maybe even begin to think someone had it out for them. Not Wash. He never let being rejected make him bitter or believe in himself any less. He kept doing his job.

"I couldn't make those people hire me," he explained. "But I can tell you they knew I was pretty good."

They also knew that he had strong opinions. Order him to do something, and he will do it. But if you let him make his own decision, don't be surprised if it's not what you had in mind. So for Wash to land a managerial job, it would take a fairly secure general manager to persuade an owner to give him a try. That GM turned out to be the Rangers' Jon Daniels, who hired him in 2006 to replace Buck Showalter.

Wash was ready for his close-up. He would manage the game just as he learned it at the academy, and in the Dodgers' organization.

"I pounded fundamentals from the day I arrived there," he said.

Still, there was much to learn, especially about the pitching aspect of the game. Early on, he believed in allowing his starters to work out of any jams they created. That didn't end so well at times. The more he learned about them, the less hesitant he was to give them the hook.

"Rather have them mad at me than have the whole team mad at me when we had a chance not to give up those extra runs," he reasoned.

If players ever did get mad about anything, he made sure they felt the freedom to let him know.

"If you're right," he told them, "I've got to sit here and take it. If you're wrong, you give me a chance to get back at you. Bring your baggage. Don't come here and think you don't have baggage. Because my baggage is already in here."

Even so, Wash had his work cut out for him.

"My first year there was a rough time," he said. "I tried to change the way they did things. Whatever I got on offense, I accepted, but I wanted pitching and defense. That was the attitude I had."

Soon the culture in the clubhouse started to change. Wash had been on ball clubs where there wasn't as strong a bond between players, and as the losses piled up, so did the blame. That wouldn't happen on his watch.

"There wasn't anybody on the outside in Texas that could destroy what we had in that clubhouse," he said. "When one guy screwed up and cost us something, it cost all of us. He's family, and we don't go against family. We come back tomorrow and prepare to make up for what we did the day before."

In the summer of 2009, one guy screwed up all right: Wash.

No, not on the field. There, the Rangers were making real progress; in 2009, they were on their way toward finishing 87-75, 8 games better than 2008. His mistake was using cocaine, even if, as he said, he did it just once. Once was once too many. In July, after testing positive for the substance, he was sure he'd lose his job.

He didn't. Daniels and the Rangers' president, Hall of Fame pitcher Nolan Ryan, accepted Wash's apology, and he got the counseling he needed. He took three drug tests a week and passed each one.

The crisis was averted. Well, not entirely. During spring training the following March, *Sports Illustrated* broke the story. Wash had to meet with reporters and the people he cared most about, his players. He hoped they would be there for him.

"I told my guys, before I went to the press conference, 'I don't want you to be with me because I'm your manager. I only want you to be on my side because that's what you feel in your heart you want to do,'" Wash said.

His players were by his side, all right, literally joining him at the press conference. He got through the day.

"None of them judged," he said. "They knew who I was."

If anything, the club became even tighter. It would be no stretch to suggest Wash regards his players as the children he and his wife, Gerry, never had. Little wonder the Rangers went on that season to capture their division by nine games over the Oakland A's and represent the American League in the World Series. Their opponent would be the San Francisco Giants.

"We were on the cusp," Wash explained, "but that [the players standing by him] sealed the deal. That's what we were searching for, that type of clubhouse character."

Against the Giants, however, the Rangers managed to win just one game. Wash was impressed.

"They were too good," Wash said. "The reports we got were that they were old and slow."

So much for those reports.

Losing the Series hurt, as it should. Yet he was patient. He had been through enough losses in his life—the three years he missed because of the knee injury was a major one—to know you can't rush these things. Not if you ever hope to move on. When his players took off for the winter, he was confident each man would deal with the pain of losing in his own way, in his own time.

Nonetheless, when the club got back together for spring training in 2011, Wash felt the need to discuss the matter with everybody right away. Just once.

"You did your best," he told his players. "There isn't anything we can do about it. This group in this room can still win and play good baseball, and that's what we're going to do in 2011. And if anybody's got anything to say, let's go around the room, get it out, because when this meeting is over, we're going to deal with 2011."

They were ready to go. Only they didn't seem anything like the 2010 Rangers over the first three months, being barely above .500 at the halfway mark, although that was still good enough to lead the division. Finally, just before the All-Star Game, Texas won seven straight and five more after the break, and never looked back.

In their final twenty-five games, the Rangers went 19-6. That's what you call peaking at the perfect time.

Wash couldn't have been more confident going into the 2011 World Series. The Rangers, he had no doubt, would play aggressively, even if St. Louis had the best defensive catcher in the game, Yadier Molina.

"If we were going to try to steal, we were going to steal," Wash recalled. "He [Molina] was just going to have to blow us up every night, all night long."

Easier said than done. The Rangers stole only one base the first two games in St. Louis, but, more important, stole Game 2, scoring 2 runs in the top of the ninth to win 2–1 and tie the Series. The momentum didn't last. The Cardinals took Game 3 in Texas 16–7, although the Rangers won the next two to assume a 3–2 lead. A World Series title, the first in the history of the franchise, was in their sights.

Even more so when the teams went to the bottom of the ninth inning in Game 6. With the Rangers up by two runs, they brought in their closer, Neftalí Feliz, to finish it off. Wash wasn't thinking too far ahead—baseball lifers usually don't—but he felt confident he was pushing the right buttons.

"I'm thinking situation," he said. "The matchups, in my opinion, were perfect."

Except Feliz was no Mariano Rivera, the future Hall of Fame closer for the Yankees. In three appearances in the Series, Feliz had put on the first batter he faced each time. Put on the leadoff man in this situation, and Albert Pujols, one of the greatest home run hitters of all time, would come to the plate with a chance to tie it with one swing. In the Game 3 rout, he'd hit 3 homers.

Feliz seemed unfazed by the moment. He retired the leadoff hitter this time, whiffing Ryan Theriot on a 98-mile-per-hour fastball. One down. Even if Pujols hit one out, the Rangers would still be up by a run. Pujols reached on a double to center. So the tying run would come up after all, in right fielder Lance Berkman.

Berkman, who had homered already this game, was having one heck of a World Series, batting .409. Feliz proceeded to walk him on four pitches. The tying run was on first, and the potential winning run, Allen Craig, was at the plate. But Craig struck out looking and the Rangers were now 1 out away.

The next batter was David Freese, and before long, Feliz had him in a hole, 1 ball and 2 strikes. At this point, you would figure that Wash, being the excitable guy he was, would be pacing the dugout. He wasn't.

Jackie Moore, the Rangers' bench coach, asked him, "Skip, how you doing?"

"Jackie, I'm just as calm as I can be," Wash responded. "It's in their hands. They got us here, and if we're going to win it, they're going to have to win it for us."

They seemed about to do just that when Freese hit that fly to right. Until Cruz froze and the ball took off. Just in front of the wall, he stuck out his glove but couldn't make the catch. The runners scored. The game was tied 7–7.

Wash knows what happened, and it wasn't just that Cruz misplayed the ball. He'd been instructed to play a straightway right, but, on his own, had moved in at some point during the Freese at-bat. Wash took some of the responsibility.

"Myself and [Coach] Gary Pettis took our eyes off of Nelson," he said. "We had him in 'no doubles' and missed him coming in a few steps."

Then, once Freese hit it, Cruz made his second mistake: he froze.

Feliz, and the Rangers, got out of the inning without the Cardinals doing any more damage. *No big deal,* Wash told himself. *We're still in the ball game.*

Wait, we're not just still in it. We're going to win it. That's how Wash felt after Josh Hamilton, the power-hitting outfielder, smacked a 2-run homer in the top of the tenth to put the Rangers back on top, 9–7.

"We had been waiting for Josh the whole Series," Wash said. "Josh had been playing with a groin injury, and he busts loose."

Heading into the bottom of the tenth, Wash called for another reliever, the lefty Darren Oliver. Oliver, forty-one, had been in the major leagues since 1993. The logic was sound.

"I know a lot of people questioned why I didn't send Neftalí back out there," Wash said, "[but] he wasn't in a good mental state after he gave up the tying run. They [the Cardinals] were sending up two left-handers, and Darren Oliver had a 0.70-something ERA against left-handers."

Baseball being as unpredictable as ever, though, you know what you can do with your logic. In the tenth, Daniel Descalso led off with a sharp single to right. Jon Jay followed with a base hit to left. The Cardinals just wouldn't die.

The runners advanced to second and third on a bunt. That was it for Oliver. Scott Feldman, a right-hander, came in to face the right-handed Theriot.

Wash was as calm as he was before St. Louis tied it in the ninth, as calm as one can possibly be with so much on the line. Feldman retired Theriot on a ground ball to third. A run scored to make it 9–8, but the Rangers were again 1 out away.

With first base open, Feldman walked Pujols intentionally, bringing up Berkman. As hot as he was, Lance Berkman was no Albert Pujols. He fouled the first pitch back. Strike 1. The next was inside. Ball 1. He fouled off the third. Strike 2.

No way, you figured, could a ball club come this far—1 strike away from a title for a second time—and not finish the job. Except for the 1986 Red Sox, of course.

Inside. Ball 2.

The next pitch was low, where Feldman wanted it. Berkman

couldn't do much with it, but he did enough. The ball landed safely in right center, and, remarkably, the game was tied again, 9–9. Poor Wash.

"When he hit that ball, I was going, 'I don't believe it,'" he said. "He got beat, but he put a good swing on the ball. If he had put a bad swing on the ball, maybe [second baseman Ian Kinsler] would have caught it. I looked at Jackie and said, 'Two champs, baby, nobody's giving up.'"

Somebody, of course, had to win it eventually, and it was the Cards, when Freese, who was raised in the St. Louis area, hit a lead-off homer in the eleventh off Mark Lowe. Nothing better than being a hero in the World Series in front of your hometown fans *twice, in the same game,* to keep your team alive.

And nothing worse than being on the other end of such heroics.

"We were supposed to keep the ball in on him," Wash said, "and we let one get out over the plate."

Wash had a tough assignment now. He had to find the right words, and quickly, for a group that could practically taste the champagne. They had to be hurting like never before, and Game 7 was less than twenty-four hours away. That's when the clubhouse culture he worked to create paid off in a big way. Wash wasn't the only one to be a leader.

"My guys stood up and were rallying each other," he said. "Kinsler got up and said, 'Hey, we've been a good team all year. We knew this was going to go seven.' [Texas's first baseman] Michael Young said something similar. Hey, we believed."

No one believed more strongly than Wash. Just as he believed he'd rebound from the torn knee, however long it took.

"It's no big deal," he urged his players. "We've come back from this type of stuff before."

The clubhouse cleared and everybody headed back to the hotel . . . to ponder what might have been, no doubt. Wash had dinner with his wife and went to sleep. Any thoughts of how close he and his team had come—well, let's just say he was better off without them.

"If I would have started thinking like that, I wouldn't have been able to sleep," he explained. "I knew I had another game to play."

That game was here before he knew it, and the only question was: Could the Rangers regroup? The answer, at least in the early going: Yes.

They scored 2 runs in the top of the first inning against the Cards' gritty Chris Carpenter, and had a man on second with 1 out, the dangerous Adrián Beltré at the plate.

"We had it set up," Wash said. "We should have blown it open."

They didn't. Carpenter struck out Beltré and got Cruz on a grounder. Those were the only runs the Rangers would put on the board all night. Final score: St. Louis 6, Texas 2. The Cardinals were the one and only champions.

Those 1986 Red Sox now had company. Wash wasn't thinking about any of that. He had another speech to give, this one even tougher than the last. It should come as no shock that he knew just what to say.

"I went up there and I rallied them," he said. "I expressed how proud I was, that there were two champions out there on the field."

Shortly afterward, Beltré stopped by his office.

"Skip, I'm so sorry this got away from you," Beltré said.

"No, no, this got away from *us*," Wash said. "It didn't get away from me. We were all in this together."

"Yeah, but I wanted it so bad for you," Beltré went on.

"And I wanted it so bad for you guys."

Wash had done his job. He was strong in front of the men who needed him to be strong. The next day, however, meeting in Texas with the owner, general manager, and the scouts, he couldn't keep his emotions in check any longer.

"It hit me hard," he remembered. "I talked about my team, about the loss. Finally, finally, it came. I was crying for me and them."

So there *is* crying in baseball, and Wash was better off for it. Because, unlike Calvin Schiraldi, he didn't put up walls that would imprison him for decades. He allowed himself to grieve, and he allowed those around him to see how much pain he was in. He and his Rangers didn't simply lose the World Series. Lots of teams do that. They lost the Series after twice being just 1 strike away. Try to imagine anything in baseball—in any sport—more heartbreaking.

Wash went home that night, and into the off-season, feeling a heck of a lot better.

"Once I got it all out of me in that room, that was it," he explained. "I did my everyday thing and never reflected on it. I was focused on the next year."

It helped quite a bit that there were no regrets. He didn't miss a field goal or attempt a risky maneuver or allow his man to make the winning shot at the buzzer; all his decisions, from one batter to the next, had been deliberate and carefully plotted out in the manner that the slow pace of baseball allows. Wash put the right people in the right spots, hoping they would perform as they did all year long. The fact that they didn't wasn't his fault.

"We never gave anything to St. Louis," Wash pointed out. "It just wasn't meant to be."

Nor did he have a bad word to say about Nelson Cruz. Remember the academy. One. Always one.

"We said that when we lose, we all lose," he said. "I'm not putting any blame on Nelson. We wouldn't have been there if it wasn't for Nelson Cruz."

Perhaps not—Cruz hit 29 homers and knocked in 87 runs that year—but the fact that he has escaped the ridicule Bill Buckner suffered from his error in the 1986 World Series seems unfair. Buckner made one mistake; Cruz made two. Again, history tends to beat up on certain victims while giving a pass to others. You can bet if Cruz had been playing right field for the Red Sox, given their fan base, and not the Rangers, he would have been judged more harshly.

In any case, how the Rangers would react the next season would say a lot about the clubhouse character Wash was so fond of and his skills as a motivator. Coming a strike away from winning it all is not something you forget about in a few months.

Safe to say that clubhouse character was as strong as he claimed it was. The Rangers made the playoffs in 2012, and although they lost in the wild card game, they gave themselves a chance, and you can't ask for much more.

"In this business, you have to be able to move on," Wash said, who was determined to maintain "the mind-set that we had the past three years. I was confident we were still in a good position to make a run at this thing again."

Even when he was reminded of how close his team had been in 2011, it didn't get him down.

"In baseball [during the World Series], how many teams were sitting at home?" he said. "Twenty-eight, and if I had to go through the rest of my life being number twenty-nine, I'll take it."

Wash is happy these days. That's because he's back in the only world he's ever known and loved. He's again the third-base coach for the Oakland A's.

He'd resigned from the Rangers during the final month of the 2014 season. Not because of his team's performance, though the ball club would finish under .500 that year, but because he had messed up once more. He cheated on his wife of forty-two years and was now afraid of losing something more important than his job: his marriage.

"I was totally worried," Wash recalled. "My wife is a true Christian. I just knew she was going to leave, but she stuck by me."

Once again, as in 2010, when the cocaine story broke, he came out in public and admitted his mistake.

"I didn't want people out there speculating and guessing," Wash said. "Nobody did anything but me. So I thought it was best I take the blame, the darts and the arrows and the knives and everything else."

After the press conference, we didn't hear much from Wash for the longest time. He needed to come to terms with what he'd done, and it would take a while. He couldn't forgive himself even when his wife told him to. Wash couldn't forgive himself until he was ready, until he had faced, in his own soul, the full extent of the loss: the lost trust between himself and the woman he adored, the lost trust he'd fight like hell to earn back. The way he fought for everything he earned his whole life.

"I just woke up one morning," he said, "and I was at peace."

Well, not completely. Peace wouldn't truly come until he was back in baseball, and given the shame he brought on himself and the organization in Texas, many people weren't willing to give him that chance. Not yet.

"I called a lot of friends," Wash said. "I called in a lot of favors, and the only one who had the balls was [Oakland A's then GM] Billy Beane. I knew what position I was putting them in. I wasn't angry."

Wash joined the A's in May 2015 and, as usual, works with the infielders on their fundamentals. They are the fundamentals he learned at the academy, and in the Dodgers' organization. Baseball has changed a lot in forty-five years, and not one bit.

He has changed, however. No longer, when he's on the road, does he go only from the ballpark to the hotel and back to the ballpark. Last fall, in New York City, he went for the first time to the Statue of Liberty and the World Trade Center Memorial Plaza. In Chicago, he visited the Navy Pier.

"When you sit at home and you feel like you've lost something, it's a different animal," he said. "I get to go to these cities for free."

He feels a similar appreciation for his years in Texas, despite the heartbreak of 2011.

"I was part of something special," Wash said. "Texas got turned into a baseball town by the way we went out and played, the attitude we brought, the commitment we showed."

Whether Wash will ever manage again is unclear. He turned sixty-four in April 2016. He has, as he would put it, a lot of baggage. He also has a lot to offer. If he does receive a second chance, you can be certain he'll manage the same way he managed in Texas. With aggression. One.

He may never get to another Series, let alone be a strike away from winning it all. The fly ball Nelson Cruz couldn't catch might be the closest he ever comes. Whatever happens, Wash will be just fine. He discovered early on that losing was a part of life, and baseball was no exception. He also learned that he could overcome any loss, as long as he faced it head on. That included losses of his own doing, as well as the ones out of his control. He never ran from them, and he's not about to start now.

8

SLAMMED!

APRIL 4, 1983

The defense was doing everything it was supposed to do in a tie game with just seconds left. Closing off the passing lanes. Stopping the dribble penetration. Keeping the shooters from getting in good position. You can't play defense in college basketball any better than that, especially given everything that was hanging in the balance. The game was clearly headed for overtime.

"Coach [Guy Lewis] made a great defensive adjustment," Reid Gettys recalled, "and we went to our half-court trap. It dictated where the ball was being swung, and the specific passes that were thrown were exactly the ones they were supposed to throw. That's why they ended up with such a desperation heave."

Reid, at the time, was a point guard for the University of Houston Cougars. You probably know them better by their nickname, Phi Slama Jama. No team at the college level had ever played the game quite the way the Cougars did during the early eighties, running and dunking nonstop for forty minutes. Miss one possession, and you might miss something special—a dazzling pass, a blocked shot out of nowhere, a thundering slam—everyone will be talking about for days.

Now, thanks to the suffocating defense they were playing against North Carolina State, they would still have an excellent chance to do what many expected when March Madness kicked off a few weeks earlier: win the national championship.

They were too talented *not* to win it. Seriously, check out these two studs who were on the 1982–83 squad:

- Akeem Olajuwon, the gifted seven-foot sophomore center from Nigeria who could score, rebound, and block shots. Olajuwon was still relatively new to the game of basketball and in his first season as a full-time starter. Man, wait until he really knew what he was doing on the court.
- Clyde "the Glide" Drexler, the junior forward who could slash his way to the basket seemingly at will.

Olajuwon and Drexler would go on to become superstars in the NBA, each named among the fifty greatest players in history.

But the Cougars were much more than a two-man team. They were deep at every position on the floor, with Benny Anders, Michael Young, Alvin Franklin, Larry Micheaux, and Reid Gettys.

The unit Coach Lewis put together ended the season as the no. 1 team in the nation with a record of 27-2, winning their last 22 in a row. Early on, the NCAA tournament was proving to be just as easy. The Cougars beat Maryland by 10, Memphis by 7, and Villanova by 18 on their way to the Final Four. Then, in the semis, they ran into what would clearly be their toughest challenge, the University of Louisville Cardinals.

With their own nickname, the Doctors of Dunk, the Cardinals were the one team athletic enough to keep up with the Cougars. Louisville finished the season at no. 2 in the polls, with a roster that included Milt Wagner, Billy Thompson, Lancaster Gordon, Charles Jones, and the McCray brothers, Scooter and Rodney.

The hype before the game, to be played at the Pit in Albuquerque, New Mexico, was huge, and with good reason. To many, this was the *real* national championship game. Whoever won would be a heavy favorite in the title game against either of the surprise squads that would come out of the other bracket: North Carolina State or Georgia.

Reid and his teammates couldn't wait for the opening tip.

"All season long," Reid pointed out, "our preparations included how other teams were going to try to take us out of what we did, how they were going to slow the game down and turn it into a half-court grind. And for the first time, our preparations included preparing for an opponent that wanted to play the game exactly the way we wanted to play. I can't tell you how exciting it was preparing for that."

To play in that game was even more exciting, because if there ever were a Final Four matchup that lived up to the hype, Houston vs. Louisville was the one.

Louisville gained the early edge and led by 5 points, 41–36, at the break of a tension-filled opening half. So tense that Coach Lewis was assessed a technical foul for tossing a towel at Scooter McCray after he stole the ball.

Lewis claimed the towel "slipped" out of his hand. Sure it did, Coach.

Both teams were sprinting down the floor as if they were being timed by Olympic judges, and this was in the days before college basketball had a shot clock.

The second half was even more of a track meet. There was one dunk after another. The Cougars had 14 in all, 10 in the second half, 5 from Olajuwon. Four of the dunks came on four straight possessions! Olajuwon also grabbed 15 rebounds and blocked 4 shots in the final twenty minutes. Phi Slama Jama literally ran Louisville out of the tournament with a 58–40 second half to win 94–81.

However, playing at that kind of pace, in an altitude of approximately 5,000 feet no less, took a toll. So Lewis decided on a lighter practice than usual the next day, Sunday. Not that anyone figured it would make a difference. The sacrificial lamb—sorry, opponent— for the championship game on Monday night, as it turned out, would be North Carolina State.

The Wolfpack, after all, already had ten losses, and in the first round of the tournament trailed Pepperdine by 6 points with under a minute left in overtime before winning in double overtime. *Pepperdine*. Talk about a slam dunk.

But a funny thing happened on the way to the coronation. NC State, coached by the charismatic Jim Valvano, was better than people realized. Meanwhile, the Cougars, for whatever reason—the altitude, overconfidence, a letdown after the Louisville thriller, who knows?—chose the worst time to play their worst game of the tournament, and of the season.

Yet here the two teams were, tied at 52–52, and all Houston needed was to execute during these final seconds, then take care of business in the overtime, and no one would ever care how the Cougars won the title. Just that they did win it.

With only five seconds left, Wolfpack guard Dereck Whittenburg had the ball more than 30 feet from the hoop. Whittenburg was no Steph Curry. All he could do was throw it somewhere near the rim and pray.

Maybe, just maybe, he would pull off a miracle and the ball would go in. But, far more likely, once he missed, overtime it would be.

Reid Gettys, from probably the day he learned how to dribble, dreamed of going to Texas Tech, where his father, Marshall Gettys, was an outstanding offensive and defensive tackle in the late forties. Reid bought posters, T-shirts, blankets, comforters, anything he could find that came with a double T.

"I had more red and black than any human being ever had," he said.

The way Reid saw his future in college sports, there was Texas Tech and nowhere else.

So imagine his disappointment when Gerald Myers, the university's basketball coach, who attended Reid's last high school game in early 1981, told him on the court afterward that he wouldn't be offering him a scholarship.

The dream was gone, just like that. Reid, who played for Memorial in Houston, couldn't believe it. Texas Tech was where he was certain he belonged, with the other six-foot-six white guys. Now what?

Reid wouldn't have to wait very long to find out. Only a few minutes, as a matter of fact. That's when Guy Lewis, who had been sitting next to Myers at the game, told Reid something he didn't expect to hear: "You can play for me."

For *you*? For the University of Houston? With all due respect, was Coach Lewis out of his mind?

"I don't fit in with run and gun," Reid thought.

Lewis obviously thought otherwise. Besides, it wasn't as if Reid was inundated with other options.

"I had one scholarship offer," he said. "I didn't have a junior college. I didn't have a Division II or a Division III. I had two choices. I could play for the University of Houston, or I was going to play for the Sigma Chis [intramurals] at Texas."

Houston it was, although the feeling of not quite fitting in didn't go away in those first few weeks of practice. So one day he decided to play the game the way his more athletic teammates did. He quickened his pace and worked on breaking whoever guarded him off the dribble. Let's just say practice didn't go as he planned.

"I was humiliated," Reid remembered, "and he [Coach Lewis] did it intentionally, to teach me a lesson. He could have stopped it immediately."

Afterward, Lewis told him to come into his office.

"Let me ask you a question," the coach said. "That crap I saw today, all the dribbling between your legs and the crazy passes. What the hell are you doing? Why are you playing that way?"

"It's the way I always play," Reid assured him.

Lewis, the Houston coach since the mid-fifties, knew better.

"Son, do you think I offered you a scholarship and never watched you play?" he asked. "I watched you play a dozen times. I've never seen any of that. So why would you show up and try to be like everybody else? I need you to be you. Leave it to me to put it all together. But if you try to be like everyone else, I don't have any need for you."

About a month later, once the season started, Reid had a similar chat with another older man he respected, his father. Reid told him he wasn't receiving enough playing time.

"The challenge," Marshall Gettys said, "is for you to make it difficult for your coach not to play you. So what are you doing in practice? How are you shooting the ball?"

"I'm shooting the ball really well," his son responded.

"Can anyone else shoot the ball?"

"Yeah, a lot of people can shoot the ball."

"Well, apparently, that's not the answer. What is it that nobody else is doing?"

The answer was clear. Nobody else passed the ball, and that was a top priority for Guy Lewis. So much so that, during intra-squad scrimmages on Saturdays before the season started, with officials present, he sat in a chair near half-court and kept tabs of just two numbers: assists and charges. He revealed the final totals after the scrimmage.

"You'd think he'd keep track of dunks and scoring," Reid said.

The messages from his coach and father sunk in, and from then on, Reid worked hard to be the best passer he could be. That meant getting to know his teammates, their strengths and weaknesses.

"There are two qualifications to a good pass: where you throw it and who you throw it to," Reid explained. "So I began to study: When is Mike Young at his best? Where is Clyde most comfortable?"

He became so good at knowing his teammates and their tendencies that he'd end his career with the most assists in school history, 740.

Learning from his father was nothing new to Reid, no lesson more valuable than the one about competition itself, what it meant, and what it didn't mean. Marshall Gettys loved to compete. He couldn't have accomplished what he did at Texas Tech, excelling on offense and defense, if he didn't. However, he felt strongly that the football field was only one field in life, and certainly not the most important one.

"He had the firmest foundation of any human being I've ever seen, in any walk of life," said Reid, one of three brothers. "From the beginning, we were taught sports is what you do, not who you are. You have to place your priority in something that will stand up to defeat. And sports doesn't stand up to defeat."

Other lessons came from men his own age, the impact just as profound. Such as during a practice freshman year when one of his teammates challenged him to a fight. Reid backed down. Eric Davis, another player on the team, watched the heated exchange and couldn't contain himself.

"He was so pissed off at me," Reid said. "He grabbed me and said, 'If you ever do that again, you're done. You look him in the eye and you tell him you are going to kick his ass.'"

The next day, he was challenged again, and this time, he didn't back down.

Reid got his ass kicked, not the other way around—he wasn't used to fighting—but Davis was proud of him. Two other teammates, Larry "Mr. Mean" Micheaux and Lynden Rose, also took a liking to him, and Reid is convinced he wouldn't have stuck around without the support of all three.

"We were all Houston kids, but I was a kid from the suburbs," he said. "Because they accepted me, everyone did."

Fights became as routine as layup drills at Houston practices. There was, believe it or not, a fight on the floor of the Superdome in New Orleans the day before the game against Michael Jordan and North Carolina in the semifinals of the Final Four in 1982. The Tar Heels beat the Cougars 68–63 and won the title, over Georgetown, two days later.

"Hakeem threw a punch and missed Benny and hit me," Reid recalled.

Coach Lewis wasn't upset. Far from it.

"We're ready," he told his players. "Let's go."

"If we didn't have blood or a fight," Reid said, "it wasn't a very good practice."

Guy Lewis and his staff didn't overlook North Carolina State, that Reid will always be sure of, no matter how many "experts" may suggest the opposite. They weren't in the team meetings or in practices. He was.

"Coach Lewis told us they were the best team at the Final Four," Reid insisted. "When they had all their guys healthy, they went through the ACC with [only] two losses."

No doubt the Cougars were feeling pretty good about themselves after the Louisville game. But now they needed to *forget* about the Louisville game. That game was not the real national championship. The next one was.

"Because of what happened Saturday, and what everyone is saying about that game, don't buy it," Lewis told his players. "This game [against NC State] will be harder."

He was right about that. The championship game was a dogfight from the opening tip, and it never got easier.

NC State showed absolutely no fear, playing at a speedier pace than anyone predicted to grab a quick 6–0 lead. The Wolfpack then suddenly got cold, missing 10 shots in a row, but with just over twelve minutes left in the half, Houston down, 10–7, Drexler committed his third foul. Lewis would have no choice but to take him out, and pray that the deficit didn't grow too large before he could bring him back, probably not until the second half. This was no time to gamble.

Try telling that to Guy Lewis.

"We were playing so poorly that Coach was just hoping," Reid said. "That's why Clyde was left in. Clyde doesn't need much to get going. One steal, one dunk, and we're off and flying."

Maybe, but one more foul and the Cougars would be in trouble, and with about three minutes to go in the half, that's exactly what happened. Still, Lewis left him in again. He was really taking a big chance now.

At the break, the Wolfpack were ahead by 8 points, 33–25. Their leading scorer was forward Thurl Bailey, with 15 points. The Cougars, on the other hand, had made only 10 of their 32 field goal attempts. They couldn't shoot much worse.

To their credit, there was no panic in the Houston locker room and no harsh words from Lewis. He believed in his guys as much as ever. And, more important, they believed in themselves.

"We weren't at our best," Reid recalled, "and there we were, still with a chance to win."

The Cougars began the second half on a 6–0 run, and that was with Drexler on the bench. Anders made a jump shot and followed with a runner in the lane. Olajuwon then hit from close range. The lead, just like that, was only 2.

Better yet, the way the Cougars were executing, Lewis didn't have to put Drexler back in and risk a fifth foul. No telling how critical that might be as the game wore on.

Trying to regain momentum, Valvano called timeout.

Didn't work. Houston scored back-to-back baskets to take the lead, 35–33. Finally, Whittenburg hit from long range to break the drought. But a hoop from Olajuwon and a jump shot by Young put the Cougars up 40–35. The run was now 15–2, and Houston had dominated the boards 12–2 since the break.

Valvano called another timeout.

Soon there were only ten minutes left, and the Wolfpack, just 1 of 11 from the field, were stuck at 2 points *for the half*. It looked as though all of those pregame predictions might come true.

On the other hand, the Cougars had expended a lot of energy to come back, not to mention the energy they had spent in the Louisville game. Yes, they were leading, but the clock couldn't move fast enough.

"There's no question we were gassed," Reid admitted. "We have no rhythm on either end of the court, and we get a lead, and it's almost like you look up and think, 'Holy cow, how are we winning this game?'"

So, with about seven minutes left and a 44–40 lead, in an effort to conserve energy, Lewis chose to roll the dice once again. He went against everything his team had always done and decided to slow it down on offense. Reid had no objection to the strategy then, and doesn't now.

"Very little was going right," Reid said. "We were in foul trouble. We weren't making free throws. Coach Lewis had the courage to try something different. It wasn't like go with what got you there. Because nothing got us there!"

Tired or not, the Cougars kept NC State at bay. Olajuwon was having another monster game—he would finish with 20 points and 18 rebounds—and Drexler was back in. After Drexler converted a pair of free throws, Houston was up 52–46 with 3:20 remaining. Just keep up the defensive pressure, and, barring a dramatic turnaround, the Cougars would be national champions.

While the Houston strategy was to slow it down, Valvano's plan was to foul the Cougars on almost every possession. If the team had one weakness all season, it was that it converted only 61 percent of its free throws.

Valvano's plan worked, especially when it came to fouling Michael Young. Young, already 0 for 3 from the line, missed the front end of a one-and-one with 2:55 to go.

Meanwhile, Whittenburg and the other starting guard, Sidney Lowe, combined for three straight jumpers, and in less than a minute, NC State tied it at 52–52. You expected that from Whittenburg. Lowe, not so much. He hit several huge shots in the second half to keep his team in range.

On the next possession, Alvin Franklin, Houston's freshman guard, went to the line after he was fouled by Whittenburg with just over a minute left. He'd have 2 shots, as long as he made the first. The odds weren't the greatest. Franklin was just a 63 percent free throw shooter, and this would be his first try of the night. He had to be nervous.

The players weren't the only ones feeling the pressure. Lewis buried his head for a moment in the red-and-white polka-dotted towel he always held—now, no doubt, more tightly than ever.

There would be no second free throw. After Franklin missed the first, the most important rebound of the game was secured by NC State. Without a shot clock, the Wolfpack could hold the ball for the final shot. They called time with forty-four seconds to go.

Reid was replaced by Anders. As much as he wanted to stay in the game, he knew it was the right move.

"I would have made the same substitution," Reid said. "Benny was twice as fast, his arms were twice as long; he was ten times more athletic."

Lewis went with the half-court trap. NC State appeared out of sync, throwing passes that were far from crisp, Drexler coming close to a steal with twelve seconds left. Then a few seconds later there was another shaky pass, from Bailey in the corner toward Whittenburg, who was between the top of the key and half-court. Anders made his move. A steal, and game-winning hoop at the other end, was a real possibility.

"That defense," Reid said, "was set up to force a trap and a steal. It wasn't set up to force a trap and deny a pass. You invite the very pass that they threw, and then it's Benny's responsibility to run through that pass."

Which explains why Olajuwon, when he saw Anders go for the ball, headed toward the other end.

"Everyone wants to suggest the mistake was Hakeem taking off and running down the court," Reid said, "[but] he was doing exactly what he was supposed to do. He saw the trap, he saw the pass, and he saw Benny go. He's busting it to follow the play down the court."

Only there was no play down the court. Anders missed the ball by a matter of inches, but it might as well have been a mile.

"I emotionally collapsed when Benny didn't get the steal," Reid said. "I can close my eyes and see it today."

All didn't seem lost, however. Whittenburg was still too far from the basket to have a decent look.

That's when we saw an ending unlike any other in an NCAA title game.

Whittenburg's shot fell short of the rim . . . and right into the hands of NC State's Lorenzo Charles, suddenly by himself in front of the hoop. Olajuwon watched helplessly as Charles gently dunked it.

The buzzer sounded. The final score: 54–52. The Wolfpack were national champions. After leading 52–46, the mighty Houston Cougars didn't score a single point in the last three minutes, and the irony of it all was a team that had lived by the dunk, lost by a dunk, and the most unlikely dunk you could imagine: off an air ball.

To suggest the Cougars were stunned doesn't begin to describe the extent of their disbelief.

"You see the play and you think, 'Let's call timeout and run a play,' and then you realize the clock is over," Reid said. "Wait, we could not have just lost the national championship on an air ball. We did everything you could possibly do right and we lost the national championship."

After Valvano looked for someone, anyone, to hug—how many times have we seen that clip during March Madness?—Reid looked for a place to be alone. He took a seat on the stairs that went up from the locker room to the main concourse. Reid might have sat on those steps for thirty minutes. Who knows? He was so distraught, he wasn't counting. For everything his dad told him about putting losing in its place, his dad never lost anything as big as this.

"I didn't want to be around anyone," Reid said. "I didn't want to talk to anyone. I didn't want to see anyone."

At first, you think maybe he shouldn't feel so bad. There was nothing he could've done. He wasn't even on the court during that final possession. Reid doesn't see it that way. Not being in the lineup actually made the loss harder to accept. He was like every other player, believing that if he had been out there, the outcome would have been different.

He then quickly added, "That's not saying I would have made the play."

In any case, Reid couldn't sit on those stairs forever, as much as he may have wanted to. Believing his teammates had left the Pit, and that he could get dressed quickly and go with his parents back to the hotel, Reid finally got up and entered the locker room.

His teammates hadn't gone anywhere.

"It got really quiet," he said.

It was also quiet in those first few days back on campus.

"It was [similar to] when someone suffers a real tragedy and you don't know what to say to them," Reid said. "The classes, which were almost pep rallies when you left [for the Final Four], you walk in and people are afraid to talk to you and check on how you're doing."

Reid did have one thing going for him. He had two years of eligibility remaining, and with much of the core group returning, including Olajuwon, the Cougars would be a strong bet to make another deep run in the NCAA tournament.

Lewis told his players every fall he would be at the Final Four, one way or the other.

"I'd love to take you with me," he said.

In March 1984, for the third year in a row, he did just that.

The road was rockier than it was in 1983, each of Houston's first three games in the tournament decided by 8 points or fewer. In the semifinal, Houston squeezed by the University of Virginia in overtime, 49–47, a far cry from Phi Slama Jama vs. the Doctors of Dunk.

No matter. The Cougars were back in the championship game.

Reid would now get a chance for redemption one year later, just as Mike Lantry got the chance against the Buckeyes in 1974. Just imagine what Craig Ehlo or Lou Michaels would have given for a similar opportunity so soon after their crushing losses. And just imagine how differently their lives might have unfolded if they'd been able to take advantage.

In Reid's case, too bad the Cougars' opponent would be the Georgetown Hoyas, coached by John Thompson and led by a star center of their own, Patrick Ewing. The Hoyas, competing in the difficult Big East Conference, had lost three games the entire season, each by 4 points or fewer. No one would ever accuse the Cougars of taking this one for granted.

"It was the first time in at least two, if not three, years that I walked on the court thinking, 'We're the underdogs. These guys are better than us,'" Reid said.

They sure were. After falling behind early, Georgetown pulled away to win 84–75. Reid finished with 6 points and 7 assists. That would be his last real chance to win a title.

By Reid's senior year, Olajuwon was gone, as were Young and Anders. Every game was a struggle, the Cougars finishing 16-14. Reid became so frustrated that, in a game against SMU, he decided he couldn't take it anymore.

"I've never told anyone, but I intentionally fouled out," he said. "I got three fouls in two minutes late in the second half."

Reid didn't have to tell Lewis. He knew.

"Didn't want any more of that, did you?" the coach asked.

"No, sir," Reid said, "I didn't."

Shortly after the Cougars lost in their conference tournament, Reid, still in uniform, was sitting on the floor in the large, open shower room, alone, he thought, until he heard a noise. It was Coach Lewis. He was sitting down in his suit on the opposite side of the room, leaning against the wall.

"You know we're going to get a bid," Lewis said.

"To the NCAAs?" Reid asked.

Lewis shook his head no.

"The NIT?"

That was correct.

"Do we have to take it?"

"Boy, I hope not."

They took it, of course, and then took it again, from the Lamar Cardinals, who beat the Cougars 78–71 in the opening round. At least the season was over.

So ended the college basketball career of Reid Gettys, on the campus of Lamar University in Beaumont, Texas, about as far away as you could get from the Final Four.

As for moving on to the next level, Reid, chosen by the Chicago Bulls in the fifth round of the 1985 NBA Draft, summed it up: "I had a great NBA career. I got there [for training camp] on a Tuesday and was gone on a Wednesday."

Jerry Krause, the Bulls' general manager, gave him the news. "I hate this part of the job," Krause said. "We're going to let you go."

"Do you think I can make it in the league?" Reid asked. "Should I keep trying?"

Krause was blunt. "Son, you're really slow," he said.

"Yes, sir," Reid said.

"You're not very athletic."

"Yes, sir."

Once Krause was done putting him down, Reid asked, "Is that *it*? Did you not watch me in college?"

Reid went on to play for Athletes in Action, a faith-based team that traveled across the United States, and then hooked up with the Albany Patroons of the CBA, basketball's minor leagues, in the late eighties for one final try to make it to the NBA.

He has his share of stories from his CBA days, none better perhaps than the time he was watching television in a bar at the airport in Casper, Wyoming. Sitting with him was his teammate Sidney Lowe, the former Wolfpack point guard. The two had never said a word to each other about the NC State game.

Suddenly, there it was—the Whittenburg air ball, the Charles catch and dunk, the title that was taken away.

Why did they have to show this *now*? And why in front, of all people, Sidney Lowe? Reid tried to regroup.

"I'm thinking, 'Don't look at him,'" he said.

Don't look. Don't look. Don't . . .

He looked.

When he did, Lowe was "rolling his ring."

Unlike his tryout with the Bulls, Reid didn't need anyone in the CBA to tell him the truth. He figured it out on his own. He asked a trainer one day to tape his ankles.

"There's tape over there in the corner," Reid was told.

For someone whose ankles had been taped for him since he was in high school, it was time to move on.

Sure, the loss to NC State hurt for some time. If it hadn't, he wouldn't have been the competitor he was. Even today, despite all the great things in his life, and the perspective he has about winning and losing, there are still moments when the pain comes back and hits him in the gut. In late 2015, he found a bunch of old VHS tapes at his father's house and watched games he hadn't seen in more than thirty years. But there was one game he couldn't bring himself to watch.

Then there was the time he was interviewed by ESPN for a *30 for 30* episode that would be aired in 2013, around the thirtieth anniversary of the game.

"They pulled the monitor over and ran that last play, and it literally angered me," Reid recalled. "I felt trapped and tricked. Nobody has a right to make us watch it, and I have no interest in watching it again."

His reaction shows Reid hasn't totally gotten over the loss. Rather, he has learned how to live with it. He might never totally get over it.

"I went to five or six Final Fours after I was finished playing," Reid explained. "But I almost can't watch national championship games because of the losing bench. When they pan down those faces, to this day, it stings. I know that feeling."

At least the feeling doesn't last very long, and for that, he can again thank Marshall Gettys and the lessons he passed on to his three sons. Without that kind of solid foundation from the start, Reid might never have come to terms with the loss to NC State.

"A tragedy is a fourteen-year-old kid getting a brain tumor," Reid pointed out. "None of this was a tragedy. It was a hard, heartbreaking, emotional loss, but in the grand scheme of life, not so much."

These days, Reid works as a litigation attorney for ExxonMobil in Houston. He wins some, he loses some. The losses in the court-room can be as tough to absorb as the losses were on the court.

"We got popped up in New Hampshire for $236 million in 2013, and we just had the appeal last month," he said. "And every time I think about it, man, does it sting."

For two years, Reid coached his middle son's high school basket-ball team. As busy as he was, he couldn't turn down the chance to help his son grow, and help the other kids, too. He pushed the boys to compete hard on every possession, to play the game the way it was meant to be played, the way he learned how to play.

"That was my number one goal," he said, "to help them realize you can be a good sportsman, you can be a Christian athlete, and still knock somebody's head off when they come in the lane."

Reid also wanted them to understand that the rewards that come from belonging to a team don't depend on how many wins you have.

"I have three Final Four rings and I don't know where they are," he told them. "They're in some sock drawer somewhere. They mean nothing to me. What means something to me is what I was a part of, and what we stood for. You spend the rest of your life trying to create that same setting aside of yourself for something that's bigger than yourself."

His son's high school team, as it turned out, won back-to-back state championships. A few years later, two of the players stopped by the house to visit Reid's son.

"How often do you wear your rings?" Reid asked.

"What rings?" they said.

Perfect answer.

Rarely does a day go by in which someone doesn't ask him about Phi Slama Jama, and it can be in the most unexpected places. Such as when he was arguing a case in McAllen, Texas, about 350 miles southwest of Houston. The two sides were about to take a lunch break when the judge told Reid to approach the bench.

"I've been sitting here, and what I don't understand is, why stall?" the judge asked.

Reid was confused. "Judge, I'm putting witnesses on as fast as I can," he responded. "I dropped two of the defenses, and some of the exhibits, and I'm not going to bring in two experts."

"No, no, no," the judge said. "Why stall?"

Reid finally got it. "NC State?" he asked.

"Yeah," the judge said, as if it couldn't possibly be anything else.

On April 4, 2016, the NCAA title game between Villanova and North Carolina was played in Houston. Reid was there. The game, as you probably remember, was a thriller, Nova winning 77–74 on a three-pointer by Kris Jenkins at the buzzer.

As Reid was filing out of the arena, he got into a conversation with a few North Carolina fans. They had no idea who he was.

"Can you even imagine losing a game of that magnitude on a play like that?" one of them said.

Reid didn't miss a beat:

"Yeah, I can imagine that."

9

715

The fastball wasn't sinking, and for a major league pitcher, there may be nothing more frightening than a fastball that doesn't sink.

The hitter, if he's any good, and most hitters are—that's how they got here—will hit the ball hard and, more often than not, a long way. The hitter in this case wasn't just good, he was great. He was one of the greatest of all time.

No wonder Al Downing, the Los Angeles Dodgers' left-hander, knew he was in trouble.

The hitter was Henry Louis Aaron. Most people knew him better as Hank. And, on this April 1974 night in Atlanta, Georgia, he was trying to do something no one had done before.

Al doesn't recall too much about another night, three decades earlier, the night his life changed forever. He recalls his aunt waking him and his two brothers, sobbing and hugging them tightly. His mother was dead.

She was killed when the car she was riding in, driven by his father, Dover, was hit by another driver about ten miles from the couple's home in Trenton, New Jersey. Al's parents were returning from a Saturday night out. His father didn't talk about the accident, and Al didn't ask, then or ever.

He was just seven years old. Not surprisingly, upon losing his mother and not knowing how to channel his emotions at such a young age, he became angry. Al needed an outlet for that anger, and maybe sports would be it, particularly baseball and basketball. He loved to pitch. He loved to throw a rubber ball as hard as he could against the wall on the handball courts at the Boys Club. Or toss the ball against a roof and catch it before it fell to the ground.

Al was angry for years. In pickup games against his teenage sisters and their female friends in the neighborhood, if he ended up on the losing side, he sometimes would take the one bat and go home, or accuse the other team of cheating. What really ticked him off was when the girls rubbed it in by chanting *"Our team red-hot, your team been shot."* Al would even chase them with that bat. So out of control was his behavior that his father hesitated when Al asked for permission to try out for the Police Athletic League.

"I'm not going to let you play because you might embarrass the family," his father said. "Are you going to act like you acted in those games?"

"I told him I wouldn't," Al recalled, "and he let me do it. I made the team."

When Al began to pitch, he had a little trouble finding the plate, but throwing the ball against the wall did wonders for his control.

By the time he was fourteen years old, he was getting guys out on a regular basis in the extremely competitive Babe Ruth League. Al and his teammates were so good that, in 1955, they found themselves just one win away from a trip to Austin, Texas, to play for the national championship. For kids that age, it would be like going to the World Series.

Al, who was playing first base that day, remembers the game well. His team was in the field, leading a team from West Virginia by a run in the last inning. The other team had runners on first and third, and there was 1 out.

The batter hit a ground ball in the hole between first and second base. Al, playing behind the runner, took a step to his right. He just had to pick the ball up and start what had a chance to be a game-ending double play. Texas, here we come.

Not so fast. Al suddenly stopped and retreated to first base. He assumed the second baseman, who was closer to the ball, would field it and get at least one out, maybe two.

You can guess what happened next.

The second baseman didn't field it. The ball went through the hole into right field. The batter made it to first, the runner on third made it home, and the runner on first scored later in the inning. Al and his teammates never made it to Texas.

"Maybe no one else knows about it, but I do," Al said. "If I had just taken three steps to the right . . . I always tell kids, 'If you see a ball come your way, and your mind-set is to go get the ball, go get it, because once you start after it, the other guy is going to stop. So if you stop, now the ball is going to go between you.' I should have made the play."

Even though they didn't hurt as much, there were other losses, too. Yet Al always knew he couldn't take those troubles home. His dad wouldn't care. As a single parent raising eight kids, he had bigger things to concern himself with than the outcome of his son's baseball game.

Feeding, clothing, and housing Al and his siblings left no money in the Downing household for the luxuries most kids take for granted. There was no bicycle. There wasn't even bus fare. So Al had to walk about two miles to the ballpark and back home. On those walks, when he was the losing pitcher, he would try to make sense of what took place: *What did I do wrong? How can I improve?* Al would usually have some ideas by the time he got to Pennington Avenue. He had to. That's close to where Mrs. Brown lived, and Mrs. Thomas, and Mrs. Davis. They all knew he was Dover's boy, and if he didn't say hello, he'd hear about it from them.

Those walks did Al a ton of good. The next time he took the mound, he was, more often than not, a better, smarter pitcher.

In high school, people took notice, including Bill Yancey, a scout for the Yankees, who signed him for $16,000 in December 1960. Al was concerned that, at five-foot-seven and weighing only 155 pounds, he wasn't big enough for the majors. *Nonsense,* Yancey assured him. *Be patient, you'll grow.*

Besides, in those days, being a skinny kid was the least of his issues. Being a skinny *black* kid was a bigger one.

Even though more than a decade had gone by since Jackie Robinson broke the color barrier, blacks still had to endure a lot of abuse if they were going to keep chasing their dream of playing in the bigs as well as staying in the bigs.

"You're going to make a lot of people mad," said Yancey, who had played in the Negro Leagues. "A lot of people are not going to like the fact that you're up there. Don't let it bother you. Your job is to play ball and to win games."

That became a greater challenge when the kid from New Jersey, who played for the *Yankees,* was sent to the South, to Richmond, Virginia, in April 1962 for an assignment in the minor leagues. In Richmond, he wasn't even a black player. He was a colored one, and the only one on the team.

On some days, being called "colored" was probably the nicest thing he heard. But Al recognized he had no choice. He had to accept the abuse, or he might find himself back in Trenton, where the only ball he'd be tossing was a rubber one at the Boys Club.

"You knew you couldn't afford to get in trouble down there," Al said. "'I can't fight everybody,' I told myself. 'I will just go out here and strike out a couple more batters.' I could throw hard then. If I got a little mad, I threw a little harder. Just let them know I could fight the battle my way, but I wasn't going to act foolish."

The lesson Al learned from his father about not getting angry paid off. So did his ability to put any unpleasant truths behind him quickly, which he had learned during those long walks home from the park. He had to in order to survive.

In his own way, Al represented the black community that was still living under the rules of the segregated Jim Crow South. On Sunday afternoons, they showed up at the ballpark to sit under a tin roof in right field to watch him pitch. They didn't choose the tin roof for the shade. They sat there because blacks weren't permitted in the grandstands where the white folks sat.

One man in particular was very supportive. His name was Walter Banks, seventy-five, who, get this, according to Al, had founded a bank.

"The first part of the year, I was getting racked," said Al, who rented a room from him. "There were no lights in front of the house, but I could smell that pipe of his, and as I made the walk to the porch, he said, 'Sit down, how did you do tonight? How are you feeling?' He taught me to be patient, and that things would work out."

They certainly did. Al, who had been first called up by the Yankees in the summer of 1961, returned to New York in June 1963 for good. He won 13 games and lost only 5 that season, and became the first black pitcher to start a World Series game for the Yankees, against the Dodgers. Al struck out six in five innings in Game 2 but gave up 3 runs in a 4–1 loss. The Dodgers swept the Yanks in four games.

The next year, he got another chance, against the St. Louis Cardinals in Game 4 of the Series at Yankee Stadium. Like the time he didn't make the play on the ground ball in the Babe Ruth League, there was a moment in Game 4 Al would love to have back.

He was pitching a gem, the Yankees ahead 3–0 in the fifth inning. The Cardinals had just 1 hit, a bloop single. Finish this one off, and the Yanks would go up three games to one and, in all likelihood, win another championship. But, in the top of the sixth, St. Louis loaded the bases with Ken Boyer, the cleanup hitter, coming up. Elston Howard, the catcher, signaled for the fastball. Al shrugged him off.

"When Ken came up, I said, okay, these guys [were] jumping on first-pitch fastballs in the first game I pitched against them, when I came in relief for Whitey [Ford], and in my game, so I have to change," Al recalled. "And my second best pitch was not my curveball; it was my changeup. Then, if I can get a swing and a miss on the first pitch, that sets up my second and third pitch."

Boyer swung, all right, but didn't miss. He crushed it. A grand slam. The Cardinals grabbed a 4–3 lead, which proved to be the final score. They went on to beat the Yankees in seven games.

"I was in total control of that game," he said. "I made one bad pitch."

Al never had a problem with the pitch selection. The execution—well, that was a different matter.

"If I didn't try to get too fancy, I could have gotten him out," he recalled, "but I tried to fool with a pitch rather than throwing it. I didn't get the proper amount of what we call 'kill' on the ball, so that you kill the speed on the ball halfway to the plate. It came in a little hotter than it should have. I took the Boyer home run very hard."

The next memorable pitch he'd throw wouldn't come for another ten years.

The fastball that didn't sink.

It was the first week of the 1974 season. Al was running wind sprints in left field on the outfield grass in Los Angeles when the Dodgers' pitching coach, Red Adams, approached. Adams was sent over by the manager, Walter Alston.

"How you feelin'?" Adams asked.

"I feel fine," Al told him.

"We're going to move you back [in the rotation] and have you start Monday instead of Sunday," Adams said.

That was okay with Al. He'd be ready whenever the manager wanted him. He always was.

Aaron had hit home run no. 714 during the season opener in Cincinnati against Jack Billingham to tie the mark set by George Herman Ruth, the Babe—without question, the most hallowed record in all of sports. Alston needed somebody he was certain could handle not just the hitters but the moment as well, as Monday's game would be anything but a routine early April matchup.

Aaron had wanted to sit out the next two games to break it, hopefully, in Atlanta. But that didn't go over so well with Commissioner Bowie Kuhn, who insisted he play on Sunday, the final game of the series. Aaron complied, though he didn't get a hit that day. Come the Braves' opener on Monday, he would get a chance to do it in front of his fans.

The pressure would be no problem for Al. Remember, he'd started two games in the World Series for the Yankees. When you pitch in the Series, you know what pressure is all about.

"Walter was a wise man," he said. "He did not like young pitchers. When the Dodgers got me, the first thing he said was 'Good, I have a veteran pitcher who knows how to pitch.'"

Al approached game day on April 8, 1974, like any other game day.

He took a nap in his hotel room. He stayed away from other people. And, in his mind the night before, he had plotted out the pitches he'd throw to each batter. The Braves had as powerful a lineup as any in the National League. In 1973, they had three sluggers—Aaron, Davey Johnson, and Darrell Evans—who each hit at least 40 home runs. That had never been done before.

Finally, around 5 P.M., Al arrived at the park. He walked into the clubhouse and put on his blue Dodgers uniform.

Al knew how big this night was, of course—who in the entire city, in the entire country, didn't?—but as he watched the fans file in and felt the buzz in the air, the magnitude of the moment really hit him for the first time. In all, nearly fifty-four thousand fans were in the crowd that night.

He had first met Aaron during spring training in Florida in the early sixties. Elston Howard, who was the Yankees' first black player, handled the introduction.

"Hank," Howard said, "I want you to meet Al Downing. He's our young left-hander."

"I heard about you," Aaron said. "If there is anything I can do for you, let me know."

In extending such a generous offer, Aaron had already done plenty. Al was still adjusting to life in the major leagues, and making it was about a great deal more than knowing which pitches to throw. Just as critical was knowing which players to trust. Al knew he could trust Aaron.

"He was a gentleman right off the bat," he explained. "Hank was in the second wave of black players coming into the major leagues. He felt a responsibility to the younger players coming up behind him, to give them some guidance."

As the years wore on, with Al in the American League and Aaron in the National, they saw little of each other—there was no interleague play back then—except in spring training, when the teams were based within an hour of each other in Florida. That all changed after Al was traded to the Dodgers before the 1971 season. From then on, he was faced with the same, unenviable task that frustrated many other pitchers of his era. How the heck do you get this guy out?

Al won his share of the battles, but so did Aaron. In April 1973, he hit a homer against Al in Los Angeles. Two months later, he hit another off him, in Atlanta. That gave him 693 for his career, and by the end of the season, he was up to 713. Heading into 1974, the question was when, not if. When would he break the record? And which pitcher would be the unfortunate victim?

The game was so special, it would be the only one on prime-time TV the whole season, not including the playoffs and World Series. The Braves gave out hundreds of credentials to the press. They probably could have given out hundreds more.

The one person who wasn't credentialed for the game was Commissioner Kuhn. Not that he needed one, of course. It's just that he didn't show up. For what could be the biggest record-breaking moment in baseball history, the commish took a pass, his office claiming he had a "previous commitment" in Cleveland.

Whoever was there, Aaron would get his chance . . . that is, if the game would ever begin. One band after another marched on to the field. Was this a baseball game or the Rose Bowl parade? Finally, after Pearl Bailey, one of America's top entertainers, sang "The Star Spangled Banner," the Braves took their positions.

The Dodgers batted first and were retired in order. The Braves also went down one-two-three.

Aaron, hitting fourth, came up in the bottom of the second. He walked to home plate the way he always did, his helmet in one hand, dragging his bat in the other. Not until he arrived at the plate did he put his helmet on. Pitchers, you see, aren't the only players with a routine.

Al had given a lot of thought to how he would pitch to him. He would throw two-seam fastballs down and away, one after the other. Trying to get Aaron to chase something low and inside would be a waste of time.

"A pitch inside," Al said, "was not going to intimidate him, because he knows that would only be a show-me pitch. Never try to get cute with good hitters. They don't think. They just execute. They just wait for that one area where they know they can handle a pitch."

A pitch in the area Aaron was looking for didn't come. Not during this plate appearance. Al walked him on five pitches.

The fans booed. Watching their hero jog to first base was not what they paid good money for on a Monday evening in early April. Al wasn't pleased, either. He hated to walk any batter at any time.

"They really weren't good pitches," he recalled. "Nobody to blame for that but myself."

Aaron would come in to score that inning, the run breaking the NL record for runs he'd shared with none other than Willie Mays. One legend down, one to go.

By the time Aaron came up for a second time, in the bottom of the fourth, the Braves were trailing 3–1 and had a runner on first. Al's goal was to get him to bounce into a double play. Which meant, again, he would throw fastballs down and away.

"That's the most reliable pitch a pitcher has," Al explained, "because all you have to do is throw it in one location. It's not going to go more than three inches away from where you throw it. But it's going to be going in the direction away from the batter, which is what I wanted."

He went into the stretch, checked the runner on first, and let it go: Fastball, in the dirt. Ball 1.

More boos.

Al didn't pay attention. He was focusing on Aaron, who was as imposing a hitter as ever—the year before, at age thirty-nine, he'd smashed 40 home runs and batted over .300—although his strategy at the plate was different than earlier in his career.

"When Hank got to [home run number] six hundred," Al recalled, he said "that he had to change his approach to hitting, that he was no longer hitting the ball straightaway. He was trying to pull the ball since it was easier for him to hit home runs that way. I thought, 'That will play right to just what I'm trying to do, fastball down and away, fastball down and away.'"

Al, let's be fair, wasn't the player he'd been during his prime. He was thirty-two, and after tearing a tendon in his pitching arm in 1967, the velocity in his fastball fell from the mid-90s to the low 80s. That's a pretty sharp decline. He was able to stick around in the big leagues for as long as he did by relying on a changeup that fooled hitters. He fooled a lot of them, even winning 20 games in

1971, his first season in Los Angeles, when he was the National League Comeback Player of the Year.

At the same time, he didn't abandon the fastball. Not entirely. He couldn't. Otherwise, hitters would have patiently waited for the changeup and teed off on it.

The plan was to throw Aaron another fastball. Al wanted this one up a bit, starting maybe around knee-high so that when it sank, it would no longer be in the strike zone.

"If you throw a pitch down in the dirt, your next pitch has to be up," he explained. "You have to get a strike," but "you are pitching to the outer five inches of the plate. It will be in that outer five-inch zone, but away from him."

Al went into the stretch and fired again.

The first sign was when Al saw where the ball was as it approached the plate. "Wrong spin," he realized. "Sometimes, you'll choke the ball rather than throwing it freely, so you don't get that good spin on the ball."

The second sign was when he heard the sound of the bat meeting the ball. He knew. Pitchers always know.

Still, he turned around to watch. The ball was going a long way, there was no doubt. But perhaps it wouldn't go long enough. Perhaps the left fielder, Bill Buckner—yes, *that* Bill Buckner—would chase it down and even climb the chain-link fence to make the catch.

Buckner didn't have a chance. The ball was gone, over the 385-foot sign in left center, retrieved in the Braves' bullpen by relief pitcher Tom House. Gone as well was the record that had stood for almost forty years.

"I tried to guide the ball too much," Al acknowledged, "and any time you try to guide the ball, you don't get the right release point between your wrist and your arm. That pitch stayed straight. The ball wound up being almost on the inside part of that zone, which is not where you wanted it."

There was nothing to do now except watch Aaron round the bases, where he was congratulated by the Dodgers' infielders. Some later questioned if this was the proper way for players on the opposing team to behave while a game was still in progress.

Hogwash, this was history!

"You might not see this ever again," Al said.

He took a seat in the dugout. He and his teammates were told ahead of time that if Aaron were to hit one out, there'd be a ceremony on the field.

There certainly was. Aaron was honored by teammates, relatives, and friends. Monte Irvin, who worked with Commissioner Kuhn, represented him.

Al sat and waited. What was he thinking? Perhaps that, because of one pitch, this would now be how he would always be remembered? Not for leading the American League in strikeouts in 1964. Not for making the All-Star Game in 1967. Not for his 20 wins in 1971. For this. Only this.

Actually, no. His legacy was the last thing on his mind. What he wanted to know was: When the celebration is over, and it has to end at some point, would he be able to get loose again? "Once I hurt my arm," he explained, "I never had that feeling I could bounce back as quickly."

He figured Alston would use him for one more inning, perhaps two, to spare the bullpen as much as possible. The game, now tied 3–3, was still only in the fourth inning. Al would do whatever was necessary to help his team. When the time came for the game to resume, he would also have to decide if he should go back to the bullpen to warm up or use the mound on the field.

He chose the mound on the field. The bullpen, behind the right field fence, was too far away, and he didn't want to waste time.

Whichever mound he used might not have mattered. After the break, Al walked the first two batters, Dusty Baker and Davey Johnson. He wouldn't be asked to face a third.

Al went right into the clubhouse, took a shower, and was approached by Arthur E. "Red" Patterson, the Dodgers' PR guy. Patterson told Al there'd be a press conference after the game, but he didn't need to hang around. If he had any comments about the home run, Patterson was happy to pass them on to the reporters.

No, thanks, Al said, he had nothing for the press. Not yet.

"I'll talk to Hank tomorrow," Al told him.

He took a cab to the hotel, and believes he watched a movie—no, he doesn't remember which one—before falling asleep around 2:30

A.M. He wasn't the least bit curious to see how the game would turn out. He'd given up 5 runs in three innings, as the two men he walked after the delay came in to score. That wasn't going to change no matter what.

"It was another start I did not complete," Al concluded. "I had seen the home run."

By the time he woke up on Tuesday morning, he wasn't thinking about the game anymore. Just like he used to move on from any poor performances during those long walks back to his home in Trenton. That's what big-league pitchers have to do. Otherwise, they would never be ready for their next start.

Upon arriving at the stadium that afternoon, one of his first tasks was to congratulate the game's new home run king.

"Send the batboy over to tell Mr. Aaron I'll meet him by the cage," Al told a clubhouse attendant.

Al and Aaron didn't meet for long. There was another game to play that night.

Aaron, despite everything that was going on around him, checked to see how Al was doing. Aaron had been around baseball since the mid-fifties. He knew the damage one pitch could do to a pitcher's ego and reputation. He didn't want that happening to Al.

"Don't feel any shame," Aaron told him. "You've had a good career."

Al appreciated the kind words. Aaron always seemed to know what to say and when to say it.

"It shows you the kind of person he was," Al said.

Aaron also told him how relieved he was that the pursuit of Ruth was finally over. He had received hate letters and death threats from those incensed that a black man would dare to break a record held by a white man.

Al, in his own way, can relate. In the early sixties, he and Elston Howard received their share of ugly mail. Al didn't let the letters bother him, just as he shut out the slurs from racist fans in the South. He knew the letters and slurs came from the same place prejudice always comes from: ignorance.

"There were people who did not believe that two black guys, one pitching and one catching, could be successful. '[It would be] the downfall of the Yankees,'" he said.

Some even suggested Al, because he was black, was secretly hoping for Aaron to hit a home run against him. Anybody who knew anything about Al, and how much he cared about winning, knew that was ludicrous.

"If it was up to me, he would have hit into a triple play," he said.

What was up to him was how he would cope with his new place in the sport's history.

Fortunately, Al had spent a lot of time around someone who handled a similar situation as well as could be expected. That was his ex-teammate on the Yankees, Ralph Terry. Terry gave up the walk-off homer in the ninth inning to the Pittsburgh Pirates' Bill Mazeroski in Game 7 of the 1960 World Series.

"I learned a lot from Terry," Al said. "It never bothered him. We were together last week. He never talks about it."

Al then referred to the two seasons Terry posted after the Mazeroski homer. In 1961, Terry finished 16-3 with a 3.15 earned run average; in 1962, he led the American League with 23 victories.

"So, obviously," Al pointed out, "it wasn't wearing on his mind."

Another Ralph he learned a lot from was Ralph Branca, the Dodgers pitcher who also gave up a game-ending home run, maybe the most famous of all, to the New York Giants' Bobby Thomson, which decided the 1951 National League pennant.

"I used to see him in Vero Beach all the time, throwing batting practice," Al said. "He never acted as if he had to walk around with his head down."

Not that Al ever went looking for solace, from Terry or Branca or anyone, for that matter, although, he admitted, "it's nice when you talk to your peers and they let you know 'he [Aaron] is a tough guy to pitch to.'"

If anything, Al appears to almost embrace his role, not much different really from how Aaron Krickstein learned to appreciate being associated forever with Jimmy Connors and Craig Ehlo with Michael Jordan. Plenty of pitchers surrendered home runs to Hank Aaron. Al just happened to be the pitcher who surrendered *the* home run, the home run that Al and everyone else knew in April 1974 was inevitable.

Yet, because of that one pitch, some fans would never look at him the same way again. Such as that guy at the ballpark in Philly later in the 1974 season.

Al was hanging out near the fence during batting practice when a kid reached over and asked for an autograph. As usual, he was ready to oblige, until the youngster's father pulled him away.

"You don't want his autograph," the man told his son. "That's Al Downing. He's a bum."

Al was taken aback. He couldn't let them leave without a response.

"Wait a minute, come here," he told the father. "I'm pitching in the big leagues. You ever pitch in the big leagues? Don't ever tell your kid that. A guy is doing something you can't do, and you're calling him a bum. That is not the way to bring a kid up."

Al wasn't sure he got through to the father, but he was sure he got through to the son.

Not long afterward, the "bum" was chosen by Walter Alston to start Game 3 of the 1974 World Series against the Oakland A's. So what if Al had won only five games the whole season and thrown just 98 innings? Alston again needed someone he knew could handle the moment, and not just the hitters.

Too bad it wasn't Al's best outing. He gave up 3 runs in 3⅔ innings, and the Dodgers lost the Series in five games.

"One play at home plate killed us," Al said. "I thought I pitched very well."

In 1977, he announced his retirement after seventeen years in the bigs. He may have been able to pitch another season or two, but he wasn't the type to stick around for a paycheck. Al was there to get outs.

He went into broadcasting, working for the Dodgers in Los Angeles from 1978 to 1991. Over the years, he and Aaron would run into each other at various functions. The home run came up, naturally. Aaron gave Al a ton of respect.

"At one luncheon, a writer was trying to pigeonhole him into saying that he really wore me out," Al recalled. "'No,' he [Aaron] said, 'I think I hit [only] 3 home runs off you. Al was one of the toughest left-handers I ever faced.'"

With the record-breaking home run coming late in his career, Al was fortunate. He'd proven himself already. He wouldn't have to prove himself ever again. "I'd gone through three World Series, an All-Star game, led the league in strikeouts, had won twenty games," he said. "I'd had a career."

And what it took for him to have that career in the first place—well, no wonder one home run, as historic as it was, didn't affect him as it might have other pitchers. Just think about all he went through:

Losing his mom at the age of seven. Going to the minors. Hearing racial slurs. Suffering a major injury to his arm. As you go on, you start to understand why he was proud of who he was and why he coped so magnificently with what happened that night in Atlanta. Al had learned how to come to terms with adversity long before, and this setback wasn't nearly as difficult as some of the others.

One may wonder, then, how Al would have responded if he had been twenty-two years old when he gave up the Aaron home run instead of thirty-two, before he had proved a thing to anyone, including himself.

Al doesn't wonder one bit. He's certain he would have responded the same way, looking toward the future, not the past, and there's no reason to doubt him. In 1965, the year after he gave up the homer to Ken Boyer in the World Series, he won 12 games for a Yankees ball club that finished under .500 for the first time since 1925!

Don't forget. Pitchers are a different breed. They have to be. There is no past, only the present and future.

"People always ask me what I was thinking when he [Aaron] hit the home run," Al said. "I thought, 'The game's tied 3–3. Now we're starting all over again.'"

The pitch to Aaron isn't what Al thinks about these days, either. The play he thinks about is the ground ball he didn't try to field in 1955.

That tells you everything you need to know about the man. The only person he let down in Atlanta was himself. So what if the Dodgers lost the game? They went on to win 102 games that season, the most in the major leagues, and made it to the World Series. Besides, that night wasn't about Al Downing. That night was about Hank Aaron and history.

You can't say the same about the game in 1955. That was about a group of teenage boys whose dreams of going to Texas and playing for a championship didn't come true.

"That play affected everyone on our team. That game would have cemented our belief that we were as good as any other team our age," he said. "We were walking around singing 'Yellow Rose of Texas.' When we went home, we were all crying."

10

THE UNFORGETTABLES

MARCH 28, 1992

Deron Feldhaus doesn't recall everything that took place during those final tense moments in Philadelphia. Maybe he's fortunate. That was a long time ago, and besides, there are some moments he's probably better off not remembering.

What he does recall, and quite vividly, are two words that his coach, Rick Pitino, said to him in the huddle and again before Deron walked back onto the court: "Don't foul!"

The message was hard to miss: Don't foul Christian Laettner.

That's who Deron, a six-foot-seven forward, would be covering on the inbounds pass, and that's who the Duke Blue Devils, down 103–102 with 2.1 seconds left in the 1992 NCAA East Regional Finals at the Spectrum, wanted to take the last shot. Think about it. Who else, except Laettner? He was literally perfect the entire game: 9 for 9 from the field, 10 for 10 from the free throw line.

As always, Deron, the son of a coach, did what he was told. He didn't foul Laettner. He didn't come close to fouling him.

Nor did John Pelphrey, the other Kentucky player who would keep track of Laettner. John, also six-foot-seven, roamed the court similar to a free safety in football. His job, if necessary, would be to break up a Hail Mary, which was pretty much what it would take for Duke to win the game.

"I was backing up to catch the ball," John said. "I was Ronnie Lott [the Hall of Fame NFL safety]."

Both Deron and John came from small towns in the Bluegrass State. Deron was from Maysville, on the Ohio River; John was from Paintsville, near the foothills of the Appalachians. And both, from the time that somebody put a basketball in their hands—in the crib, perhaps—dreamed of the day they'd put on the University of Kentucky uniform. Come to think of it, it was *every* Kentucky boy's dream.

Getting to Lexington wouldn't be easy for either of them, nor would staying there. But they'd done it, and now, on this March evening in 1992, they were on the verge of fulfilling another dream: playing in the Final Four.

The Wildcats had come a long way in the last three years, further and faster than anybody believed was possible. From the dead, one could say, with little exaggeration. Now if they could just finish what they started and do what they had to do in these final 2.1 seconds.

"Don't foul!"

A sk Deron and John to remember the first loss that hurt, and their answers will be the same: The 1987 state tournament. Ballard High.

Ballard High was the school in the Louisville area where Allan Houston, then only a sophomore, was the main attraction. Houston would go on to become a star at the University of Tennessee and play twelve years in the NBA.

So when Mason County, Deron's high school team, took on Ballard in the quarterfinals, he realized it would be a battle for the whole thirty two minutes. Which it was. With just a few seconds left, the game was tied, and Ballard had the ball. Houston was sure to take the final shot.

Houston took it, all right, but the shot was blocked. If Mason County could just get the rebound, the game would go to overtime.

Mason County didn't get the rebound. A Ballard player did,

a player Deron had been covering but left free to go for the ball himself. The kid, to Deron's recollection, hadn't made a basket the entire game. He made this one, and Mason County was out of the tournament.

Deron was devastated. Not only had he lost the game, and the chance to win a state championship he could cherish for the rest of his life, especially in a state as basketball crazy as Kentucky, it was also his last game in high school.

John knew exactly how he felt. The game his team, Paintsville High, played against Ballard in the next round, the semis, was also his last. Up by 1 point heading into the final quarter, Paintsville missed about 10 shots in a row, including a few layups. John and his teammates made a late run, but each time Paintsville crept a little closer, Ballard responded with a clutch free throw or basket.

"There was no doubt in our mind that we were the best team in the state," John said. "Funny how sports is. You have to finish games."

Yes, you do. However, John and Deron didn't stay dejected for long. There was too much to look forward to, in basketball and in life.

The trip to Lexington wouldn't be a very long drive for each, but they were about to enter a new world. Their games would mean more than ever, and the whole state would be watching them.

Basketball *was* the University of Kentucky, thanks to Adolph Rupp. Rupp was the coach who led the Wildcats to four national titles between 1948 and 1958. Deron had known all about Rupp since he was a boy. His father, Allen, played for him in the early sixties.

John was just as familiar with the UK tradition, though there was a time when he was willing to give up on his dream of playing there. He was angry. He wanted to commit to Kentucky early in the recruiting process, after his junior year, but the school was waiting to hear from a few other players and wouldn't make any promises.

"I felt like I was misled," John said. "It inspired and motivated me to where I told the coaches, 'I'm going to win Mr. Basketball, and I'm going to go somewhere [else] and play ball.'"

So, six months later, after he did what he said he would do, winning the award for the top player in the state, and with the school now offering him a scholarship, John went to Lexington with one thing in mind.

"I want to tell these people no to their face," he told his father.

In the end, not surprisingly, after he met with Coach Eddie Sutton and the rest of his staff, and had a few days to think it over, John couldn't say no.

This was Kentucky and this was his dream.

John redshirted his freshman year and so did Deron. There was still a lot to learn about the game and about college life.

Besides, given the talent on the 1987–88 Wildcats, who won the SEC and made it to the Sweet Sixteen, they would have spent most of their time on the bench anyway. Once that season was over, though, the two couldn't wait for the next one. Sure, there would be plenty of holes to fill—the team's five top scorers left in 1988—but others, including John and Deron, would step up.

Only there was more to learn than either could imagine. After going 13-19 in their first season in uniform—apparently, not enough players did step up—John and Deron found out that nothing is guaranteed. Not even at Kentucky.

In May 1989, the Wildcats were placed on probation for three years because of a series of recruiting and academic violations. Worse yet, the school was banned from participating in the NCAA tournament for two years.

Deron was beside himself. Losing to Ballard High was one thing; you know you're not going to win every game. Losing two years of having a chance to be a part of March Madness was another. You have only four chances to begin with, and one was gone already.

"Why me?" Deron wondered. "Here's my dream. This is the worst thing that could happen."

Changes had to be made, and they were.

Out went Sutton, who had been the coach since 1985. In came Rick Pitino, most recently the coach of the New York Knicks in the NBA.

Pitino was seen as someone who could turn around any program, in college or the pros. He took Boston University to the NCAA tournament for the first time in twenty-four years, and Providence to the

Final Four only two years after the school went 11-20. As for the Knicks, they had just won their first division title since the seventies, only two years after he took over a team that lost nearly 60 games.

Well, if there was ever a program in college basketball that needed to be turned around, it was the University of Kentucky, and not only when it came to the number of wins and losses. The violations had caused a lot of damage to the school's reputation.

With so much uncertainty, no one would have blamed Deron or John one bit if either had transferred to another program. This was not what they signed up for.

Deron dismissed the idea right away, even knowing the Wildcats would be basically starting from scratch. If he were to transfer, he'd have to sit out another year. Sitting out the one year when he was redshirted was more than enough.

John didn't consider leaving, either. Sanctions or not, he loved everything about the place. That's why he got over those hard feelings and took the scholarship. He would have never forgiven himself if he didn't.

"The feeling was that we did not want to be known as the guys who were at Kentucky when Kentucky was not very good," John recalled.

What the Wildcats did have going for them was a tremendous work ethic. No coach in college basketball demanded more of his players—in the weight room, on the track, on the court, everywhere—than Pitino. There was no mystery to his plan. If he didn't have the most talented players, he sure as heck would have the most fit ones.

As long as they didn't quit first.

Deron's parents grew worried when they saw the sunken expression on his face, and they wondered if his body could absorb the punishment. He was told to shed 15 pounds, going from 220 to 205. Plain turkey on white bread and cereal with skim milk, that was his diet for breakfast and lunch. He wasn't crazy about it.

John didn't fare any better in the beginning.

"Running around a track is not in my DNA," he said.

Pitino required that each player run two miles in twelve minutes or less, or he wouldn't be able to take part in Midnight Madness at

Memorial Coliseum. Midnight Madness was huge in Lexington, as it was at many campuses. That was when each team, at the stroke of midnight on October 15, could officially begin practices for the upcoming season. Fans camped out for hours to get a seat. The building was, as usual, sold out.

The pressure was on Deron and John. To miss Midnight Madness—well, you just couldn't.

"If [your family] comes down and you're not out there, how are you going to explain that to them?" John said.

Fortunately, they both finished the two miles in time, John on the last possible day, and barely.

"You just made it by the grace of God, 11:59," Ray "Rock" Oliver, the team's strength and conditioning coach, told him, though, to this day, John wonders if "I made it or not, or he just felt this guy can't run any faster."

Whether he did or not, Kentucky was soon on the road back to being . . . well, Kentucky. Pitino got the players to buy into his brand of basketball, game after game, possession after possession—running, pressing, running, pressing some more.

Said Deron, who was able to get rid of those fifteen pounds—and a few more—in less than a month: "You felt like you would never get tired. We were in so much better shape than anyone."

The Wildcats won 14 games in Pitino's first season. Many thought they would win about 5. Deron was one of those who had his doubts.

"We didn't have many points from last year over on the bench," he said. "We were pretty thin."

Whoever was on the roster, Pitino was always positive. That's what Deron remembers the most about the day he first met him.

"He said, 'We will win,' and that gave you a little excitement."

There were some low moments, to be sure, the lowest a 150–95 loss at Kansas. There were some highlights, too, like the win at Rupp Arena over LSU, 100–95. Deron scored 24 points and pulled down 10 rebounds against the Tigers' All-American big man, Shaquille O'Neal.

"We had to guard him," Deron said, referring to Shaq, "but with our style of play, he was going to have to guard us."

Pitino was just getting started. The next season, the Wildcats won 22 games, and lost only 6, and they would have been the SEC champions (14-4) had they not been ineligible because of the NCAA sanctions.

"We had a ticker-tape parade with fire trucks through town," John recalled. "Everyone knew we were the best team [in the conference]."

As for anyone who dared suggest the Wildcats weren't the true champions, you would certainly hear about it from the Kentucky fans.

"People on campus started selling T-shirts that said KISS OUR ASTERISK," John said.

Then came the fall of 1991. John and Deron were seniors. The years in college sure went by fast. The best player on the team was now the sophomore forward Jamal Mashburn. He was also one of the best players in the nation. He could shoot from the outside. He could score in the post. He could play defense.

Jamal Mashburn could do everything.

"Our team was devastating on offense," John said. "We were unguardable. Jamal was the biggest reason. You had to play him with two people."

Little wonder Kentucky went 23-6 in the regular season and won the SEC title—for real, this time. Even so, Pitino was as hard on his players as ever. Such as the time he took the four seniors to a charity function a day after one of those 6 losses. A chance to get away from the gym and kick back, you might assume.

Not with Rick Pitino.

"He had the game film and he just ripped us," Deron said. "I broke a bigger sweat [that day] getting reamed than I did [all year]. But once he did that," and got it out of his system, he held no grudge.

The tough love worked. The Wildcats defeated Vanderbilt, LSU, and Alabama to win the SEC tournament. They then beat Old Dominion, Iowa State, and Massachusetts to advance to the NCAA East Regional Final.

Next up was a date with Duke, the defending national champions.

"We'd never gone to the NCAA tournament," Deron said. "We wanted to go out in a big splash."

The Blue Devils were the favorite, no one could argue that. They had Laettner, guards Bobby Hurley and Thomas Hill, and forwards Grant Hill, Brian Davis, and Antonio Lang. We missing anyone?

Oh, yeah, the coach, Mike Krzyzewski, who would one day become the winningest coach in college basketball history, that's all.

The Wildcats were impressed but not intimidated. No team with Rick Pitino in charge ever is.

"I think we can get this done," Deron told a friend on the bus before the game.

It sure looked that way early on, as Kentucky jumped to an 8-point advantage. The champs rallied and then some. Duke took a 5-point lead into halftime and extended it to 12 with about eleven minutes left. That's a 20-point turnaround. Hard to imagine a team with their experience, talent, and coaching letting go of a lead that big.

But the Wildcats staged a comeback of their own. All those hours in the gym, and on the track, were paying off, and it couldn't be at a more opportune time.

"Coach Pitino, that's what he always stressed," Deron recalled, "[down the stretch]: 'We're going to make our run. We're going to wear them down.'"

In the meantime, they were riling them up—at least Laettner. Of course, it didn't take much.

While underneath the basket on one possession, Laettner, known for being a dirty player, stepped on the stomach of Kentucky freshman center Aminu Timberlake as he was lying on the floor. Years later, Laettner would admit he did it on purpose to get revenge for being shoved too aggressively a few possessions before.

Laettner had been shoved, all right, but it was Deron who shoved him, not Timberlake. In any case, the officials gave him a technical, which sent Kentucky to the line for two free throws. Many felt they didn't punish him enough.

The Wildcats tied the game with about five minutes left. The teams went back and forth the rest of the way, the game tied 93–93 at the end of regulation.

Going into overtime, like the fifth-set tiebreaker in the Connors-

Krickstein duel at the U.S. Open six months before, was only fitting. This game was too good to be settled in forty minutes.

The OT was just as dramatic, neither Duke nor Kentucky going up by more than 3 points. This was, officially, a game to remember, and we were far from done.

However, Kentucky got a bad break when Mashburn fouled out with fourteen seconds to go in the extra session. He was playing as well as Laettner, with 28 points and 10 rebounds.

"That was a killer," Deron recalled.

Little did he know how much of a killer. Laettner made the two free throws to put Duke up by 1 point. Kentucky quickly brought the ball to the frontcourt and called timeout with 7.8 seconds left. With Mashburn out, who would take the biggest shot of the Wildcats' season?

Sean Woods, the senior guard, that's who, and the shot he got off, a high floater in the lane—over Laettner, by the way—was not exactly what you would consider a high-percentage shot. Yet it somehow found the bottom of the net, and the officials allowed it, even if Woods forgot to call bank.

"It was a little bit of a lucky shot," John admitted. "Sean was clean, and then all of a sudden, here comes [Laettner], so he had to throw the ball higher, which caused it to bank in."

Kentucky 103, Duke 102.

Duke called a timeout, while the Kentucky players went nuts on the bench. In their minds, and you couldn't blame them, they figured the game was theirs.

"Oh, you know it," Deron said.

John was equally convinced.

"Good for Sean," John thought. "He's going to make the shot that puts us in the Final Four."

A bit premature, to be sure. Especially against a team that had won it all the season before and had most of that talent still on the court, and Mike Krzyzewski on the sidelines, with time remaining on the clock. Even if Duke did need a miracle, the Wildcats couldn't afford to get cocky.

Confident, yes. In college, unlike the pros, when teams call a timeout after a made basket, they don't get to automatically advance the ball to the midcourt. That meant a Duke player would have to throw an almost perfect pass, about 75 feet, from the opposite end of the court.

That was just for starters. Another Duke player would then have to catch the pass, bring the ball down, create some space, and get a shot off—all in *two* seconds. Sorry, *2.1* seconds. And on top of all that . . . that player would have to make the shot, too.

Which may explain why Pitino was worried about fouling Laettner. Putting him on the line was probably Duke's best chance, perhaps its only chance.

"He's not going to miss a free throw," Deron said. "He didn't miss a shot the whole damn game."

The huddle broke up, and the players went back on the floor. Guarding Grant Hill, who would attempt to throw that perfect pass, was . . .

Nobody! To place an extra defender in the forecourt, Pitino chose not to put anyone on Hill and the inbounds pass. Many were shocked, wondering, and justifiably so, what in the world Pitino was thinking. He was making it much easier for Hill to throw the pass.

John, who would become a college coach himself, wasn't one of those who questioned the move.

"I would have played it exactly the way he had it," he said. "When you go the length of the floor, and you put everybody on the ball, it's like man-to-man. There are plays that you can run. You can screen, you can roll, you can do all kinds of things. But when you take the guy off the ball and stick him back there, now it's five against four. That's good odds. You're going to take those in Vegas every time."

Deron also didn't have a problem with the decision.

"To this day," he said, "I'd never second-guess that guy's coaching."

Perhaps not, but there's no doubt that Pitino's plea—"Don't foul!"—was on Deron's mind when he got back on the floor, and that it had an effect.

"That put the scare in us more than anything," he pointed out. "We played it totally soft instead of being aggressive and maybe going for the ball."

Of course, if Pitino could've had his way, he wouldn't have assigned Deron to guard Laettner and instructed John to help out. He would have given the job to Mashburn. Deron was right. Mashburn fouling out *was* a killer.

The official handed the ball to Hill. The count got under way. Hill, with a clear look at the entire court, took several steps to his right and let it go.

"Clock, go off," Deron thought as the ball hung in the air. *And, whatever you do, don't foul!*

John, meanwhile, played free safety, ready to break up the play. Given how much time was remaining, that would surely end the game.

Except, the pass was perfect. Tom Brady couldn't have thrown it any better.

"We had rehearsed that defensive possession throughout the course of the year," John said, "and we were always able to prevent the team from catching the ball. This time, we were not."

Laettner caught the ball a few feet behind the free throw line. Pitino didn't have to worry. There would be no foul. Laettner then did something that surprised Deron and a lot of people in the Spectrum. He took a dribble.

"I really didn't think he would get it off in time by putting the dribble down," Deron said.

But he did. He stepped to his right, jumped, and fired away, the ball leaving his hands with 0.3 seconds left. Talk about cutting it close.

Deron knew right away, just as Al Downing knew when he heard the crack of the bat.

"It was dead on," Deron said.

Duke 104, Kentucky 103.

For the record, just over a week later, the Blue Devils beat Michigan, 71–51, to capture their second straight national championship. That game wasn't nearly as unforgettable.

Deron and John knew the feeling all too well. Senior year, Ballard High, the state tournament. Only this time, it felt worse, much worse.

"It was literally like death when we lost," John said.

John was in denial at first. Not about the outcome itself but the part he played in it.

"I felt like the guy took the ball out of my hands," he said. "I had this sensation of my hands actually touching the leather. It wasn't until several days later that I realized that I never got close."

When you think about it, Deron and John could probably second-guess themselves on what they did in that final possession until doomsday. Yet no matter what they did, or didn't do, they would have to find a way to cope with the loss, then and forever.

They couldn't hide, that's for sure. The state of Kentucky isn't large enough. Heck, planet Earth isn't.

"When I finished school, I ended up getting married and playing in France for a month or two, and in Spain for six and a half months," John recalled. "I'll never forget being in a little northwest corner of Spain. The phone rings and [a reporter] wanted to write an article about that game, and it's been that way ever since."

How, then, did they cope?

One way was through the values they'd picked up at home, the same values that helped Reid Gettys deal so well with the heartbreaking defeat to North Carolina State in 1983. Winning meant a great deal, but it didn't mean everything.

Another was knowing how much they had given to their team and their school. They couldn't have given one ounce more.

Pitino sure knew it. In the locker room after the game, he showed his guys a copy of the memorable May 29, 1989, *Sports Illustrated* issue, which had hit the newsstands once the sanctions came down. The words on the cover: "Kentucky's Shame."

"This is where we started," Pitino told them. "There's no reason to be ashamed of what you all accomplished."

No reason whatsoever.

Only you couldn't expect young men who had invested so heavily to feel that sense of accomplishment. Not yet, anyway. Not when they hadn't even taken their jerseys off. The pain of what they had failed to accomplish was still too raw.

"We weren't ready to hear that," John said.

They would be soon enough. That's because they weren't "the

guys who were at Kentucky when Kentucky was not very good," as John once feared. They were, rather, the guys who had revived the program, one of the most glorious in college basketball.

"I still consider us winners," Deron said.

The fans felt the same way. Deron, John, Sean Woods, and Richie Farmer, the other senior in 1992, became known as "the Unforgettables," and to those folks who live and die with Kentucky basketball, that's who they'll always be. No team in Lexington, or anywhere, that did *not* win a national title has been more beloved.

"I have people come up to me and say, 'You're still my favorite group,'" Deron said. "They got to know us."

The scene in town when the team arrived home from Philly said it all.

"From the airport to Wildcat Lodge, there were people all along the sides of the road just standing and waving," John said.

The Unforgettables felt the love again a week or so after the loss. They showed up at Rupp Arena for what, they assumed, was a routine awards ceremony. But as C. M. Newton, the athletic director, was giving his remarks, John saw four covered banners hanging in the rafters.

Banners? For what? And why four?

Suddenly, he got it.

"Deron, I think they are going to retire our jerseys," John said.

"No way," Deron answered.

Yes way.

"I couldn't believe it," Deron said. "I never dreamed of that. Every time I go there, I have to take a peek to still believe it. And when I take my son—that's where the state high school basketball tournament is—that's pretty special to see him looking at the jerseys up there. I know we didn't win; we got beat by Duke. But to have our jerseys retired, that's about as high as you can get."

We often talk about how a fan base can support its team while a game is in progress—the "twelfth man" in football—but here was an example of the support fans can provide *after* a game, and how much it can help the ones who hurt so deeply cope with their disappointment.

"Just like they knew we needed help to compete at a higher

level," John said, "they also recognized we needed them to kind of overcome the devastation that took place when that ball went in the basket. One thing the fans did for us, they started the healing process."

"Started" is the key word. Those fans, as supportive as they were, could only do so much. Their focus, understandably, would soon be elsewhere.

"There's always another group of freshmen," John pointed out.

The values the Kentucky players learned from day one with Coach Pitino also went a long way in helping them begin to heal.

"I don't think anybody ever felt like a victim," John said. "We were given the support and the foundation and the fundamentals to be able to handle something like that."

The rest of the healing was up to the players themselves, including the four seniors who were getting ready to leave Lexington and go their separate ways. They hung out with one another as often as possible in the last month or so of college.

"Our greatest strength was together," John said.

Nonetheless, the pain of losing to Duke didn't go away. During the summer of 1992, John, who hadn't been drafted, attended a rookie camp held by the Philadelphia 76ers. He wasn't optimistic about his chances but gave it a go.

"I flew into Philly and didn't think anything of it," he said, "but as we started our descent, I looked out the window and saw the Spectrum. It just leveled me."

As the years went on, though, John and Deron coped very well. Like many who found themselves on the opposite side of a historic sporting moment, real life had taught them that the toughest losses aren't tallied on a scoreboard.

Deron first learned that lesson as a freshman in high school. His parents got a divorce. He lived with his mother and saw his father, also his coach, at practice. Deron promised himself he'd never get divorced. Sure enough, he did, and when it happened, there was another child left to deal with the consequences, his three-year-old son, Jake.

Jake, who is now eight, has adjusted well, considering, just as Deron feels he adjusted when his folks split up. In any case, Jake is what he cares most about, not a basketball game from another lifetime, no matter how often people bring it up.

"I kind of blow it off big-time, don't I?" he said. "I guess that's why I don't go back and watch the game. It's not that big a deal."

What is a big deal is what John went through off the court. His story will break your heart.

The loss, in his case, was that of his son, John Patrick, who died at birth in 2003 from a rare blood disorder. John made a very important decision right away. He would put his trust in the Lord.

"We're not going to let this take us to a place where it becomes destructive for us," John told Tracy, his wife, "for our marriage, for the people around us and our two children."

Easy to say, almost impossible to do. Their faith, as strong as it was, had never been tested like this.

"It is very difficult to stay in the moment and not ask why," he said, "and not to lash out and be angry and depressed. It's never fun to go and pick out a casket the size of a shoe box. Do I buy the whole plot or do I buy half of it? You kind of look at each other: 'Are we really doing this?'"

With their love for each other and the trust they placed in God, John and Tracy survived the test and never went to those destructive places he was so worried about.

"It helped me grow as a human being and as a man," John said. "A lot of times, it can split families up. That didn't happen to mine. Our relationship grew deeper."

John and Tracy set up a foundation that, among other things, helped raise money for the neonatal unit of a children's hospital in Arkansas.

"It was important for us to help somebody else out who had gone through the pain of what we went through."

John wasn't done with experiencing loss. None of us ever are.

In 2011, he was fired after four seasons as the basketball coach at the University of Arkansas. His record, 69-59, wasn't really that bad, and the class of freshmen he had recruited for the incoming season was one of the best in the country. None of that mattered. He was out.

John was crushed. Just like at Kentucky, he loved everything about the school—the community, the students, the logo . . . everything. For the first time in his professional career, he felt like a failure. He tried to figure out what he did wrong and why he was unable to finish the job. Now it was his faith in himself that would be tested, and severely.

He passed, again.

"I thought if I lost my job," he recalled, "I would die. I didn't do that. It doesn't make you bad if you lose your job. There were a lot of people who lost their jobs, in a lot of areas, who were spectacular."

In April 2016, John was hired as an associate head coach at the University of Alabama. Perhaps he'll be back in the NCAA tournament before too long and even help lead his team to the Final Four. Whatever happens, the loss to Duke will always be there. Because as much as the support from the fans, the lessons from Pitino, and the perspective of time made coping with the loss a lot easier than it might have been, it's too much to expect the men whose hearts were broken when Laettner made the shot to ever be completely over it.

But don't be sad for John and Deron. On the contrary, be happy. Realize how fortunate they were to care so intensely about their team and one another, even if the ending wasn't what they wished for. They went to the school of their dreams, in the state they loved, and remain, to those who followed them, well . . . unforgettable. You can't ask for more than that.

"If you're a warrior and you're in the battlefield and you get slashed, bruised, whatever, that scar is not going to go away," John said. "There's a story to that scar."

What a story it is.

11

THE CHOKE

JULY 18, 1999

Anyone who happened to be in the gallery on that day along the eastern coast of Scotland, or watched those fifteen minutes or so on TV, still can hardly believe what they saw. Golf can be a cruel game, that we knew. Play it just once, and you'll see for yourself.

We just didn't know *how* cruel, until we were introduced to Jean Van de Velde.

For those who might not remember, Jean was the French golfer who stepped to the tee at the seventy-second, and final, hole of the 1999 British Open, one of the game's four major championships, at Carnoustie Golf Links, with a lead that would soon be 3 shots. As long as he got no worse than a double-bogey six, the trophy would be his. Not bad for somebody who, let's face it, no one expected to be in this position.

When the final British Open of the twentieth century got under way on July 15, the list of favorites included:

- David Duval, the former top-ranked player in the world
- Ernie Els, the two-time U.S. Open winner
- José María Olazábal, the reigning Masters champion

And, of course, Tiger Woods.

None of the experts brought up the name Jean Van de Velde, and why would they? Since turning pro a decade earlier, he had played almost all of his golf on the lesser-known European Tour and had just one win, the Roma Masters in 1993. The only reason he even got into the field at Carnoustie was by winning a qualifying tournament the Sunday and Monday before. He bogeyed the first two holes before he rallied to shoot 67-67.

"Just shows you what an incredible game it is," Jean said.

He played Carnoustie the next day, and then on Wednesday, he hit a few balls on the driving range and worked on his chipping and putting. As hard as the wind was blowing, there was little to gain by going another nine or eighteen holes. Besides, he said, "I had played it once. I'd seen what I had to see."

He felt good about his chances.

"First, I was playing very well," Jean said, "and second of all, I was putting extremely well. Where you're going to be at the end of the week, you never know. I could put four rounds together, that I knew."

Maybe, but it sure didn't look that way once the British Open got started. He shot a 75 the first day, which was four strokes worse than par. He tired down the stretch and it showed, as he bogeyed three of the final four holes.

"I was fuming at myself," Jean said.

His mistake was expending too much energy early in the round. He wouldn't make the same mistake the next three days. He'd pace himself to be as fresh as possible when he reached the fifteenth tee.

"I knew that the course was so long that I accepted any punishment that was going to come my way," he said. "I didn't try to fight it."

Typically, when you shoot a 75 in the opening round of a major golf tournament, other than the U.S. Open, it means you have very little chance to win. You will have to rally, and quickly, just to qualify for the last two rounds, on Saturday and Sunday. In this event, only those players after thirty-six holes who were tied for seventieth place, or better, from a field of 156, would get to compete all four days. But this wasn't a typical major. The course was extremely difficult, even by British Open standards, the fairways narrow and the greens fast. Everyone was getting punished. The best round of the opening day was a 71. So, despite his rough start, Jean was still only 4 shots behind.

He rebounded on Friday, shooting a 68 to take the lead by one. In the stretch from the fifteenth through the eighteenth hole, where he messed up on Thursday, he went two under par. He'd used his energy wisely.

Jean was just getting on a roll. On Saturday, he fired a 70, including a most unlikely birdie on the eighteenth when he sank a 45-footer. That wasn't the only bomb—the term for a long putt—he made. The other was from 70 feet on the fourteenth hole; he also knocked in a 25-footer on the seventh. Jean was as hot as Christian Laettner in the Duke-Kentucky game. He couldn't miss. He was up by 5 strokes. Jean Van de Velde! The British Open!

No wonder, after having dinner and a glass of wine—he's French, remember—he barely got any sleep. Two hours maybe, max.

"I was thinking about the day I had ahead of me," he said.

In doing so, he knew how important it would be to stick to his game plan: where on every hole he hoped to put the ball, and where he hoped *not* to put it. In golf, where you miss your shot is often more crucial than the ones that reach their target. Bogeys usually won't kill you. Double bogeys will.

Jean hoped to shoot around even par, maybe a shot or two higher. That ought to do it.

"I knew nobody was going to shoot sixty-five at Carnoustie," he said. "No matter what. No matter what!"

The other thing he had to control was his mind. He couldn't think of how winning the Open might change his life, either immediately or for the long term. There were too many holes to be played. Besides, those kinds of thoughts backfired more often than not.

Come Sunday, he was ready. Unfortunately for him, so was Australia's Craig Parry, who shot four strokes better over the first nine holes than Jean. Just like that, his lead was down to only one, and then it was gone entirely. Parry was up by a shot after eleven holes, and Justin Leonard, the 1997 British Open champion, was only three back.

Jean could have easily been discouraged by this abrupt turn of events. He wasn't.

"I knew I had the mental strength and quality of game to get past that," he said.

Which he did, going even par the next five holes while Parry, who made a triple bogey on the twelfth, was six over. Paul Lawrie made the move of the day, finishing with a 67, but he was still three back when Jean got to the final tee. Leonard, meanwhile, was now officially in second place, two behind, although he was facing a putt for bogey on the eighteenth green. He, too, appeared to be out of it.

Jean knew early on golf was the game for him, and he didn't mean minigolf, which his parents brought him to twice a day for a month or so. He wanted golf without windmills and artificial carpets. So he kept bugging his father to take him to a regular course.

His father finally gave in. "This is silly," he said. "This has to stop. Let's go over to the real golf and see what's happening."

Conveniently, "the real golf" wasn't far away. His parents had a summer home in the South of France next to one of the country's better courses, the Hossegor golf club. Jean, six at the time, was excited. Safe to say the head professional, Martin Hausseguy, didn't share the boy's enthusiasm.

"He's too small," Hausseguy told Jean's parents. "Come back next year and we'll see if he's grown and if he's stronger."

Next *year*? Jean had already waited long enough. He started to cry. The pro felt bad for hurting his feelings and said he could hang around for a few hours. Jean loved it. When the pro returned from a lunch break, he brought Jean a club he'd cut in half and put half of a new grip on.

"I had tiny hands," Jean explained.

The same day, Jean received his first lesson and a putter, also cut down to his size.

"I stayed there every single day," he said. "Whenever I wasn't on the putting green, I was running back and sitting next to him, listening to him teaching."

He played every chance he could, from the beginning of spring until the end of fall. By his early teens, he was good enough to make the French national team. He was fortunate to have parents who could afford to do their part. Golf is never cheap.

"My father built a putting green in the garden and a chipping area and a bunker," he said. "How many people have that in their house?"

Even so, when Jean decided to turn pro at age twenty, giving himself two years to make it, his father, who sold engineering products, had his doubts. Jean didn't blame him one bit.

"It was a world he didn't know," he said.

While still an amateur, Jean had gotten a chance to caddy for an American, Lee Trevino, at an exhibition in Paris. Trevino was in his mid-forties by that point and not the same player who won five major championships in the late sixties and early seventies. He was as talkative as usual—that was his MO—but even in an event that didn't mean anything, Jean saw another side to him.

All that smiling and chatting "was just a façade," he said. "The guy was highly concentrating. I remember him saying he wanted to play like he was in a golf tournament. He had to prepare for the following week."

That he did, shooting in the low 60s. Trevino took the time to tell Jean why he hit certain shots with one shape and other shots with a different one.

"He was aggressive and he was such a good putter," he recalled.

That would also describe the one-of-a-kind player from Spain, Seve Ballesteros, who won the British Open three times and the Masters twice. Jean watched Ballesteros in person as a kid and was in awe, like so many others, of how he seemed to always find a way out of trouble.

Many years later, while a player on the European Tour, Jean was on the putting green at a tournament in Scotland when he heard a familiar voice:

"Can you please have a look?"

The voice belonged to Ballesteros, who was speaking Spanish.

Jean turned around. The great Seve Ballesteros couldn't be asking him to check out his technique.

Yes, he was. No one else was on the green.

"It was unbelievable," he said. "We spent forty-five minutes talking about his putting stroke. I don't know if he used any of it."

What Ballesteros and Trevino had in common was more than winning the most prestigious tournaments. Both had a tremendous passion for the game, which you couldn't possibly miss. They also were very sure of themselves.

"If they thought it was the right thing to do, they went for it," Jean noted.

Jean, thirty-three, was set to make his own mark in the game as he arrived at the tee on eighteen. Only not the history he, and everybody else, thought he was going to make.

The list of his troubles would end up being a long and painful one, but it started right there, when he grabbed the driver. The driver was the *last* club Jean should have been using with such a big lead; it meant that his ball, if he didn't hit it accurately, could wind up in "Barry Burn," a stream that winds through the course connecting the Scottish Hills to the North Sea. End up there, it's a one-stroke penalty, and suddenly that lead wouldn't look so big anymore.

"I'm not sure this is right," remarked Peter Alliss, the legendary commentator for the BBC.

Jean *was* sure.

"I just wanted to play the hole the way I liked to play it," he said.

Besides, being fearless is what got him this far, this week and his whole career, the same self-confidence he admired so much in Trevino and Ballesteros. Now he'd display it. Not because he was cocky, but because it was who he was.

Only this tee shot, the most important of his life, was off line right from the start on the 487-yard par-4, and it looked as if the ball might find the Burn. Fortunately, it didn't, though Jean had hit the ball so far right it was close to the seventeenth tee.

"You lucky little rascal," Alliss told his viewers. "Some golfing god is with the young man at this moment."

If some golfing god was with this young man, it didn't stick around for long.

The smart play for his second shot, and everybody knew it, was to go with a shorter club, maybe a wedge, to put the ball safely in the fairway. That would set up a good chance to get it onto the green with his third, and even if it took him three putts, he would be the Open champion. The odds, to be sure, were still overwhelmingly in his favor. His name, as a matter of fact, was already being engraved on the championship trophy.

At this point, forget finishing in style. Jean just needed to finish with a score at least one stroke less than anyone else.

Even so, needing about 185 yards to get over the Burn in front of the green, he chose to go for it. Out came the two iron. That's a long club, and the longer the club, the harder it is to control.

Similar to the tee shot, the ball veered right immediately. This time, he was *un*lucky. The ball struck a metal railing in the grandstand, deflected off the stone wall that borders the Burn, and bounced backward into a patch of nasty rough. If only it had stayed in the grandstand, he would've gotten a free drop, and been in a better position for his third shot.

"It was a fluke," he recalled. "The piece of metal was the size of a golf ball."

Jean looked at the lie. It wasn't just bad; it was horrible. So horrible he thought about hitting the ball sideways. He decided against it.

"I didn't know if I was capable of hitting that ball onto the fairway," he said. "It might stay in the rough."

The next shot, with a wedge, was his worst yet. The ball ended up, as it had seemed destined to from the tee box, in the Burn. Jean Van de Velde was coming apart as no golfer ever had on a stage this large. And it looked like he had no idea of how to pull himself back together.

The BBC's Alliss summed it up best: "This is so, so, so, so sad—and so unnecessary."

Jean would now have to take the ball out of the water and accept a penalty stroke.

Or maybe not.

Much to the crowd's delight, he took off his shoes and socks and rolled up his pants. Club in hand, he hopped down into the water. Standing between walls nearly six feet high on either side of the Burn, he could see that the top part of the ball remained above the water, just enough to make him believe he could hack it out of there. What we were witnessing couldn't have been more dramatic, or more bizarre.

"I was definitely going to hit that ball," he said.

In other words, conventional wisdom be damned, he was going to keep playing his way.

But, unlike other sports, golf gives you time to think, and the longer he did, the longer he stood barefoot in the water, the more he realized how unrealistic—"absurd" might be a better word—the whole notion was. Even for Jean. He needed to have entered the water almost immediately.

"The problem was that the tide was going up," he said.

Craig Parry, who was playing with Jean, joked, "If you wait about eight hours, you might be able to hit it."

So he took his drop and was now lying four. To finish with a six on the hole and win the tournament, he would have to hit his next shot onto the green and sink the putt. The way he was unraveling, no one thought there was a chance in you-know-what he could pull that off.

He didn't. The ball ended up in the bunker adjacent to the green. Jean would have to chip it on, and make the putt just to *tie* Leonard and Lawrie, and get into a playoff. Forget about winning; now it was about survival.

Parry, meanwhile, had found the same bunker. He played first. So what does he do? He knocks the ball into the hole! Exactly what Jean needed to do.

All Jean could do was smile. The odds of two players holing out from the bunker on the same hole are—well, you don't want to know.

"You going to throw something else at me?" Jean wondered.

He pulled himself together, at last, and hit a decent shot of his own, the ball ending up roughly 8 feet from the cup. Given the pressure, you couldn't have expected him to do much better. Eight feet wasn't far, although it had to feel like 80 feet after what he'd been through the past fifteen minutes or so.

A lot of players would be too rattled to believe in themselves.

Not Jean. Confidence was never his problem.

"I'm still in it," he told himself. "Come on, you can make it."

He made it, all right, for a triple-bogey seven, and celebrated with a fist pump. He was battered and bruised, but not broken.

Too bad the golfing gods were merely giving him a reprieve.

The playoff between Jean, Lawrie, and Leonard, which took a while to get started, was set for four extra holes.

Except for those who follow the sport closely, no one remembers who won—it was Lawrie—just as no one remembers who won the 1991 U.S. Open after Jimmy Connors beat Aaron Krickstein.

All anyone remembers is the man who lost. No player in golf, in *any* sport, ever lost quite like this.

If anybody should be haunted by falling apart on the big stage, you'd think it would have to be Jean Van de Velde. Like Aaron, there was no teammate to blame, though there was one key difference. Aaron was beaten by a great player on a great run. Jean beat himself.

So when he showed up at a Paris restaurant one morning during the fall of 2015, one would expect to see signs of the pain that must still be in there—in his expression, his words . . . somewhere. Yet there were none anywhere. Jean long ago made his peace with Carnoustie. He thinks it's about time you did, too.

"It's a sports event," he insisted. "We're not running the world. We're not deciding on climate change or deciding on poverty. This is trivial, man, as trivial as it gets. Let's talk about Syria."

What mattered to him in 1999, and still does today, is that, like the players he admired so greatly, such as Ballesteros and Trevino, he was true to himself on the golf course. That he was the kind of player he wanted to be, win or lose.

"For some people, winning is everything," he said. "They will even cheat to win. I played golf for myself, for the pleasure that golf gave me, and if I believed I could hit a golf shot, I hit it. I don't need to justify myself. If I want to hit driver three times in a row, I'll hit driver three times in a row. If I want to hit a two iron, I hit a two iron. If I want to lay up, I lay up. I'm accountable to myself."

Nor would he let anyone else's expectations affect how he would cope with the outcome. He would cope his way, as usual.

Don't get him wrong. Jean wanted to win the British Open. He wanted to win badly. And there's no telling how differently his career—and his life—would have gone if he'd scored a six or better on the final hole.

"I happened to lose that tournament that I had in the middle of my hands, basically, so, of course, I was sad, I was devastated, whichever word you want to use," he said. "It meant a lot to me."

Sadness, yes. Shame? Absolutely not. Never.

"At least I feel like I touched them [the fans], whether it's a positive way or a negative way," Jean explained. "It's nice to see that you trigger a reaction in somebody. Why do we play sport? Why do we watch sport? For the emotion that is conveyed to you, or just for the sake of it? You want those who actually play the game, whatever kind of game, to trigger joy or pain in you."

Even so, he was asked if he would change any of his decisions on eighteen—choosing the driver, hitting the two iron, walking into the Burn; there was a lot to pick from.

There was one thing. On the third shot, he would have tried to hit the ball out of the rough sideways and hope he reached the fairway. Even if it remained in the rough, he said, "the lie was very likely to be much better" than the one he faced at the time.

Other than that, no regrets whatsoever.

"I'm going to ask you a question," he said. "Who won the Open in 1907? Who won in 1963?" He doesn't care about the answer. His point: "Does it really matter?"

Fair enough, but, if not haunted, he couldn't have been very thrilled with some of the things that were said about him, and not just by Peter Alliss. Curtis Strange, a two-time U.S. Open champion who was doing the analysis for ABC, said Jean's decision making was "the most stupid thing I've ever seen." Ouch.

Here, again, give Jean credit for having the right attitude. Plenty of guys would carry a grudge.

"At the end of the day, I don't care," he said. "Everyone is entitled to have an opinion. There are a lot of people who said those things on the spot because it meant so much to them. They could associate with the pain. It was like it would've happened to them. But then, you give them five years or ten years, and many of them don't use the same words. They had time to understand it wasn't them. It was somebody else."

Knowing him, it was no surprise he even found a way to poke fun at his collapse.

He was having dinner a month later at the PGA Championship in the Chicago area when he said he could have scored better on the final hole if he'd used just his putter. Almost immediately, Jean and everyone at the table agreed: *Let's find out.*

So, in December, he went back to the scene of the crime and filmed a commercial for a company that makes putters. Lo and behold, on his third attempt, he got the six he could have used in July. His "tee shot" traveled 160 yards in the air and another 100 or so on the hard and icy ground.

By this point, he was no doubt looking ahead to the 2000 season and beyond. Okay, he messed up the final hole at Carnoustie, and okay, it was the most important hole of his life. But it was still just that . . . one hole. He had come out of nowhere to lead the British Open going into that hole, and no one could take that away from him. He just needed to finish things off the next time.

"There was going to be an Open next year and another one the year after," he said. "I proved to myself I could be in that position. It was just a matter of re-creating it. Why couldn't I do it? I *had* done it."

Only he never would be in that position again. Not in a major.

Though Jean did have his moments on the course. In 2000, he came in second at a tournament in Reno, Nevada, missing a 12-foot birdie putt on the final hole of regulation that would have won it. He lost, eventually, to Scott Verplank on the fourth playoff hole. That's as close to victory as Jean would ever come against the top players in the world.

Not to trivialize things, but his career was certainly affected by the events of September 11, 2001. He was in position to secure his spot on the PGA Tour in the United States for the 2002 season, but after the attacks, he dropped out of the remaining events and flew back to Europe.

"If something, the following week, were to happen in Europe," said Jean, who was married at the time, "I wanted to be next to my loved one. Did you know what was going to happen? Were we going to enter into a war? Nobody knew."

The fact that he gave up his chance to play in America because of real-life events says as much about Jean Van de Velde as anything else. To him, golf is just a game. Lots of athletes say that. Jean means it.

He resumed playing in Europe in 2002, but that same year, he had to undergo two knee surgeries, the problems dating back to a ski accident in the early nineties. For more than two years, he could barely walk. Even today, the knee bothers him, and he limps whenever the weather is nasty. Being away from the game he loves that long made him appreciate it even more.

"I was wondering if I was ever going to be able to play at the level I wanted to play," he said.

He was, thank goodness, and in June 2005, he was in contention to win a tournament that meant as much to him as the British Open—the French Open, at Le Golf National near Paris.

With just one hole to go, Jean was leading by a stroke. You won't believe what happened next. Maybe you will.

He knocked the ball into the water and had to go to a sudden-death playoff with another French player, Jean-François Remésy. It gets worse. On the first extra hole, he hit it into the water again and ended up losing the tournament. The golfing gods apparently weren't done with him just yet.

Now it's history's turn, and history, so far, has been just as cruel.

Every time a golfer is in danger of blowing a big lead down the stretch of a big tournament, you can almost count on somebody bringing up Jean's name. No other example compares. That's how he'll be remembered, and there's nothing he can do about it. His reaction was exactly what you would expect.

"That doesn't bother me," Jean said. "Why would it bother me? It's a fact. So I have no problem."

What would have bothered him, on the other hand, is if he had gone against who he is.

"Put it this way, if I would have hit a wedge and then another wedge and shanked my second wedge, or not find the fairway with the first wedge, and not won," he said, "*then* I could not have lived with myself."

Saying good-bye to Jean at the restaurant in Paris, you can't help but ask yourself: Is this guy for real? Does he honestly believe that, except for one decision, he wouldn't change a thing about how he navigated the last hole? Seriously, wouldn't he rather have been the Open champion instead of the golfer who *blew* the Open Championship?

Yes, he is for real. The fact that we might have trouble believing him is our problem, not his, and only points out the fundamental differences in how we look at life and losing. He would never wish for himself to lose, but he doesn't run from it, either. Losing is simply another part of being alive.

"I feel extremely blessed in the satisfaction I've received from it [golf]," Jean explained, "and in receiving, I'm not only talking about trophies. Receiving is the full spectrum of emotion, from extreme sadness to extreme joy. It's like love and hate, they're together.

"You need to love life for what it is."

Calvin Schiraldi has coached at St. Michael's Catholic Academy in Austin, Texas, since 1996. The Crusaders have won two state championships so far. *Courtesy of Ohga Gilmore*

Part of the joy Calvin gets out of coaching high school baseball is the impact that he can have on so many young lives. *Courtesy of Ohga Gilmore*

Calvin's wood-paneled wall of memories is dedicated to the high school teams he's coached, not to his days as a big-league pitcher. *Courtesy of the author*

The Cleveland Cavaliers signed Craig Ehlo to a ten-day contract in January 1987. He stuck around for seven years. *Courtesy of Craig Ehlo*

Craig's wife, Jani, knew little about basketball when they were honeymooning in Tahiti in 1985, but she quickly became his strongest defender over the years—on and off the court. *Courtesy of Craig Ehlo*

Whether at Disney World in 1992; on the beach in Destin, Florida, in 1994; or in the sometimes tumultuous years since, Craig's family has always been what brought him back to reality. *Courtesy of Craig Ehlo*

Even during his high school days in College Park, Georgia, Bill Curry was undersized for an offensive lineman.
Courtesy of the Fulton County Public School System

His family and faith have meant the world to Bill, who, as the years went on, learned that there is a lot more to sports than winning and losing.
Courtesy of Bill Curry

Having worn the number 79 during his playing days, Lou Michaels found a special way to celebrate his seventy-ninth birthday with his team in retirement, his family. *Courtesy of Ed Michaels*

Johnny Unitas was the first guy to welcome Lou after he was traded to the Baltimore Colts. A fact Lou remembered over the years.
Courtesy of Judy Michaels

Even as a two-year-old, Lindsey Jacobellis was quite the athlete.
Courtesy of Anita Jacobellis

The Winter Olympics were a lot closer than it looks here as four-year-old Lindsey took her first ski lesson with her older brother, Ben.
Courtesy of Anita Jacobellis

Starting as an eleven-year-old, Lindsey naturally took to snowboarding. The trophies began piling up that very first year.
Courtesy of Anita Jacobellis

Lindsey won a national title at the United States Ski and Snowboard Association's giant slalom competition at age thirteen, and has been considered one of the best in the world ever since.
Courtesy of Anita Jacobellis

Mike Lantry in 1969. Vietnam was a long way from his hometown of Oxford, Michigan. *Courtesy of the Lantry family*

After his days in the military were done, Mike walked on to the University of Michigan football team, where he might have been the toughest-looking kicker in America. *Courtesy of the Bentley Historical Library, University of Michigan*

Though proud of his service to his country, Mike was more than happy to leave army life behind. *Courtesy of the Lantry family*

One of the best junior players ever in American tennis, Aaron Krickstein began hoisting the hardware at an early age. Here he is as the eleven-year-old winner of the twelve-and-under division of the Junior Orange Bowl. *Courtesy of Aaron Krickstein*

Aug 6, 1981

DAD,

My Attitude and my mind has finally changed I think. I Know it won't be easy but I finally understand what you've been telling me for 4 years. Everytime I walk on the court I'm going to try to drive myself and give 110% effort every minute I'm out there. The drive must come in conditioning too. I feel with this drive and effort I will not wine and cry on the court again. And also, I am not a babie anymore! And next year the 1982 Kalamazoo champion is Game - set - match - KRICKStein

Love, Aaron

The letter that Aaron wrote to his father, Herb, which helped propel his young career. *Courtesy of Aaron Krickstein*

Aaron won his last forty-five matches as a junior, including defeating Patrick McEnroe in the final to win the National Championship in Kalamazoo at age fifteen. *Courtesy of Aaron Krickstein*

Ron Washington talks defense with Nelson Cruz during Game 2 of the 2011 World Series. Cruz's defense became a big factor later in the series. *Ezra Shaw/Getty Images*

Throughout his baseball life as a player, coach, and manager, Washington has always been ready to greet you with a smile and a laugh. *Rob Tringali/Getty Images*

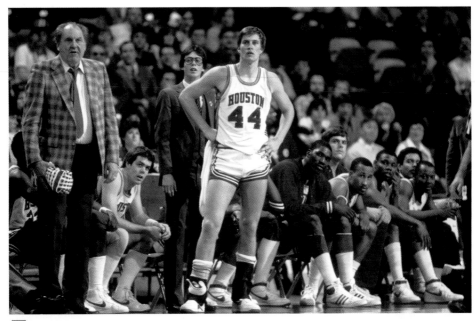

Early on, Coach Guy Lewis instilled in Reid Gettys that his talent was far different—and in some ways, more needed—than those of his celebrated teammates. *Rich Clarkson*/Sports Illustrated/*Getty Images*

Hugging his son, Reid passes down the lessons he learned from his father, Marshall, about the role of sports in life. *Courtesy of Reid Gettys*

The still-baby-faced Al Downing returned to the New York Yankees for good as a twenty-one-year old in the summer of 1963. He went on to pitch for the Yankees in the World Series that year, and the year after.
Kidwiler Collection/Diamond Images/Getty Images

The moment after THE MOMENT.
Herb Scharfman/ Sports Imagery/ Getty Images

To make sure they would truly be "the Unforgettables," John Pelphrey, Coach Rick Pitino, Richie Farmer, Sean Woods, and Deron Feldhaus were all inducted into the inaugural class of the University of Kentucky Athletic Hall of Fame in 2005. *AP Photo/Lexington Herald-Leader, Jonathan Palmer*

John and Tracy Pelphrey focused their lives on family, and helping others, after losing a son at birth. *Courtesy of Tracy Pelphrey*

F rom his ill-advised decision to use a driver off the tee, Jean Van de Velde almost seemed destined to find the Burn, which he did on his third shot. *David Cannon/Allsport*

J ean was planning to hit the ball out of the water on the final hole of the 1999 British Open at Carnoustie, but the longer he stood in Barry Burn, the more he realized the idea was not a good one. *Photo by Phil Sheldon/Popperfoto/ Getty Images*

D espite it all, Jean has maintained his sanity—and sense of humor—as he realizes some things are more important than golf. *Pete Fontaine/WireImage*

She burst onto the scene in the early seventies as Little Mary Decker, and she was to become the best middle-distance runner in the world, breaking all kinds of records. *Bettmann/Getty Images*

For Mary, getting married to Richard Slaney in 1985, and having a daughter, Ashley, showed her there was a lot more to life than running. *AP Photo/Adam Stoltman*

Because of arthritis, Mary can't run these days, but she enjoys competing on the elliptical bike. *Courtesy of ElliptiGO, Inc.*

Junior Seau and Rodney Harrison shared so much more in common than just Pro Bowl–level playing ability. Rodney loved and admired his teammate on both the Chargers and Patriots. *Courtesy of the San Diego Chargers*

One of the few times you won't see Everson Walls with a smile on his face. Sure, he was an eleven-year-old MVP, but his team lost the league championship game. Right after this picture, he cried. *Courtesy of Everson Walls*

With Mom—and those infamous braids—in the Bahamas at age fifteen. *Courtesy of Everson Walls*

Everson always wanted to look his best for his mom. Especially on Easter Sunday 1972. *Courtesy of Everson Walls*

RONALD REAGAN

February 18, 1994

TELEFAX FOR DAN JANSEN
              U.S. GOLD MEDALIST
              LILLEHAMMER, NORWAY

FROM: RONALD REAGAN

I jumped out of my seat when I saw you cross the finish line today!! It's like they say, good things come to those who wait!

Your nation applauds you, Dan, for your outstanding sportsmanship, your courage and your fighting spirit!

Congratulations and God bless you.

Ronald Reagan

THE WHITE HOUSE
WASHINGTON

March 1, 1995

Mr. Dan Jansen
Greenfield, Wisconsin

Dear Dan:

Congratulations on winning the Sullivan Award from the Amateur Athletic Union.

I understand that you weren't able to fly to Indianapolis to pick up your award because of bad weather, but ice seems to bring out the best in you. Your dedication and perseverance are a source of inspiration for all Americans.

Hillary and I wish you every future happiness.

Sincerely,

Bill Clinton

After finally winning gold, Dan Jansen received letters from four U.S. presidents. *Courtesy of Dan Jansen*

GEORGE BUSH

March 5, 1994

Dear Dan:

I am pleased to add my heartiest congratulations to the many good wishes you have received. Like all Americans, I am very proud not only of what you accomplished, but the way you accomplished it.

In winning the Gold Medal in Lillehammer after several bouts with disappointment, you demonstrated the rare ability and determination that had already made you a great champion. Yours was the perfect example of the Olympic spirit, and Barbara joins me in commending you.

Sincerely,

G. Bush

Mr. Dan Jansen
West Allice, Wisconsin

JIMMY CARTER

March 6, 1994

To Dan Jansen

Rosalynn and I are pleased to offer our congratulations on your return home as an Olympic Gold Medalist. You have truly personified the Olympic spirit with your determination and positive attitude. Your fine example is an inspiration to young people around the world.

With warm best wishes for continued success in all of your future endeavors,

Sincerely,

Jimmy Carter

Growing up in West Allis, just outside Milwaukee, Wisconsin, Dan was the youngest of nine children. The last three in the house, Jane, Mike, and Dan shared a special bond. *Courtesy of Dan Jansen*

Speed skating was big even when the Jansen kids were little. In the front yard after a meet in 1973 are Dan (age seven), Mike (age nine), and Jane (age twelve). *Courtesy of Dan Jansen*

Jane, who died the morning of his famous fall in 1988, seemed to know that some day her little brother Dan was going to be a big fish. *Courtesy of Dan Jansen*

12

FALLING SHORT

For once in her life, Mary Decker decided, she would allow someone else to take the lead. With the pace quick enough for her liking, she'd hang back in the pack with the other ten women and make her move in the final lap or two.

The race, at 3,000 meters, just shy of two miles, was for the gold, and it was the biggest race the best middle-distance female runner in the world had yet to win. Something always seemed to get in the way when it came to Mary Decker and the Olympics, and it was never her fault.

In 1972, Mary was too young to compete in the Games even though she was as fast as many other women hoping to represent their countries in Munich.

In 1976, she was injured. She watched the Olympics, held in Montreal, on television. It killed her not to be there.

Then, in 1980, she wasn't too young and she wasn't injured. She was unlucky. That was when the United States, with Jimmy Carter as president, decided to boycott the Games in Moscow to protest the Soviet Union's invasion of Afghanistan in December 1979.

Finally, here at the 1984 Games in Los Angeles, there was nothing, and no one, that could stop her.

She was coming off one of her most successful seasons yet, winning the 1,500 and 3,000 at the first-ever 1983 World Championships in Athletics. They even came up with a name for what she accomplished: the "Double Decker."

Later in 1983, she received an honor no one saw coming, and that included Mary, the *Sports Illustrated* Sportsperson of the Year. No woman had won the award since tennis star Chris Evert in 1976, and no woman, in an individual sport, would win it again until Serena Williams in 2015.

"I was blown away," Mary recalled. "Track and field? Seriously? And a woman?"

Now if she could only take home the gold medal she'd been pursuing—forever, it seemed.

Mary started running at the age of eleven by accident, really. She received a handout one day in school about something to do with cross-country that coming weekend at a park near her home in Huntington Beach, California, just south of Los Angeles. She and a friend decided to give it a try.

"Neither of us knew what cross-country was," Mary said. "We had no idea it was running."

The race went for three-quarters a mile, and much to her surprise, she outran all the other girls. No one in her family was a runner. And the way she played basketball and volleyball—let's just say Mary hadn't shown signs of being much of an athlete.

After the race was over, the coach of a girls' track club up the coast in Long Beach asked her if she wanted to join. Sure, Mary said. She didn't realize running could be so much fun and so easy.

"It felt completely natural to me," she said. "When I found running, I found what I felt I was meant to be doing. I found out I was way better than a lot of people."

Way better, indeed, and it wasn't long before she was running faster than women twice her age. By the time Mary turned twelve, her mind was set: she wanted to become an Olympian.

Running was also a place for her to escape from the tension at home, if only for a few hours. Her parents were having problems and would wind up getting a divorce.

"I started running before all the chaos in my life happened," she said, "so, obviously, it wasn't a catalyst. But I think it was one thing I felt was mine, no matter what happens with the family situation."

She ran as often as she could, against others or on her own. There was nothing she enjoyed more, except perhaps winning.

One race that stands out wasn't even a real race, though it sure was satisfying. Mary was supposed to run against a boy in her school, Alex (not his real name), who had put her down in front of the other kids. It began in typing class when there was an announcement over the loudspeaker about a world record she'd set the previous weekend in Los Angeles.

"That's not such a big deal," Alex blurted out.

"Well, let's see how big a deal it is," the teacher said.

The teacher suggested a mile race for the following day at lunchtime between Mary and Alex. They both agreed.

The news got around fast. Everyone at Portola Junior High School turned out to see what would happen, "even the kids who would go in the bathroom and smoke at lunchtime," Mary said, laughing.

Except Alex never showed up at school that day. So, for fun, she ran instead against two boys from the track team. Each boy would race 800 meters as part of a relay, while she would go the entire mile. She won easily.

"I was a skinny kid, gangly, and not a popular cheerleader type or anything," Mary recalled. "I had my couple of friends. What I got out of that was I did something all my peers respected. It made me feel like I belonged more, as opposed to being this little outsider that was good at running."

Winning that type of competition in junior high, with all of those people watching, is how legends are made, my friend.

"For years," Mary said, "anybody who went through Portola Junior High heard that story."

There would be plenty more stories to come. Eventually, everyone affiliated with track and field in the United States would hear about the ninety-pound girl known as Little Mary Decker. She'd have an excellent chance to qualify for the 1972 Games in Munich.

One problem: the minimum age to make the Olympic squad was fourteen. With Mary's birthday falling on August 4, by the time the

Games actually got under way in late August she would have been old enough. However, since she was still thirteen when the trials were held in late June, she wasn't allowed to participate. Mary was asked if she could ever see any merit to the other side's point.

"Hell, no," she said emphatically. "I had the fastest time in the country for women in the 880."

Then, in 1973, at a U.S.-Soviet meet in Minsk, Belarus, she won the 800 meters, defeating the woman who had earned the silver medal in Munich.

"It was a big moment," Mary recalled. "At fourteen, I didn't know how big. I guess I surprised a lot of people back then."

Herself not included.

"I knew that I could be one of the best in the world at the distances I ran," she said.

She soon began to get excited about Montreal. They wouldn't be able to keep her off the team again. Too bad her body let her down, and it would not be the last time. Not even close. The pain was in her shins. She tried resting, therapy, you name it, but the pain didn't go away. Montreal was out.

"My injury problems started a year before that," she said. "And they persisted and persisted."

At least she would have no one to blame this time. Besides, Mary felt certain she would have more opportunities—quite a few, in fact. She was only eighteen and a long way from her prime.

Then came the U.S. boycott in 1980. Even after President Carter's announcement, she continued to hope that something would happen at the last minute to change his mind. She took part in the U.S. Olympic Trials and made the "team." But nothing, unfortunately for Mary and the other athletes, changed Carter's mind. Mary was in Italy when she watched the Olympics on TV. Watching other women compete where she should have been was becoming a bad habit.

Yet that wasn't the worst part. The worst part was what took place back in the States. First, there was a special meet for the team in Philadelphia. "That was our Olympics," Mary said. A week of events in D.C. followed, capped off by a ceremony at the White House.

Upset or not, when the president of the United States invites you to 1600 Pennsylvania Avenue, you go. So there she was, having to greet President Carter and his wife, Rosalynn, in the long receiving line, unable, of course, to say what was truly on her mind.

"You just had to go through it," she said.

The only upside was she got to meet athletes from other sports who, after the sacrifices they made, year after year, were just as heartbroken as she was. Probably more.

"The thing which struck me was I felt I was young and I had another chance at the Olympics," she recalled. "I met a lot of people in a lot of sports that this was it."

Besides losing a chance to go for the gold, Mary lost something else. She lost a little faith in the Olympics and what they supposedly stood for.

"It's so political. It's not what sports should be," she said, "and 1980 proved that, to a very large extent."

Maybe, but running was still her passion and winning a gold medal her goal, and it wasn't long before she started to look forward to the 1984 Games in Los Angeles.

First came the World Championships in Helsinki. Mary went to Finland with a lot to prove, not to herself but rather to those who doubted her. She had posted excellent times in a wide range of distances, her critics gave her that. In 1982, Mary set eleven world and U.S. records. What they weren't as sure of was how she would fare against the best runners in the world. You prove that in the Olympics, and she hadn't had that opportunity, not yet. The criticism was perhaps unfair, but she couldn't ignore it.

The reality was not that Mary wasn't good enough. She was actually *too* good. Being in front of the other women in many of her events, she didn't have to think through how she'd adjust if she found herself in what's known as a tactical race, where everybody is bunched together close to the lead. In tactical races, you have to know the right time to make your move because it's very easy to make it at the wrong time.

In any case, she didn't plan on having that problem in Helsinki. You see, no matter what others thought of her, she'd run *her* race, not theirs. Which meant she wouldn't hesitate to take the lead in the first lap or two.

"My attitude going into '83 was, well, the Russians, the Romanians, the East Germans are all amazing," she said, "but I [decided] it wasn't going to be a tactical race. They're going to have to race a relatively respectable time to win. I did not want to come out of the race thinking that it was ten seconds too slow, and why did I do that?"

Their times were respectable enough. Her times were better. In the 3,000, which she ran first, she took the lead early on and then held off the USSR's Tatyana Kazankina, who had won two gold medals in Montreal and another in Moscow. Four days later, in the 1,500, Mary went ahead once more, but was passed with less than 200 meters to go. Trailing down the stretch for a change put her theory to the test. No sweat. She found another gear, edging Zamira Zaitseva in a thrilling finish. So much for those who doubted her.

"I beat people nobody else thought I could beat," Mary said.

That year, she won every race in which she made it to the finals, twenty races in all. She was ready for the 1984 Games.

Mary couldn't have asked for anything more. The Games would be hosted at the Coliseum. The track would feel like home and the fans would be on her side. That wasn't all. The Russians and the other Eastern Bloc countries, except for Romania, boycotted this time to get back at the United States for skipping the Games in 1980. A number of the top runners in the world came from those nations.

Even her body, for a change, was in pretty decent shape. She injured her Achilles tendon during the Olympic Trials a few months before and had to take a little time off and train in the water. Maybe that would be to her benefit. Better to be hurt in June than in August, although the injury would lead to her skipping the 1,500 meters in Los Angeles.

At last, on August 10, a typically gorgeous summer day in Southern California, Mary stood at the starting line for the 3,000—twelve years later, perhaps, than she hoped to be in an Olympic race, but here, nonetheless.

Winning the gold, despite the records she'd set and the absence of the Eastern Bloc runners, would be no sure thing. There were still talented women who could beat her. One to keep an eye on was Maricica Puică from Romania, who came in seventh in the 1,500 meters at the 1980 Olympics. Two years later, she broke Mary's world record for the mile with 4:17.44. She missed the event in Helsinki because of an injury but was good to go for the Games. Another was an eighteen-year-old from South Africa, Zola Budd. Budd weighed less than ninety pounds and ran barefoot, but, man, could she fly.

Budd almost didn't make it to Los Angeles. South Africa was barred from the Olympics due to its racist apartheid system, but with a grandfather born in England, she was quickly granted British citizenship—too quickly, in the view of many, although that hardly mattered now.

The gun sounded, and they were off.

Right away, Mary was in a familiar place: in front. The pace for the opening lap was brisk, at sixty-seven seconds. There were six and a half laps to go. Running closely behind her was Budd. The race went on like this for a couple of minutes, until the fifth lap, when Budd made her move and took the lead.

Mary would try to take it right back, you'd assume. She knew no other way. Her coach, Dick Brown, as a matter of fact, used to come to her room and give her a breakdown of each runner she would be competing against: her weight, racing record, how she ran, and so on. He was wasting his breath.

"To me, it was like I didn't really want to hear any of it, so it went in one ear and out the other," she said.

Brown would go into what plan A should be, and just to be safe, he'd move on to plan B. He may as well brought up the Dodgers, for all she cared.

"To me, plan A and plan B was just him talking," Mary said. "I can't even remember what plan A and plan B were because it didn't take, as far as what was in my mind, and that was to run my race the best I could."

That didn't stop Brown. As long as he was Mary's coach, he would go over strategy with her. Needless to say, this race, as big as it was, would be no exception.

"If someone wants to take the lead for a couple of laps, let them," Brown suggested a day or two before the race.

As usual, she didn't make any promises. Except this time, his advice didn't go in one ear and out the other.

"It was just there, in my brain," she said. "With all his statistics, I knew I was probably the fastest speed-wise at the end of the race. Typically, going into the last lap, I liked to either be in front or feel like I'm in control. I would slowly pick it up, especially into the last lap. I always wanted to feel like I had more left coming down the home straight, so I could run with whoever was coming or trying to go."

Now, with Budd in front, the time had come for Mary to make her decision, and more went into it than just strategy.

"I had been chasing the Olympics for a long time," she explained, "and I wanted to do it right. You have a coach for a reason."

So, she stayed right where she was, although it wouldn't be for long.

The runners soon approached the end of that fifth lap. Budd was still ahead, Mary right behind her, Romania's Puică in third. The gold was very much up for grabs.

And then it happened, out of nowhere, the moment that, more than the races she won and the records she broke, is what we think of when we think of Mary Decker: Mary fell. Onto the infield turf. Her right foot collided with Budd's left calf, just above the Achilles tendon. She rolled over on her back, grabbed her left leg, and couldn't get up. So went her chance for the gold, or any medal.

The race went on, but everyone's eyes were on Mary. The fans booed as she remained on the ground, helpless, in agony. A minute or so later, on the next lap, Budd and the other runners raced by, Mary still lying on her back, being attended to by medical personnel. The race was soon over, the winner, as if anyone cared, Maricica Puică. Budd faded, finishing seventh.

Mary rose and began to walk with some assistance, until she was picked up and carried away by her boyfriend, Richard Slaney, a discus thrower on the British team, who is now her husband. She was in tears, and no doubt, so were the fans at the Coliseum and those watching at home.

"When I tried to move," she said, "there was physical pain, but what made me cry was the disappointment of what occurred. I couldn't finish what I started, to just get back on the track. And then there was the realization of another Olympics that was gone."

She went right from the track to the hospital to get X-rays on her leg. At the hotel later that night, her leg packed in ice, she watched some of the other track and field events on television. She was thinking ahead, to races that would be coming up in Europe. Unfortunately, the injury, a torn muscle in her hip, was too severe. Her season was over. Instead of competing, she'd have to sit with the fall and the damage it caused—to her body, her legacy, her dreams. To everything.

"You didn't get back at it," she said. "You didn't train. You had all this bottled up."

Much was made, at the time, of what Mary said after the fall. When Budd came up to her in the tunnel after the race to apologize, Mary told her, "Don't bother." What happened to her was cruel, there can be no denying that, but did she have to be so unforgiving? Budd didn't trip her on purpose, that much was clear. All these years later, Mary regrets her response.

"I would not say that again," she insisted.

On the other hand, don't expect her to apologize. For one thing, she doesn't feel what she said, given the frustration of the moment, was that horrible to begin with.

"All the things people say now, I think it was pretty mild," Mary said.

Second, she wants everyone to keep in mind where she was in her life at that time.

"People need to realize that when you're looking at athletes in their twenties, they are young people," said Mary, who was twenty-six.

In any case, she harbors no ill will toward Budd, who was disqualified at first for obstruction but quickly reinstated by the officials once they looked at the film.

"There is no blame," Mary said. "Where do you put blame? She was inexperienced running in a group, and, quite frankly, I was inexperienced running in packs."

If anyone was at fault, Mary indicated, it was her. She shouldn't have listened to her coach. She should have done what she did over and over for years—run *her* race, from start to finish.

"I made a tactical, stupid decision, and I never did tactics," she said. "I just ran."

Back home in Eugene, Oregon, where she has lived since 1979, the next few months were as tough as you might imagine, though not being back on the track was, in one way, a blessing. She was able to grieve. If only Craig Ehlo and Calvin Schiraldi had done the same.

"Initially, I cried a lot," she said.

She also pored through letter after letter from fans, and there were thousands. If there were people who felt she overreacted, well, they were not the people who wrote to her.

"I can't honestly remember reading a negative letter, as far as my actions," she said.

She was overwhelmed by how many said they were at the Coliseum and that they cried when she fell. She felt she'd let them down. Speaking of crying, it bothered her to no end that she was taken to task for becoming so emotional that day. By contrast, she asked: "How many times have you watched football or basketball players cry? 'Oh, they're so sensitive,' people say. A young girl cries, and she's a crybaby."

What also disturbed her was how the media suggested there was a feud between Mary and Budd. There was no feud, she said. Not then. Not ever.

"You can talk to Zola, and she would say the same thing," she said.

The two, as a matter of fact, wrote letters back and forth for several months. Both were stuck in a nightmare that wouldn't end. Budd even received death threats.

"We didn't get into the race itself, ever," Mary said. "We both realized it was an accident. We just wanted it to be concluded in everyone else's mind, to go on with our lives."

You've got to give Mary credit. Being as honest as she was with herself about the mistake she made in the race allowed her to come to terms with the fall in Los Angeles much sooner than she might have otherwise. At the same time, there was still more healing to do. You don't invest as much as she did, physically and mentally, and be able to then let it go in a few months, not to mention how the latest disappointment only added to the earlier ones. To help her move past 1984, she looked forward to a new beginning in 1985, on and off the track.

Mary wasted no time. On January 1, she married Richard Slaney.

"[The date] was specifically chosen because we wanted to start the new year off on a positive note," she said.

Later that year, she got pregnant with their only child, a daughter, Ashley. No wonder 1984 didn't seem like such a big deal anymore.

"Instead of your whole life being about track and field, there's real life," she said. "Once you have a child—you don't realize it until you actually have the child—that becomes the single most important thing in your life."

Of course, as competitive as she was, finding bliss at home wouldn't be nearly enough. She needed to prove herself again in competition, and in 1985, boy, did she, setting U.S. records in the 800, 1,000, 3,000, and 5,000. By the way, Mary also broke the world record in the mile with 4:16.71 in Zurich, Switzerland. She didn't lose one race the whole year, including in England, where she ran against Budd for the first time since the Games. Budd finished fourth. In none of those races did Mary hang back. She ran *her* race each time, and she excelled because of it. Lesson learned.

"I wanted to prove to everyone in track and field that I could have won [the gold]," she said. "I can't remember getting on the track, not once, no matter what the distance was, and not feeling like 'nobody's beating me.' After that I was good." If she hadn't had a year like that, "I probably would have continued to be frustrated over '84."

She was able to get beyond 1984, not just because of what she did in 1985 but also because she was sure she'd have more chances to win the gold. Except something always got in the way. Naturally.

In the summer of 1988, just weeks before the Olympics in Seoul, she began to have more health problems. Mary blames the heat at the trials in Indianapolis in mid-July.

"It was one hundred twenty-five degrees on the track, and the humidity was in the nineties," she said. "You couldn't warm up, and then they take you straight into drug testing when you finish and they keep the room cold. I remember shivering and shivering for hours. You know something's wrong when they have IVs lined up around the entire track."

Mary didn't fully recover in time. In Seoul, she finished eighth in the 1,500 and tenth in the 3,000.

"You go off," she said, "and within the first lap, you realize it's gonna suck."

Looking back at her misfortune in 1988, Mary started to laugh.

"You kind of have to," she said. "Otherwise, you'll go crazy. By that point, I realized I'm just not meant to be a great Olympian."

Mary gave it another go in 1992, the Olympics set for Barcelona, but was injured again. She underwent surgery for plantar fasciitis and failed to make it out of the trials.

Then came the 1996 Games in Atlanta, when she qualified for the 5,000 meters at the age of thirty-eight. But while training that summer, she started to experience a shortness of breath and numbness over her arms and legs.

"I thought I was having a heart problem," she said.

Her heart was just fine, thank goodness. The diagnosis would later turn out to be asthma. Mary was surprised. She didn't realize there was a history of asthma in her family.

She ended up competing in the 5,000, but her time in her heat was 15:41:30, nowhere near fast enough to qualify for the final.

"I [physically] felt horrible," she said.

To make the year even worse, a test showed too high a ratio between testosterone and epitestosterone in her system. Although she argued that the results were unreliable because she was taking birth control pills, and was eventually cleared of any wrongdoing, the damage was done.

"I had always been opposed to performance-enhancing substances," she said. "Never did I think you could be called out for something you never did."

In any case, 1996, once and for all, ended her pursuit of the gold. She knew when she was twelve years old that she wanted to be an Olympian and that she was. No one could say Mary didn't give it everything she had, and for close to twenty-five years. She didn't feel, as others might, she needed a gold medal to redeem herself. She redeemed herself with that incredible season in 1985.

"I don't have a bad life because of 1984," Mary said. "I don't have a bad life at all. I have a really nice life. I have a wonderful husband and a wonderful daughter."

Besides, as she approaches sixty, she no longer puts the Olympics on the same pedestal as she did when she was growing up, and it's not just about the politics.

"You think it's the greatest sporting event in history," Mary said. "I don't believe that anymore. You can't have all the best athletes competing because each country is allowed only so many. Individual sporting events in individual sports are far more what sport is about than the Olympics."

She also has a problem with the win-or-else-you're-a-loser mentality that people have about the Games.

"Athletes who actually *make* it to the Olympics should feel like they're winners. Period."

As Mary sees it, there's too much emphasis placed on what happens in a single day of competition. Something totally out of a person's control could go wrong, which she knows as well as anyone. What she did over the her entire career, all the wins and records she compiled, more than makes up for that time she fell in front of the world.

"You throw away every other day of the year, for years, and say they mean nothing," she said, "all the training, all the races . . . everything. And the only thing that counts in your life is that one day."

Yet there is still the matter of her legacy, and she knows the day at the Coliseum will follow her to her grave, as it did with Lou Michaels and the kicks he missed in the Super Bowl.

"The only thing that has bothered me over the years, every now and then, that's not how I want to be remembered in the sport," Mary said. "I want to be remembered for the accomplishments I had."

If she has any regrets, perhaps she pushed herself too hard for too long.

"When you're young, you feel invincible," she said. "And I'm also the type of person that, if I am going to do something, I want to do it well, and I don't do it halfway."

As for any sense of loss she might feel at this stage of her life, it has nothing to do with not having a gold medal. The loss she feels is much deeper: the loss of the pure joy she used to get from running. The joy she felt that day she ran for the first time, when she had no idea what cross-country was. The joy she felt beating the boys on the track team in junior high.

She yearns for the time she felt that joy, win or lose. But because of arthritis, which prevents her from running, Mary knows she will never have that feeling again.

"I would trade any of my competitions, any of my results," she said, "just for the privilege of being able to run without pain, to just have it be a part of my life. Because that's what it meant to me.

"I miss running so much."

13

THE HELMET CATCH

Rodney Harrison figured he was pretty much over that awful day in Arizona.

Boy, was he wrong.

The moment he saw Seattle Seahawks wide receiver Jermaine Kearse make a miraculous, juggling catch while lying on his back, with just over a minute to go in Super Bowl XLIX in 2015 against the New England Patriots, giving his team a first down on the 5-yard line, Rodney recalled, it felt "like a knife in my heart."

One can understand why.

Rodney, you might recall, was at the same stadium in 2008 for Super Bowl XLII, between the Patriots and New York Giants, when something similar happened, too similar. He was still a player back then, a safety for the Patriots, who were chasing more than just their fourth Super Bowl title in seven years.

The winners of eighteen straight games, counting the regular season and playoffs, the Patriots were chasing history. No NFL team had ever finished a season a perfect 19-0. And no team still has. The Giants, thanks in part to another miracle catch with a little over a minute remaining, pulled off a stunning 17–14 upset.

"That [Kearse catch] play made me rehash every single moment in that Giants game," Rodney said. "I was sick."

195

All he could think about over the next few minutes of the 2015 game was how cursed his Patriots must be.

His Patriots.

Because even though he was now an NBC Sports broadcaster who was covering the game, there was no doubt which team he was rooting for.

Thanks to the Kearse reception—he caught it after it apparently had been broken up by the Pats' Malcolm Butler (remember that name)—the Seahawks, trailing by 4, were in position to take the lead and deny New England another ring, just as the Giants did in '08. Even Al Michaels, who was doing the play-by-play, assumed it was incomplete at first. Quarterback Tom Brady shook his head in disbelief on the sidelines.

"For that receiver to make that catch," Rodney recalled, "I said, 'Oh my goodness, the game is over.' That was the most negative feeling that you can feel."

Well, not exactly.

Heading into the 2007 campaign, the Patriots had gone two full seasons without winning a Super Bowl, and for a franchise that thought of itself as a dynasty, that was a long time.

The most painful year had to be the one before. New England was leading the Indianapolis Colts 21–3 in the AFC Championship game, and teams that were coached by Bill Belichick, and had Brady leading the offense, don't blow leads that big, especially not with a ticket to the Super Bowl going to the winner.

They blew this one, falling to Peyton Manning and the Colts, 38–34, Indy scoring the winning touchdown with about a minute to go.

In 2007, though, the Patriots were more dominant than ever, most of all on offense. They scored 34 or more points in each of their first eight games, winning by at least 2 touchdowns every time. In Week 6, they thumped the Cowboys 48–27 in Dallas. The next two games, they put up 49 points against Miami and 52 versus Washington.

Much of the credit belonged to Brady's new target, wide receiver

Randy Moss. That year, Brady to Moss was as dangerous a combination as Joe Montana to Jerry Rice, if not more. Moss would go on to score 23 touchdowns, the most ever by any receiver in a single season. And to think, not everybody felt the Patriots knew what they were getting themselves into when they traded for Moss in the off-season. Moss, who had spent most of his career in Minnesota, wasn't exactly a candidate for NFL Man of the Year.

"A lot of questions surrounded Randy," Rodney said. "Can he still play? How will he fit in? How will his personality go with Bill? Will he be a pain in the butt?"

Any doubts were put to rest in a hurry.

"He worked his butt off, and I think that's the thing that people don't realize," Rodney said. "He was a great physical specimen, but every day I looked up and he was doing something in the weight room."

Moss wasn't the only option Brady had. Just as dependable was his slot receiver, Wes Welker, also in his first year with New England. Welker, acquired in a trade with the Miami Dolphins, would catch 112 passes that season, tied for most in the league. Between Moss and Welker, that's what you call being loaded at the wide receiver position.

"You saw this jubilation in Tom Brady," Rodney remembered. "It almost took him back years. He was a kid with all these different, new toys to play with."

The season became more special by the week, and not only on Sundays.

"We were very competitive in two-minute drills and stuff like that on Fridays," he said. "It became heated. It wasn't like guys were taking plays off. Guys were trying to intercept Brady, and there were a lot of F-bombs and stuff like that."

The Patriots, to be sure, were tested down the stretch. They won them all, though, and finished 16-0. Three more victories in the post-season, and they would match the 1972 Miami Dolphins (17-0) as the only teams to go undefeated throughout the regular season and playoffs.

The fans, the media, everyone was talking about the streak—everyone, it seemed, but the players themselves.

"I never sat down in a hot tub or at lunch or at dinner with a guy and talked about [going] undefeated. We were so brainwashed by Belichick, one game at a time," Rodney said. "That's his gift as a coach, his ability to keep you focused on the moment, and that's what we did."

The next moment was the postseason, and after having a bye in the first round, the Patriots hosted the Jacksonville Jaguars. The game was close most of the way, the outcome not certain till late in the fourth quarter, the Patriots winning 31–20. Brady was nearly perfect, completing 26 of 28 for 262 yards and 3 touchdowns.

One week later, in the AFC Championship game, their opponent was, thank goodness, not the Colts, who lost to the San Diego Chargers the week before in the divisional round. Any time you could avoid Peyton Manning was a reason to celebrate.

Yet San Diego, like Jacksonville, kept things interesting. Brady was far from perfect this time, tossing 3 interceptions. The running game, with Laurence Maroney rushing for 122 yards, made up for it, leading the Pats to a 21–12 victory. New England was bound for Arizona and, perhaps, the ages.

Next up were the New York Giants and the other quarterback from the Manning family, Eli. The Giants were one of the few teams to give the Patriots a game in the regular season, falling 38–35 in the final week. Even so, New England, like the Baltimore Colts in 1969, was a heavy favorite. Heck, the Giants hadn't even won their own division, qualifying for the playoffs as a wild card. To get to the Super Bowl, they'd won in Dallas on a fourth-quarter touchdown and in Green Bay in overtime.

Whatever the odds, no matter the opponent, Rodney was ready, as always. Ready to play the kind of football he was known for. He hit people as hard as anyone in the league.

The season, his fourteenth in the NFL, was one to savor, and it wasn't just because of his team's record. Another reason was the opportunity to play alongside his buddy and teammate for nine years in San Diego, the future Hall of Fame linebacker Junior Seau. No one in the game ever meant more to him than Seau.

"When I came in [to the league], Junior believed in me," Rodney said. "He called me 'Hotrod,' because I was a young kid with a lot of energy. I couldn't believe someone with the prestige of Junior Seau would take interest in me."

Rodney wanted a ring for himself, needless to say, but he owned two already, both with the Patriots, from 2004 and 2005. Seau didn't have any, and, at age thirty-nine, this could very well be his last chance.

"We're going to win one for you," he told Seau in the locker room before the game.

"Just do your best," Seau said.

Seau didn't have anything to worry about. Rodney Harrison had been doing his best since he fell in love with football. He was six years old.

But playing football cost money, and his family, which lived in the Chicago area, didn't have much. With his father not around—his parents were divorced before he can remember—his mother took care of Rodney and two older siblings. She worked two, sometimes three, jobs at a time.

"I remember her driving a tan Chevette with a red door that had a hole in the floor," he said. "We used to put a piece of cardboard to cover up the hole. Any movement, and you could see the street as you're driving."

To join the football club in his neighborhood, the fee was forty dollars, which also happened to be the amount of that month's electric bill.

"You know what, sweetie," his mother told him, "I'm going to sign you up for football. We'll figure out a way to pay the light bill."

The sacrifice didn't go unappreciated.

"Mom," he promised her, "you're not going to have to struggle your entire life. I'm going to put us in a better situation. I'm going to buy you a new house when I go pro."

He put in the time from the start, and everything else came second.

"When everybody was out drinking and partying and chasing

the women," he said, "I was in front of my house, with my mom in her lawn chair, at nine, ten o'clock at night, running sprints."

Still, no matter how hard he worked, there was always someone in a position of authority who didn't believe in him. No problem. They were exactly what he needed.

"I thank people like that," Rodney said. "They really gave me that fire inside of me."

Rodney had hoped to play college football in the Big Ten, either at Iowa, Illinois, or Ohio State, but wound up going instead to Western Illinois University. A football factory, it was not. Yet that didn't keep Rodney from being named an All-American after both his sophomore and junior seasons. In a game against Western Kentucky, he made 28 tackles, a school record that still stands.

There was more disrespect to come. Rodney wasn't chosen until the fifth round of the 1994 NFL Draft, by the Chargers. In all, 144 players were picked ahead of him.

Again, no problem.

"All I wanted was a chance," he said, "and when you gave me that forty-five-thousand-dollar signing bonus, and it was twenty-three grand after taxes, I took it and I bought my mom a refrigerator, a TV, a washer and dryer, and paid some bills."

Once camp started, his competitive drive overrode simply wanting a chance.

"Some of the guys that they drafted in front of me, I looked at them, like 'Hey, man, you're not as good as me,'" he said.

It bothered him even more when he wasn't receiving enough playing time.

"I [could] play this game at a high level," he said. "I came with an attitude, and that fifth-round mentality stuck with me, whether it was my fifteenth year or my first year."

In that first year, the Chargers went to the Super Bowl. Only Rodney saw very little action that day.

"We're getting killed by the San Francisco '49ers," he said, "and I keep bugging [defensive coordinator Bill Arnsparger]. 'Coach, put me in. Put me in. Our safeties are getting killed.' He wouldn't put me in, and that just absolutely freakin' pissed me off. I'm going to come back stronger. I'm never going to let a defensive coach tell me that somebody's better than me."

By 1996, he was a starter, leading San Diego in interceptions with 5, and in 1998, he was named to the Pro Bowl squad. He learned a lot those first few years in the league, no lessons more valuable and lasting than the ones he picked up from Junior Seau. Rodney was blown away by how seriously Seau approached practice every single day.

"I was always taught in the pros 'don't go so hard early on,'" he said. "I had players tell me, 'Slow down a little bit, man.'"

One day, finally, Rodney asked Seau: "Junior, why do you practice so hard?"

"I get paid to practice," Seau told him. "I play the games for free. Anybody can play in front of eighty thousand people."

From then on, Rodney practiced with the same intensity, game after game, season after season, though he could never outwork Seau. No one could.

"I would come in at six o'clock in the morning and think that I'm there before everyone," Rodney said, "and Junior Seau is there at five forty-five. He'd tell me, 'Man, why are you coming in so late?'"

Similar to Jean Van de Velde with Lee Trevino and Seve Ballesteros, Rodney had found his kindred spirit. Seau was the kind of football player he yearned to be.

Though his work ethic, if admirable, wasn't always appreciated by some of his teammates.

"I even got into a fight [in practice] with Ronnie Harmon [the Chargers' running back]," he said. "He came through and I hit him. Boom! He threw the ball at me. Why is this guy trying to pick a fight with me?"

That didn't stop him, not for a second.

"Once I went to the Patriots," said Rodney, who was signed by New England in 2003, "I did the same thing there. I ran down on special teams, made the tackle, and made the special teams' stars mad at me. Belichick said, after I retired, 'He was the hardest practice player I've ever coached in thirty-three years of coaching.' I know I didn't leave it out there."

After defeating the Chargers in the 2007 playoffs, the Patriots had two weeks to prepare for the Giants, and whenever you give Belichick that much time, the other team is usually in a lot of trouble.

Except something strange went on during practice a few days before the game, and Rodney was concerned. He usually minded his own business—focusing on the defense kept him busy enough—but this time, he couldn't resist. The offense was dropping balls. The offense *never* dropped balls.

"Man, what the heck is going on?" Rodney asked one of the offensive assistants.

"Don't worry, Rodney," the coach told him. "We're going to be fine. We'll be ready to play on Sunday."

Rodney wasn't so sure.

"You can't turn it off and on like that," he explained. "I just didn't have a great feeling walking off the field after that practice. You just knew this wasn't our offense."

Whether this was an omen of things to come or just an off day, no one could be certain. But we were about to find out.

The Giants struck first in Super Bowl XLII, assuming a 3–0 lead. Better yet, on that opening drive, they held on to the ball for nearly ten minutes. That's how you stopped Tom Brady, or, at least, kept him from killing you. New York got down to the New England 14 before the drive stalled.

The Patriots, when they finally gained possession, marched 56 yards in 12 plays to go ahead, 7–3, which was the score at halftime. Neither team scored in the third quarter, but the longer the game went on, the more it became clear:

The Giants could actually win this thing.

Then came a fourth quarter to remember.

New York scored first, Manning hitting wide receiver David Tyree from 5 yards out with roughly eleven minutes to go. Giants 10, Patriots 7.

The Patriots were forced to punt on the next possession, but when they got the ball back, with less than eight minutes left, they showed why they were, well, the Patriots.

They needed a drive to save their shot at perfection, and they got it, going 80 yards in 12 plays. Moss and Welker caught three balls apiece. When Brady connected with Moss for a touchdown on a third-and-goal from the 6 to put the Patriots on top 14–10, everything in the universe seemed in order again.

Now all they had to do was stop the Giants one final time.

Rodney was confident, as always.

"We expected our offense to go down [and score], and we expected to stop the Giants defensively," he said. "Being a smart, physical team that plays well under pressure, that was our motto."

The Giants began on their own 17, with 2:39 remaining and all three of their timeouts. There was plenty of time, if they used it wisely. On the first play, Manning found Amani Toomer for an 11-yard gain. Then, after two incomplete passes and the two-minute warning, Manning hit Toomer again, but was inches shy of a first down. The Giants obviously couldn't afford to give the ball back to New England, so they went for it on fourth down. Brandon Jacobs, the burly running back, got the first. Barely.

In the next series, Manning scrambled for 5 yards on first down. On second down, trying to hit Tyree near the sideline, the ball went right into the hands of the Patriots' Asante Samuel—and, fortunately for the Giants, right *out* of his hands. The game was almost lost then and there.

Rodney couldn't believe it.

"Asante Samuel had the best hands I've seen, outside of Randy Moss, with the guys I played with," he said. "The fact he missed that? Asante? It was a shock that he dropped the pass."

Instead of an interception and game over, the Giants were still alive, with a third-and-5 from their own 44. Manning backed away from the center into a shotgun formation. As soon as he took the snap, there was pressure from the left side of the line. Adalius Thomas came through practically untouched. This forced Manning to step into the pocket to avoid the sack, and once he did, Richard Seymour wrapped his hand around the quarterback's waist, while Jarvis Green got a hold of the back of his jersey. Eli Manning had nowhere to go.

"I saw our two defensive tackles grabbing [Eli]," Rodney said. "I think the play is about to be called."

But the whistle didn't blow, and for good reason. As the late NFL Films president Steve Sabol put it, in his narration of the final drive, the Giants "needed a miracle on third-and-5. They got two."

The first was when Manning, hardly the most mobile quarterback in the game, somehow escaped the clutches of Seymour and Green. He moved to his right and, with no one in front of him, spotted Tyree in the middle of the field, just inside the Patriots' 25.

A Hail Mary? Not quite. There would still be time on the clock no matter what happened on the play. Though it sure looked like a prayer of some kind once the ball left Manning's right arm, especially with Rodney in the area. Besides, Tyree wasn't some big-time receiver. He'd caught 4 passes during the entire season! And just 1 in New York's three playoff victories leading up to the Super Bowl.

Rodney Harrison, the All-Pro, the first player to have 30 sacks and 30 picks, vs. David Tyree, the All-Anonymous. This matchup didn't seem like a fair fight, although they weren't matched up head-to-head to begin with. With New England playing a zone coverage involving two safeties, Rodney was responsible for the left half of the field on anything deep.

"All I saw was a wide receiver running down the middle," Rodney said. "I'm hauling butt over there."

He got there in time, and when Tyree jumped for the ball, Rodney jumped right with him.

"I thought I knocked it down," he said.

He didn't. Tyree pressed the ball against his helmet and held on even after Rodney wrestled him to the ground. Some have called it the greatest catch in Super Bowl history. That's debatable, but it's certainly the most memorable. Watch the play again. You still won't believe he made that catch. Rodney didn't.

"I'm on top of Tyree," Rodney recalled, "and Steve Smith, the little wide receiver, said, 'Get off of him. Get off of him. Good catch.' Good catch? The ball should be way over there."

And that's when it hit him. The ball wasn't over *there*. The ball was *here*, in Tyree's hands. First down New York on the New England 24. Fifty-nine seconds to go. Rodney then saw the replay on the scoreboard video screen.

"You got to be kidding me," he thought. Tyree "made a one-in-a-million catch. What can you say?"

The Giants called timeout. Rodney looked at his teammates and didn't like what he saw.

"They were dejected," he said. "You could just tell. All the optimism, the hopes, everything just out of them."

Rodney wasn't feeling too good, either. Still, as a captain, he knew it was his job to make everyone else believe. Before it was too late.

"I was yelling, 'Look, guys, they still got to score.' I still believed it," he said. "They still had a long way to go."

He was right. Gaining 24 more yards was far from a sure thing. The Patriots didn't go undefeated just because of Tom Brady, Randy Moss, and Wes Welker. The defense, fourth ranked in the NFL, was responsible for their success, as well.

The next play was a perfect illustration. The Pats chased Manning out of the pocket and sacked him for a 1-yard loss. New York called its final timeout.

On second-and-11, Manning went to Tyree again, who was unable to hold on this time. But on third down, Manning found Smith by the sideline to give the Giants a first on the Patriots' 13. Thirty-nine seconds left.

As the Giants went back to their huddle, the call came in from Dean Pees, the New England defensive coordinator: Blitz! The next thing Rodney saw was Ellis Hobbs, the five-foot-nine cornerback, lined up against Plaxico Burress, the six-foot-five wideout, by himself. Uh-oh.

"Junior, you got to check the call," he told Seau.

"Run it!" Seau said. "Run it!"

So Rodney did. He blitzed, to no avail. Manning got rid of the ball in plenty of time. Burress, who hadn't practiced the whole week because of ankle and knee injuries, put a fake on Hobbs and was open in the corner of the end zone.

"I didn't have to look back," Rodney recalled. "I knew it was game over."

The Burress catch and the extra point put the Giants on top, 17–14. The Patriots got the ball back with thirty-five seconds left but didn't come close to scoring. That was it. So much for history.

"I worked so hard," he said, his eyes welling up. "And not being able to make that play [the Tyree catch] . . . I was really down. I felt like I let, not only myself down, but a generation of former Patriots, people involved in the organization. We could have done something so special, that no one ever accomplished. And that's to go 19-0."

He felt he'd let Junior Seau down most of all and told him how sorry he was.

"Hey, buddy," Seau said, "there's a bunch of other guys on that field. It's not your fault."

That only made Rodney feel worse.

"Because," he said, "it *was* my fault. I'm the leader of that defense."

Seau was just as understanding the last time the two ever spoke. He reminded Rodney how fortunate they had been to be on a team that didn't lose a game the entire regular season.

In 2012, Seau killed himself. Rodney couldn't believe it. That wasn't the Junior Seau he knew and loved. Seau had shot himself in the chest so that his brain could be used for research. It turned out that he had been suffering from chronic traumatic encephalopathy (CTE), the degenerative brain disease found in an increasing number of ex-players.

"He always found a shining light in a negative situation," Rodney said, "and that's what made the irony of him taking his own life so crazy."

After the Super Bowl loss, the weeks went by, but the pain didn't go away. He worked out. He played golf. He did everything he could to put David Tyree and the game behind him. No chance. He wasn't used to feeling like this.

"I made big plays in big moments," Rodney said. "And now, all of a sudden, I was on the other side."

Nor did it help that wherever he went, someone felt a need to weigh in. As time went on, he heard it all:

"Oh, that was a lucky catch."

"Hey, man, I saw that catch."

"You're the David Tyree guy."

Those were the nice things people said. Some comments in the years since haven't been so nice. Like the one from the guy who yelled to him at New York's LaGuardia Airport: "How does it feel to fuck up a perfect season, Harrison?"

Bad enough that Rodney felt responsible for the Tyree catch. He also felt horrible about the Burress touchdown.

"In essence," Rodney said, "there were two plays I felt like I screwed up."

His mistake was either not being more assertive in getting confirmation from the sidelines on the blitz, or not, on his own, changing a call he knew was wrong once he noticed how the Giants were lining up.

"If I see Hobbs against Plaxico," Rodney said, "I know what's coming. Fifteen years in the league, I've seen it all."

The reason he did nothing, except tell Seau to check the call, was because of the tremendous respect he had for him. One also can't help but wonder if Rodney was still affected by the Tyree play and wasn't his usual confident self.

"I had the power to make the change [in the call]," he said. "Forget Junior, just check it! Belichick always said I'm a smart, physical guy that played well under pressure. Because I always prepared myself. That day, I failed."

If it had been his former teammate Tedy Bruschi, or probably any other player, he "would have checked it," Rodney believed, "but I knew that Junior wanted to go after it. Junior wanted to make a play." In any case, he wants to make one thing abundantly clear: He never blamed Junior Seau. He blamed only himself.

As the days wore on, his mood stayed in the dumps, which was hard to watch for the people who loved him. The people who, about a month after the Super Bowl, felt they had to do something about it, for his sake, and theirs.

"Look, you've got to stop feeling sorry for yourself," his mother and his wife told him. "You have been so blessed. You have Super Bowl rings. You have beautiful kids. You need to put things in perspective."

Rodney was shaken up.

"They came at me real," he said.

They asked him if he had done everything he could to stop Tyree from making the catch. Rodney gave it a lot of thought. Yes, he had. He also thought back to the two weeks leading up to the game itself. There, too, he did everything right. He went through film, lifted weights, and did nothing but prepare for the New York Giants.

Well then.

"Finally, I kind of forgave myself," he said.

His wife and his mother weren't the only ones who helped him see the broader picture. So, he said, did the Lord. Rodney got on his knees and prayed. He was searching for answers.

"I got a nice house and money in the bank," he said, "and my kids are healthy. Why am I feeling down?"

He soon got the answers, and they made a lot of sense.

"Sometimes, it's not about you," was the message he took away. "What if [God] had something else planned for someone else?" Coming to that realization "humbled the heck out of me. I said, 'You're being selfish right now. You're moping around, and you're not giving the people who love you, and the people you love, the best you can give them because you're making this all about you.'"

In those difficult early weeks, Rodney also reflected on what his coach, Dean Pees, said in the locker room after the game: "A lot of people are going to say what they're going to say . . . but the one thing they can't take away is all the hard work and all the sacrifices we made."

Pees then gave Rodney a hug.

"I love you. You're the best," Pees told him.

"I kept that with me," said Rodney, who started to tear up while he recalled their conversation. "And I keep that with me right now. He [Pees] really started the healing process for me when he pulled me to the side and said that."

Also very dear to him, needless to say, are his two Super Bowl rings. He can't imagine how he would feel if he didn't have them *and* he'd failed to stop David Tyree.

"It would have been very, very difficult," he admitted.

Don't get him wrong. If Rodney could go back in time, he would like nothing better than to knock the ball out of Tyree's hands. He would have, in all likelihood, earned his third ring, Junior Seau his first, and the 2007 New England Patriots would have secured a spe-cial place in the history of the National Football League.

"I would have been part of the greatest team to ever live," he said.

But, since he didn't make the play, he was able to see all the good that came out of it, and how much he learned about himself and what matters in life. And how, instead of breaking him, the catch, and the loss, made him a better person. Which Rodney might never have discovered if, as he routinely did in his record-setting career, he had knocked the ball out of Tyree's hands. Or if the Patriots had kept the Giants from scoring on the final drive.

"It made me realize winning isn't everything," Rodney said.

For someone who spent his whole career trying to be the best, trying to prove the doubters wrong, to admit that winning isn't everything was quite a transformation. The reason he could reach this level of understanding was because he faced the truth about his loss, and himself.

Now, as a father and husband, Rodney sees life in a way he didn't before. For example, when it comes to his two boys, who are both involved in sports, he doesn't have the same expectations.

"I don't scream at them," he said. "I don't say, 'Hey, you have all this talent, you need to get a scholarship.' I'm not pushing them. I can go to the game and I can relax. My [feeling] is 'I don't give a damn, just try your best.'"

As for his relationship with his wife, Erika, he realizes that "you're going to be disrespectful at times, you're going to do things that you shouldn't do. It's made me stronger, more mature."

After Kearse's juggling act, Rodney received about a hundred texts from his friends. Each said the same thing he was thinking: The Patriots must be cursed.

Al Michaels put it best, referring back to the Tyree reception: "This was the scene of the crime for New England."

On first down from the 5, Seattle quarterback Russell Wilson gave the ball to the bruising running back Marshawn Lynch, who took it to the 1. No doubt Lynch would carry the ball again on the next play. He was almost impossible to stop around the goal line.

We'll never know if he would have scored, of course, because Wilson threw it instead . . . into the hands of Malcolm Butler. The "drought" was over. The Patriots were the world champions for the first time since 2005.

Rodney couldn't have been more excited.

"I started yelling and screaming," he said. "When he made that play, not only did he make it for the Patriots of [that year]. He made it for me. I wanted to cry. When I got in the car, that's exactly what I did. It just blessed and touched my heart. And that made it really, really special."

He also felt empathy for the other side, especially for Pete Carroll, the Seattle head coach. That was also a direct result of the Tyree play.

"This is going to stick with him for the rest of his life," he said. "Pete Carroll, that was me at that point in time. I think Pete would have served himself best if he had said, 'Look, I made a mistake. We should have run the damn ball.'"

Rodney has no illusions. He knows that the Tyree catch will stick with him for the rest of *his* life, even if he's mostly over it, even if he feels he was actually blessed that it happened; being so candid about the catch, he believes, convinced NBC to hire him. Because something will happen, like the Kearse catch, to instantly bring him back to that painful day in Arizona.

"It [the ball] wasn't coming out," Rodney said. "It wasn't meant to be."

14

THE CATCH

JANUARY 10, 1982

One of the best running backs in the game had the ball in his hands and a huge hole in front of him. A cut here, a cut there, and no one would catch him. Run to daylight, they call it.

His timing couldn't have been better.

A touchdown would give his team, the Buffalo Bills, the lead over the New York Giants with under two minutes to go in Super Bowl XXV in 1991. All the running back, Thurman Thomas, had to do was get by one man, and that one man was somebody who couldn't match his size and speed, no. 28 in blue, defensive back Everson Walls.

Everson was well aware of what was on the line for his Giants, and, looking back, he also realizes what was on the line for him—a chance, at least in the opinion of others, to make up for what he'd failed to do nine years before. Quite possibly, his last chance.

"This was my moment to screw up," Everson recalled, "and when he broke through, the anxiety was there for me. I had to make that play just to hold off any naysayers."

Nine years before, Everson was a rookie on the Dallas Cowboys and a really good one, leading the league with 11 interceptions, the most in the history of the franchise. No player in the NFL has recorded more than 10 picks in a season since.

Yet the way he manned his position annoyed Tom Landry to no end. Landry, the head coach of the Dallas Cowboys since they joined the NFL in 1960, was as old school as they come. The dark gray hat, the striped tie and blue jacket, the unemotional look on the sidelines no matter how the game was going. A lot of things changed in pro football, American's new national pastime, between 1960 and 1981. Not Tom Landry.

"Pay attention to your man," Landry lectured Everson on more than one occasion.

Everson didn't listen. Instead of sticking to his assignment, he used to take a peek to see what the quarterback was doing in the pocket, which was how he got a large percentage of those picks. The term for what he did was "clueing." The defensive backs did it all the time in the eighties to get a better sense of where the ball might be headed. Since he wasn't the fastest guy in the world, he searched for any advantage he could get.

"He was 'my way or the highway,'" said Everson, referring to Coach Landry. "He couldn't give me the highway because I was making plays. I made a lot more plays than I gave up, but I gave up more than my coach wanted me to."

The fact that Everson was a member of the Cowboys in the first place tells you a lot about him.

Of the 332 players who were selected in the 1981 NFL Draft, Everson Walls of Grambling State University was not one of them. If that wasn't upsetting enough, he had to listen, round after round, to the names of other defensive backs he knew he was better than.

Someone wanted them. No one wanted him.

The only hope he had that summer was to get signed as a free agent. Three teams—the New Orleans Saints, Buffalo Bills, and Dallas Cowboys—showed some interest.

The Saints were out because they were terrible.

The Bills were out because Buffalo was too cold.

The Cowboys were in, and it made sense. He had grown up in Dallas and was a huge fan. Everson would still have to prove himself, and it wouldn't be easy. There were twenty-five rookie defensive backs at training camp, and only a few spots were available.

On his first day—his first *drill*—he was close to throwing away any chance he might have. After Everson took on a receiver running an out-and-up pattern, Gene Stallings, the secondary coach, got right in his face.

"Boy, what the hell is the matter with you?" Stallings barked. "Someone beats you, you get after them."

There were any number of ways for Everson to respond, and most of them, to say the least, wouldn't have done him much good.

Growing up in Hamilton Park, a black section in the northern part of Dallas, Everson was no stranger to bigotry. Because of busing, he went to an integrated school about seven miles from his house. He might have spent as much time in fights as he did in classes. In eighth grade, he watched a black friend of his get thrown down five flights of stairs at the football stadium by a white coach. The coach was angry at the black players for boycotting practice.

The kid, though he wasn't seriously injured, was scared to death, as were those who saw him hit the ground. After the boy's mom complained, the school didn't punish the coach. The school supported him.

"Of course, they did," Everson said. "This was 1972. In Texas."

Everson witnessed injustices more often than he can recall.

"Whenever we [black kids] got into trouble in high school," he said, "we were automatically guilty before we stepped into the principal's office."

Some of the trouble he got into, to be fair, was his own doing. Like the time his high school basketball coach warned him not to wear braids in his hair. Defiantly, he wore braids, anyway. The next game was to be played on his sixteenth birthday and he wanted to look his very best. A girl he knew braided his hair. On top of that, his mother was coming to the game, and it would be the first time she would see him play basketball in person. He couldn't wait to show her how good he was.

Everson never got the chance. One look at the braids, and his coach told him he wouldn't be playing. He thought he may get reprimanded, but never did he imagine he would be forced to sit out the entire game.

"I'm still pissed off about that," he said. "What's wrong with freakin' braids? I had no respect for authority, especially for rules that I thought were color-influenced."

His mother never came to another game.

A much more dangerous occasion occured when he lied to the police after two friends in high school told him they'd robbed a dry cleaner and asked him to provide an alibi. What these "friends" didn't bother to tell Everson was that one of them had forced a young woman who worked at the cleaners to give him oral sex.

When he told that lie, his mother was in the room. He saw her move around nervously in the background, though she kept her mouth shut. He could tell she wasn't buying his story for a second.

"What are you doing?" she asked after the officers left.

Everson stuck to his story. Only when he went to the police station for a second chat, and the woman from the cleaners identified him as the person who sexually assaulted her, did he tell the truth. He was willing to lie for his friends, but he wasn't willing to go to prison for them.

The others were arrested, eventually, but Everson didn't get off entirely. He was sent to juvenile hall for fifteen days while his case was being reviewed. During those fifteen days, he did a lot of thinking about his past and his future. He had been hanging around the wrong crowd, that was obvious.

"It let me know the path I shouldn't be on," he said. "I had to make a change, to stop messing around with idiots."

No wonder then, years later, when he heard the word "boy" at the Cowboys' training camp, it didn't matter what the words were that came afterward. He was back in high school, ready to defend himself and his race.

"I had been around people like that all my life," he explained.

The first word he thought of in response to Coach Stallings was the F-word. Yet as close as the word was to coming out of his mouth, it never did. He sensed the coach was testing him, and if he failed, his career as a Dallas Cowboy would be over before it ever started. Without football in his future . . . well, he might not have a future.

"Yes, sir," he told Stallings.

"He looked at me like I was crazy," Everson said. "It was one of the most important moments in my life. He was expecting an ass-hole response, expecting for me to weed myself out, to do his work for him."

There was nothing Stallings could do but let him keep playing.

"Get you *anotha*," he told Everson.

Translation: Another receiver to cover.

He was tested quite a bit in his first camp, and that was precisely the challenge he was looking for. Each time Doug Donley, a second-round draft pick from Ohio State, got up to run a route, Everson pushed his way to the front to take him on. The whole point was to get better, and it wasn't going to happen against receivers he was expected to contain.

"You think that he's good?" he thought, pumping himself up. "Doug Donley, your white lightning, big school. I'll show you what I can do."

"I challenged him on every route. I didn't give him anything."

Everson got beat at times, but he also made stops, not too shabby for a free agent facing a high draft choice. He was so certain he would make the final forty-five-man roster that he packed enough clothes for the entire six weeks of training camp.

"I could have been gone the first *day*," he said.

He wasn't. He not only made the team, but by the time the Cowboys played the San Francisco 49ers in the NFC title game on January 10, 1982, at Candlestick Park, he was as valuable as anyone on the Dallas defense, a defense that would need to be at its absolute best.

San Francisco was filled with playmakers who could catch the ball and put points on the board, such as Freddie Solomon and Dwight Clark. The Niners also had a pretty decent playmaker calling the signals behind center. You might have heard of him.

Granted, Joe Montana wasn't the Joe Montana we think of today, one of the three or four best quarterbacks to ever play the game. No one knew of him as "Joe Cool," and if you weren't a football fan, you probably didn't know him at all. He was only twenty-five years old, in his third year out of Notre Dame, and had won just one NFL playoff game, and that was the week before against the Giants.

"A gunslinger who needed help" was what Everson thought of him.

He didn't have much regard for the San Francisco team as a whole, either, even though the Niners, with Montana throwing 2 touchdowns, demolished the Cowboys 45–14 in October at Candlestick.

"We kept looking [at film of] the previous year and they weren't that good," Everson said.

Asked why those film sessions didn't focus more on the game from three months before, Everson put it simply: "Sometimes you don't want to look at something that devastating."

Still, when the Cowboys looked at footage of Montana, going back to his days in South Bend, they saw some things that gave them serious concern. One game, in particular, made a lasting impression: the comeback win over the University of Houston in the 1979 Cotton Bowl, known as the "Chicken Soup Game."

Despite suffering from the flu, and staying in the locker room at the start of the second half for extra treatment, including a helping of chicken soup, Montana was magnificent. He brought the Irish back from 22 points down midway through the fourth quarter for a 35–34 victory, hitting wideout Kris Haines on the final play of the game.

"You could see he was a guy who wasn't going to ever give up on a play," Everson explained.

The Niners struck first, Montana connecting with Solomon for an 8-yard TD to lead 7–0. The Cowboys responded with a field goal and a touchdown in the first quarter to go up by 3. From then on, one team scored after the other.

We hear over and over that defense is what wins championships in the National Football League. Not this championship, it would appear.

Montana was making plays, but he was also making mistakes, with 3 picks and a fumble. While Joe Cool was hot and cold, Everson was on fire. For a rookie. For anybody. He recovered one fumble and got 2 of the interceptions. The second pick came with about ten minutes to go in the fourth quarter, the Cowboys leading 27–21.

"We got Tony Dorsett, we got Danny White, we got Drew Pearson," he said, referring to the Dallas running back, quarterback, and receiver. "This was the nail in the coffin."

Not exactly.

On the ensuing drive, Dallas managed only a couple of first downs and punted the ball back to the Niners. Even so, the odds weren't in San Francisco's favor. Needing a touchdown to regain the lead, the Niners would have to go 89 yards in less than five minutes.

"We had the best two-minute defense in the league that year," Everson claimed. "We've got six turnovers. We're going to get another turnover. It's what we do with our dime package [six defensive backs]. Very rarely do we give it up."

Enter Lenvil Elliott.

Of all the players in skilled positions on either side one could imagine making an impact in a game this significant, Elliott would have to rank near the bottom. He was a backup running back who'd been cut by the Niners in training camp and, after rejoining the team, rushed just 7 times the entire season for 29 yards. The only reason he was playing was because the starter, Ricky Patton, was injured and didn't suit up.

Yet there Elliott was, taking the handoff on 3 of the first 5 plays of the drive, the biggest in the history of the franchise. Bill Walsh, the 49ers' coach, must have been out of his mind.

Not really. Walsh knew the Cowboys were thinking pass and he was right. Elliott gained 24 yards on his 3 runs, moving the chains, giving his team a much-needed spark.

"Walsh was ready for us," Everson said. "What got them in position was Elliott running around the end. Our linebackers were getting shut off, and our safeties had to come from half the field or deep middle to make the play because we were man-to-man in the corner. The slot guy has to come off to make the play but he also has to play man-to-man. That was the genius of that drive."

Why, then, didn't Landry and the Cowboys simply adjust their game plan? Making the right adjustments is the key to success in the NFL. Tom Landry, of all people, surely knew that. Perhaps, but you won't get Everson Walls to second-guess his coach. Not when it comes to this drive.

"You just don't bail when they start to break your tendencies," he said. "It was will vs. will. We stuck with ours and they stuck with theirs."

The Niners mixed things up extremely well between the run and the pass. At the two-minute warning, they were in good position, on the Dallas 49, with all three timeouts remaining.

On second down, he gave the ball to Elliott, who handed it to Solomon on a reverse. Another excellent call by Walsh; Solomon picked up 14 yards. The Dallas defense was bending, trying hard not to break.

The next play was one that, to this day, Everson still can't quite believe.

Montana threw it to Clark, who was running a simple out route close to the sideline. As Everson saw the play develop, he was feeling pretty good.

"I got this route," he thought.

Moments later, the football was in Clark's hands, and Everson was feeling pretty awful. First down San Francisco on the Dallas 25.

"I remember cutting underneath him. I've seen the play many times, and I don't know how I missed it," he said. "It looked like it went through my fingers. It was like he threw a curveball to a fastball hitter."

On the next snap, Montana came through again, connecting with Solomon for another 12 yards. Everson made the tackle.

Timeout, Niners. The Cowboys were bending, badly. As confident as Everson was, of himself and the dime package, he wasn't blind.

"The chains kept moving," he said.

Fatigue was getting to both squads.

"Dwight was taking all day to come out of the huddle," he recalled. "Freddie was taking all day to come out of the huddle. You just try your best to stay focused."

For Everson, that meant keeping in mind the play coming up was the only play that mattered.

"You don't think of the game as a whole," he said. "You've got to take it one play at a time. You have to. Because otherwise, you will mentally get bogged down. You remember things that happened, but you can't worry about how many plays you played. You can't worry about what time of the game it is. When it comes down to it, you've got to concentrate for four or five seconds. It keeps the fatigue factor out of play."

On first down from the 13, with 1:15 to go, Montana dropped back and looked for Solomon. Solomon, tired or not, was having his usual strong game, with 6 receptions for 75 yards. Better yet, he was open, with a couple of steps on Everson in the left corner of the end zone. For Montana, it was a routine throw, the kind we'd never expect him to miss in the years to come, especially in crunch time.

He missed this one, throwing it well over Solomon's head. Second-and-10.

No doubt the Niners would throw it again on the next down. The last thing they could afford was a third-and-long. So much for conventional wisdom. Walsh called for a sweep for, you guessed it, Lenvil Elliott. The carry was the most important in Elliott's nine-year NFL career and, as it would turn out, his last. He retired after the season. That being the case, the man certainly knew how to make an exit, breaking a tackle to pick up 7 extremely tough yards. With just under a minute left, the Niners needed 3 yards for a first, 6 for a touchdown.

Bend or break?

Coming out of the huddle, Everson made an important decision.

"I need to play this straight up," he realized. "I am not going to look back. I am going to watch my man."

His man, on this play, was Clark. The Dallas defensive backs covered a side of the field on every snap, not a particular player. That was why Everson went back and forth the whole day between lining up against Solomon or Clark.

"They used to match me up on third downs later in my career," he explained. "He [Landry] wasn't going to match a rookie up with anybody."

Everson was really focusing now.

"I wanted to make sure that I played this solid," he said. "I knew Joe was slick. I didn't want any balls zooming by my ear."

The moment the Niners lined up, Everson had a good idea of

what they would do. It turned out to be the same play San Francisco used to score on the first touchdown of the game—Sprint Option Right.

"It's a hell of a play," Everson recalled. "I'd run it every time, too."

In the earlier score, Clark was out wide to Montana's right while Solomon went into motion from left to right. The ball was snapped just as he passed the right tackle, leaving him open in the flat to beat defensive back Dennis Thurman. This time, however, the Niners put Solomon in the slot. Thurman also recognized it right away and went to cover him, leaving Clark as Everson's responsibility on the outside. If Solomon managed to get open, Montana couldn't possibly miss him. Not again.

Only Solomon slipped on the famously loose turf at Candlestick, disrupting the timing of the play.

"Can't go there," Everson said.

Where then *could* Joe go? Wherever it was, he didn't have much time to decide. The rush was coming.

As the seconds ticked off, Everson didn't bother to find out. He was sticking to his new strategy. He wasn't letting Clark out of his sight.

"I watched my man for five seconds," he said. "It felt like ten. I didn't know what was going on back there. Any other time, I would be looking for the ball. But I played it safe."

By keeping his eyes on his man, Everson didn't see Montana rolling to his right and backpedaling . . . backpedaling . . . backpedaling some more, edging closer and closer to the sidelines. The play was taking a long time to develop. Too long. His instinct told him he had to see what was happening for himself.

"It was like Lot's wife," he said.

Unlike that biblical tale, Everson wasn't turned into a pillar of salt for the punishment of looking back, although what happened did, indeed, change his life. At the exact moment he turned, he saw the ball floating in his direction high in the air. He couldn't have been more relieved.

"That's going over the back of the end zone," he thought. After the certain incompletion, the Niners would face a fourth down. If the Cowboys could come up with one more stop, they'd be on their way to their fourth Super Bowl in seven years.

Just then, however, as Everson continued to follow the flight of the ball, he noticed something else, and what he felt was definitely not relief.

The ball wasn't as high as he originally thought. It was falling. And quickly. And . . . you've got to be kidding . . . toward the hands of the six-foot-four Clark, who leaped high to pull it down in the back of the end zone, just a step or two from being out of bounds. With his body twisted because he had turned around to see what was taking Montana so long, Everson never had a chance to jump and try to knock the ball loose.

"I was still in stride," he said.

The crowd, some sixty thousand strong, the largest in Niners history at the time, went nuts. After the extra point, San Francisco was up 28–27 with fifty-one seconds left.

"We were all in the same pissed mode, kind of stunned," Everson recalled, "and when something like that happens, you're not just thinking of that play. You're thinking of the mistakes we made to get there. That's where my mind was: 'Man, we've never been driven on like that in the last two minutes.'"

He has no doubt what his mistake was. He should have looked back sooner. If he did, he would have seen Montana get rid of the ball and been able to track its flight.

"I should have stayed with my unorthodox methods," Everson said. "I am in no way trying to blame Tom Landry for my incompetence on that play. When it comes down to it, I am the one who choked. It's up to you on how you approach any particular play, especially a big play like that, and choking comes from the gravity of the moment and doing something against your nature."

Maybe, but as he pointed out, if he'd looked back sooner and his man, Clark, had broken free as a result and *then* scored a touchdown, Landry would "have never let me forget it."

Like Rodney Harrison and Mary Decker, what hurt Everson so much was that he had gone against what he knew was right. For him, at least. He had always played a certain way and, more often than not, made the big plays. Now, the one time he had failed to do it his way, it came back to hurt him.

Upon reaching the sidelines, Everson pulled off his helmet and took a seat on the bench. As a player, he was, in all likelihood, done for the day and, unless his team rallied, the season. But as a Cowboys fan, he was just getting started.

He'd followed the team since he could remember, cheering for star quarterback Roger Staubach, All-Pro defensive back Mel Renfro, and the other players who had blue stars on their helmets. Everson believed in the Cowboys then, and he believed in them now.

Never was his faith rewarded more than when Staubach connected with Drew Pearson on a 50-yard touchdown with twenty-four seconds left to shock the Minnesota Vikings 17–14 in a 1975 playoff game. The play came to be known as The Hail Mary, a term that has been around football ever since.

"This is what we do," Everson said. "This is the time to do it."

He was rooting harder than ever.

"Get me off the hook for giving up this lead," he thought.

They had gotten him off the hook before.

In October, against the Miami Dolphins, the Cowboys stormed back from a 13-point deficit in the fourth quarter to win 28–27. David Woodley, the Dolphins' quarterback, had hit the man Everson was covering for big plays.

This time, Dallas needed just a field goal, not a touchdown, to regain the lead.

The Cowboys got right to it. On first down, from his own 25, Danny White, with excellent protection, hit Pearson in perfect stride near the 50. Pearson was on his way to pay dirt and being the hero once again.

Montana to Clark would be long forgotten. White to Pearson, *that* would be The Catch.

Just then, Eric Wright, San Francisco's gifted rookie defensive back, decided to rewrite the script. He caught just enough of Pearson's jersey to drag him down at the Niners' 44.

Nonetheless, Everson was excited. White was definitely on his game, and that wasn't always something you could count on.

"We gave a lot of grief to Danny about not finishing," he recalled, "but that was the best pass he had thrown all year. Oh my God, it was so good, and that's what I was accustomed to seeing as a Cowboys fan. I knew hope was definitely alive and that we had maybe 15 yards to go [to get into field goal range]. We got Rafael Septién. These are my guys. This is the freakin' Cowboys!"

Septién, the kicker, warmed up on the sidelines. Everson was right. Another 15 or so yards might well be enough. That would make it about a 45-yard attempt, and Septién converted 7 for 12 that season from 40 to 49 yards. Get the ball 5 or 10 yards closer, and his chances would go up.

On the next play, White got the snap and went back in the pocket. This time, however, the protection broke down, Niners converging in every direction. Everson wanted to shout: "Put the freakin' ball away!"

White didn't put it away, and the ball was stripped by defensive end Lawrence Pillers. The Niners recovered and ran out the clock. That was it.

Everson wouldn't be let off the hook, then or ever.

"I don't know if Danny got distracted by the immediate rush, but he just froze," Everson recalled. "He just froze."

The mood in the locker room was as somber as you'd expect. The Dallas Cowboys, America's Team, let a great opportunity slip away, and there was no telling when the next one would come, or if it would come.

Yet, as disappointed as he was, Everson was far from discouraged. He would soon be heading to Hawaii to represent the NFC in the Pro Bowl, no small feat for a rookie from Grambling State who was passed over by every team in the league.

"I had come through so much from high school, college, and now I'm with the Cowboys," he said. "What am I going to be gloom and doom about? I felt this was the beginning of my career and the beginning of a lot of great success as a team."

Only as the weeks went by did Everson start to recognize that what took place at Candlestick was a bigger deal than he thought. The press kept asking him about the play and so did the fans, which surprised him then and, really, to this day.

"That was a great play in San Francisco, but, damn, that Pitts-burgh play!" he said, gushing over the Franco Harris catch, off a deflection, in the last seconds of a 1972 playoff game against the Oakland Raiders, known as The Immaculate Reception. After catching the ball inches from the ground, Harris, the Steelers' star running back, eluded one defender, and the out-of-bounds line, and ran it into the end zone to give Pittsburgh a win for the ages.

Clark's reception, on the other hand, was of "great significance, but didn't take any great athleticism," according to Everson.

Why, then, did The Catch become such a magical moment in NFL history?

One answer might be the photo that appeared that week on the cover of *Sports Illustrated*. Taken by Walter Iooss Jr., one of the best in the business, the picture captures the precise moment a leaping Clark gained control of the ball, a helpless Everson standing by his side. Millions saw that image or perhaps a similar one in their local papers, and it left a lasting impression.

"If you get up the next morning and see that picture, but you don't see [one of] Danny fumbling," Everson explained, "as a fan, that's what you're going to think."

Yet, while Clark caught the ball, The Catch has lived on all these years because of who threw it.

Much as The Shot became famous because it turned Michael Jordan from great to legendary, you can say the same about Joe Montana and The Catch. For both, from that point on, as long as they had the ball in their hands, and there was time on the clock, you knew that anything was possible. That's how myths are made.

Look at it another way. The Catch would not be what it is today if an ordinary Joe had been the quarterback instead of the Joe who would go on to lead the Niners to four Super Bowl victories in nine years. The *moment* is what set Montana apart from the other quarterbacks of his time—of any time—and will always define his legacy.

So what if he threw 3 interceptions in the Dallas game and lost a fumble? No one remembers that. All anyone remembers is The Catch.

"It was all about the golden boy," Everson insisted. "Who gives a damn about a rookie free agent from Grambling State University? Throw his ass under the bus."

If Everson sounds bitter, that isn't his intention. From the start, he dealt with his fate as well as anyone could, and like Mary Decker, he never again went against the way he preferred to play. In the season after The Catch, which was shortened by a players' strike, he led the NFL in interceptions again, with 7 in nine games.

"I always say I don't know how many [picks] I would have gotten if we had played an entire year," he said.

There was no mystery to why Everson was able to bounce back so well. He had bounced back before, whether it was after he spent those fifteen days in juvenile hall or after he was skipped over by every team in the draft.

"Just another brick in the wall" was how he put it, "just something else you got to deal with. Maybe if I wasn't accustomed to that, depression might have set in, anger might have set in. I knew what I brought to the table was going to outlast that play."

He was fortunate. The Catch occurred so early in his career that he would have, if he stayed healthy, years to make up for it. With Landry in command, the Cowboys figured to be in the same position many times.

They weren't. In Landry's last seven seasons as coach, Dallas made it to only one more NFC title game. Not until the 1991 Super Bowl in Tampa, nine years after The Catch, did Everson get the chance he was hoping for.

He was on the New York Giants by then, let go by Jimmy Johnson, the new Dallas head coach, who showed even less tolerance for Everson than Landry did. In November 1989, after a 24–20 loss to the Phoenix Cardinals, the Cowboys' ninth in their first ten games—they'd go 1-15—Johnson bawled Everson out after seeing him chatting on the field with Arizona wide receiver Roy Green.

"Get your ass in the locker room," Johnson said. "You're out here fraternizing with the enemy."

As usual, Everson didn't appreciate being treated that way by an authority figure, but this wasn't like the time he was called "boy" in training camp by Gene Stallings. He didn't have to say "yes, sir" to keep alive any hopes of making the team. He had been on the team for eight years. Now he just wanted to make a point.

"Don't talk to me like that," he told Johnson. "Respect."

The two cussed each other out the whole way to the locker room. To no one's surprise, Dallas cut him before the 1990 season. Getting cut is no fun, needless to say, but he couldn't have landed in a better spot, with Bill Parcells as New York's head coach and linebacker Lawrence Taylor as the leader of the defense.

In the Super Bowl, the Giants would face the Buffalo Bills, who, like the Niners in the Montana era, could score from anywhere on the field at any time, with Thurman Thomas, quarterback Jim Kelly, and receiver Andre Reed, each in the prime of Hall of Fame careers. Their defense was led by another all-time great, defensive end Bruce Smith.

Earning a ring wasn't the only thought on Everson's mind as Super Bowl Sunday crept closer. Even though he claims he had moved on from The Catch, and you believe him, the damage that had been done to his legacy, to how *other* people saw him as a football player, was still there. The only way to enhance that legacy was to come up big in a big game.

"I didn't tell anyone," he confessed, "[but] whatever happens in this game, you are not going to say that Everson Walls was to blame."

He would silence anybody who didn't believe in him. Like Bill Walsh.

In the days leading up to the game, Walsh, who had retired from coaching and was working for NBC, made a comment that got under Everson's skin.

"He said the Giants' defense didn't have the playmakers," Everson recalled. "He pointed me out as one of those guys that was going to be a deficit for a great New York Giants defense."

We'll see about that, he told himself.

His coaches asked him to call the plays for the defense, and it was just the distraction he needed. There would be no time to think about any mistakes that might have been made on the play that had just been whistled dead. The next play was the one to focus on, and with the Bills going with a no-huddle offense, the next play would be here fast.

The game was close the entire way, just as the 1981 NFC title game was. And, like the Niners, the Bills had a long way to go on their final drive, beginning on their own 10 with a little over two minutes remaining. There was one crucial difference. Buffalo, trailing 20–19, was only a field goal away from taking the lead and, most likely, winning the game.

After two Kelly scrambles, Thomas, on third-and-inches from the 19, burst through a hole in the middle of the field.

Forget about 3 points. The Bills were on their way to 6.

It was now up to Everson.

"I was the first one to see the draw," he said. "Nobody else saw it. We expected them to throw."

He would have to rely on the wisdom he'd picked up during his ten years in the league more than ever. He knew that, in the past, he'd missed his share of open-field tackles by coming to meet the ball carrier too soon and diving for his legs. That wouldn't work with the speed and power of a Thurman Thomas.

"I let him commit instead of taking a dive where he could have faked me out," Everson said, and once Thomas committed, he made the tackle. "It looked more simple than it really was."

Still, this was no occasion to celebrate. With Thomas gaining 22 yards, the Bills were on their 41, about 30 yards from field goal range, and they had plenty of time.

"I just stopped one cut," Everson said. "Lot of cuts to go."

Sure were. The Bills kept advancing, until, with eight seconds left, Scott Norwood, their kicker, was asked to be the hero from 47 yards out. As the ball was about to be snapped, Everson feared the worst: "Am I going to lose another freakin' championship?"

He was not.

The kick was no good—"wide right," the memorable call from Al Michaels—and now it would be Norwood's turn to cope with being on the wrong side of history. As for Everson, he felt he'd evened the score at last. While he had long ago come to terms with The Catch, with his performance on the field, year after year, he felt he had now proven something to those who still blamed him for the one play he didn't make.

"That's why I have a smile on my face all the time," he said.

Everson was on the cover of *Sports Illustrated* that week for the first time since The Catch, the caption stating: *"Everson Walls Exults in the Giants' Victory."*

It's no stretch to suggest there would have been no Giants victory if not for the tackle he made on Thurman Thomas.

"Do you think Myron [Guyton, the Giants' safety] would have caught him if I had missed him?" Everson asked Bill Parcells afterward.

"He would have caught him in the parking lot," Parcells responded, according to Everson.

In any case, he said his prime motivation on the Thomas tackle wasn't personal.

"The tackle was just to stop a man from scoring a touchdown," he said. "The Catch happened when I was a freakin' rookie. To try and make up for that my entire career, I never thought I had to."

However, one can't help but imagine how Everson would feel today if the Norwood kick had been good. He can't be sure. All he is certain of is the fate he was fortunate to escape.

"I didn't want to be one of those guys," he said, referring to the players who never won a championship. "I can always say that I got mine. You can talk about The Catch. You can talk about [me] being slow. You can talk about not being in the Hall of Fame. You can talk about all that crap. But when it's said and done, I got that freakin' ring, and I was instrumental in helping acquire that for my team."

He sure was, and it wasn't the first time he made a big play. He was one of the top defensive backs of his generation, leading Dallas in interceptions a record five times, and was the first player to lead the NFL in picks three times. Yet despite all that and the title he was a part of, in the spotlight of New York City, no less, The Catch is what he's remembered for. Nothing will ever change that.

"Every time I meet people who have wanted to meet me for decades, the first thing they say is, 'Man, I cried that day as a Cowboy fan,'" he said. "So I am always reminded of how I let them down. They've got to get that out. They don't ask questions so much as make statements."

He lets them vent. Without fans who live and die with their teams . . . you can fill in the rest.

"It's not like I go into convulsions when I hear about it [The Catch]," he said. "It's just a part of my life. I didn't let that define what I did from then on. I can hold my head up high. Regardless of the outcome, I gave all I had."

15

REDEMPTION

Dan Jansen felt a wonderful sense of peace while he waited on the starting line in Lillehammer, Norway. The feeling wasn't one that Dan was very familiar with, at least not in the days, nor the hours, before his most important races, when the world would be watching. Before those races, his mind wandered, at times, to thoughts of the future: What would it actually mean to be an Olympic champion? What would it mean for his career, his personal life, everything?

Because even though he was the top speed skater in the world during the late eighties and early nineties, he hadn't won a gold medal. Forget about winning the gold; Dan Jansen hadn't won *any* Olympic medals. Period. Not in 1984. Nor 1988. Ditto for 1992. And not several days earlier, during his first race here, in 1994. You see, for Dan, like Mary Decker and Lindsey Jacobellis, something always went wrong when it came to the Olympics.

This time, though, while he waited for the race to begin, he thought about skating to his potential, which was something he had never done in the Games. If he could manage that, just this once, it wouldn't matter to him where he ended up on this night or in history.

Dan started skating when he was four years old. In 1977, at the age of twelve, he missed winning the national championship by

1 point. Dan cried during the awards ceremony and on the entire drive from Minnesota to his home in West Allis, Wisconsin, a small town outside Milwaukee.

He kept waiting for his dad to say something, anything, to make the tears go away. He always did. Not this time. He didn't say a word. Not until they pulled into the driveway six hours later.

"There's more to life than skating in a circle," Harry Jansen said.

That was it. Dan could only wonder what his dad was trying to tell him. One day, he would find out.

He was fourteen when he knew he wanted to be in the Olympics. He knew after he saw Eric Heiden, his hero, win five gold medals in speed skating at the 1980 Games in Lake Placid, New York. Dan even worked out at the same track in Milwaukee where Heiden trained.

"I would watch him every day, and he was just this big god to look up to," he said.

His first chance came rather quickly, when he qualified for the 1984 Games in Sarajevo, Yugoslavia. At eighteen, the youngest skater on the U.S. team, Dan fared better than many people thought he would, missing out on the bronze in the 500 meters by only 0.16 seconds.

He wasn't disappointed in the least. Coming that close to a medal in his first Olympics, he saw himself as a winner. As a matter of fact, he was so proud of his finish he thought, when he returned to West Allis, perhaps they'd throw a parade for him. They didn't. The lesson he learned was one he'd never forget.

"This was how the outside world saw the Olympics," Dan explained. "All they see is medal counts."

Going into the Games in Calgary, he was one of the favorites in the 500. He loved the 500; it was the ideal distance for him. He could skate as fast as he wanted and be sure he wouldn't tire down the stretch. That wasn't the case with the 1,000. You needed to pace yourself more in the 1,000.

A week before, he'd captured the overall title at the World Sprint Speed Skating Championships in, conveniently enough, West Allis. Dan had never won the worlds before. He was peaking at the perfect time.

Only something was missing: his sister Jane. She had always been the one person who believed in him more than anybody else. Jane had told Dan, who was fifteen or sixteen at the time: "*When* you win the worlds . . ." Not if. Never if. Except now, Jane couldn't be there, even though the event was just down the road from her. She was fighting for her life against leukemia.

Dan drove directly from the track to the hospital. He showed her the medal from the world championships and said he'd be back in about a month, after the Olympics. If everything went the way he hoped, he'd have another medal to show her.

The two had always been close, and that wasn't easy in a family of nine kids who were always on the go.

"By the time I was five," Dan pointed out, "some of my older sisters were already off to college or close to getting married."

That didn't include Jane, who was five years older, and because of the large gap between the younger and older siblings, the two, along with a brother, Mike, formed their own tight group.

"We were the three who were always together," Dan recalled. "The family trips, which used to be everybody, became the three of us and my parents. Jane was an amazingly sensitive person. Her first thought was always about someone else. She took care of me."

Boys will be boys, of course, so there was no end to the trouble Dan and Mike caused her. Such as the time they snuck into her room and left a dozen chocolate chips on her belly while she was taking a nap. When Jane woke up, the chocolate had melted. She chased after her brothers, but forgave them. She always did.

"She went to a nursing school about ten miles from our house," Dan said. "The next year, she told my mom she wanted to come back to live at home."

"All the boys do is tease you all the time," their mom said.

"That's what I miss," Jane replied.

In January 1987, Jane gave birth to her third daughter, Jessica. A few days later, while performing a simple blood test, the doctors spotted the cancer. She would require a bone marrow transplant. Dan offered to be the donor, but, as it turned out, another sibling, Joanne, was chosen.

Jane fought hard to lick the disease, but near the end, she was concerned about how her three daughters would go on without their mother. Dan, along with the rest of the family, assured her someone would always be there for them. He was now the one giving her comfort.

In Calgary, Dan did everything possible to prepare for his two races. All he needed was to skate somewhere close to his best in the 500 and the gold medal would very likely be his.

At 6 A.M. on the day of the 500, there was a knock at the door. Dan knew it had to be about Jane. He went to take the call in the U.S. Olympic Committee office.

"I literally started shaking when I was walking down the stairs," he said.

When Dan got to the phone, he was told that his sister probably wouldn't make it through the day. Most of the family was at the hospital, except for one brother, Jim, and several others who were in Calgary to support Dan. Someone put the phone next to her. Jane, breathing through a respirator, couldn't speak, but Dan knew she could hear every word.

"That's when I told her I'd win for her," he said. Then he asked one of his brothers to give her a kiss for him.

After hanging up, Dan walked back to his room. He phoned Jim, who came over to the Olympic Village. They talked about their sister and the wonderful times they shared. A few hours later, Jane was gone.

Dan gave serious thought to skipping the race and flying home to Wisconsin. But he'd told Jane he'd win the gold for her and knew that this was where she'd want him to be. He stayed.

The next couple of hours remain a bit fuzzy, as one can understand. What stands out was what happened during the Team USA meeting that afternoon.

"Everybody dedicated their races to Jane," Dan said. "I was trying to not break down when they came forward and said that."

He didn't succeed. Soon afterward, he took a jog with one of his teammates.

"I wanted to clear my head," he said, "and try to get loose if I could, and start a normal preparation. It wasn't normal, by any means, but the jog didn't hurt. It helped me get out there and start moving."

Typically, three or four hours ahead of the scheduled starting time, Dan would go over the race in his mind. That's not what he did in Calgary. He couldn't. His mind was elsewhere, on what he just lost, not on what he might win. After his jog, Dan returned to his room for a brief rest and then took off for the track.

"Let's just go and give this a shot," he said.

When he arrived at the arena, roughly ninety minutes before the race, he went through his usual warm-ups. If the gold was still what he wanted, and it most definitely was, he needed to get his body as ready as possible, even if his mind wasn't.

Except his body, like his mind, wasn't willing to cooperate.

"I couldn't keep my legs straight," he said. "I tried to skate through it."

By this point, the race almost about to begin, Dan was aware the reporters had heard about Jane.

"There was a pile [of them] around," he recalled.

What Dan didn't know was how deeply his loss had affected so many people in the States. That, he wouldn't know until he got back to West Allis and saw the thousands of letters in his bedroom.

Finally, just after five o'clock local time, the race got under way.

Dan raced in the second heat, lining up, as always, next to another skater. Reaching the finish line before the other racer is mandatory—you can't win the gold if you don't—but in speed skating, the race that matters is the one against the clock. Beating the other guy won't mean a thing if you don't post a good time.

His time for the first 100 meters was 9.95 seconds. Dan should have been faster. Those fractions of a second mean the world in speed skating, especially in the 500, a short race. If he were to have a chance for the gold, he'd have to make up that ground immediately.

But then, after making the turn in the corner, on his second stroke his left skate suddenly went out from under him. He fell and slid hard into the rink-side pads—so hard the impact knocked a rink-side photographer's camera to the ground. There went the 500 and the prayers of a nation.

He quickly got up, took off his hood, bent down for a few seconds, and held his head in both hands before he skated away.

"I struggled a bit with my emotions that day," Dan said. "If I felt bad about what happened on the ice, it would seem selfish, so I didn't quite let myself be upset about the fall. But on the other hand, deep down, I was, of course. I had trained for it, and I was a competitor. I didn't accomplish what I set out to do."

Dan thought again about going home, but decided to stay. There was still one more race, the 1,000.

Over the next three days, when he wasn't on the ice practicing, Dan hung out with his best friend, along with his fiancée, Canadian skater Natalie Grenier, and members of his family. He was trying to accept that Jane was really gone, while also focusing on the race ahead. If this sounds like an impossible task, that's because it was.

Before he knew it, he was on the starting line again, for the 1,000. He was in the fourth heat. Dedicating the race to Jane, Dan seized the moment, recording the fastest time in the field through 600 meters. Two more efficient turns with those long strides of his, and he would soon likely be standing on the podium, a medal around his neck.

There was only one more efficient turn.

Dan fell to the ice again, on a straightaway when he rolled too far over on the outer edge of his right skate. These kinds of errors can happen, even to the greatest skaters in the world. And at the worst of times.

But why him? Why now? Hadn't he suffered enough?

After the race, Dan flew to Wisconsin for the funeral but returned the next day to cheer on his friend, speed skater Bonnie Blair, who had yet to compete in her first event. Blair would go on to capture the gold in the 500 and the bronze in the 1,000.

"At home, there was certainly nothing I could do, and it would have been dark and depressing for me to be there and try to watch on TV," Dan said. "Calgary was the best place for me."

A few weeks later, Dan felt the best place for him was Savalen, Norway, for a World Cup event. The following week, he skated again, in Inzell, West Germany.

"I just wanted normalcy, and skating was that for me," he said.

"It helped me for those first few months afterward. That was my solace."

Only he couldn't delay his grief forever.

In the fall of 1988, he went back in Calgary to train and to take a few classes at the University of Calgary. In the city where he first received the news of his sister's passing, the loss hit him harder than ever.

"It was all about Jane," Dan said. Being at the same track, walking the same routes, he remembered everything, even the smallest details that he had blocked out before. "That was a really tough time in my life."

As the months wore on, and he prepared for the next racing season, he tried his best to not think too much about the two falls, but the reporters kept bringing them up. He understood they had a job to do, but there were only so many times he could give the same answers.

So, in the spring of 1991, he decided to accept help. His agent knew just the man. He'd read an article about Dr. Jim Loehr, a sports psychologist, who worked with tennis players, including 1990 U.S. Open champion Gabriela Sabatini. Dan felt an immediate connection with the good doctor.

"He's intense, but he looks right in your eyes and you can tell he cares," he said. "That's the feeling I got from that first meeting and it never ended."

In long talks with Dr. Loehr, Dan realized for the first time why he might have fallen in Calgary: Because he didn't give himself permission to win. Because he needed to do something, anything, to deprive himself of a victory when he had lost so much. It's a theory, at least.

"I wondered if people would have thought that I didn't care [about losing Jane] if I had won," he said. "It's hard going into a race wondering if you should win or not. I was definitely confused."

From then on, thanks to Dr. Loehr, the questions concerning the 1988 Olympics didn't bother him as much. He could get on with preparing for the 1992 Games in Albertville, France.

Another thing Dan worked hard on was developing a better attitude toward the 1,000. If he were to have any chance of earning a medal at the longer distance, he'd have to embrace the challenge instead of simply putting up with it. The challenge was difficult enough already. Dr. Loehr was a big help. He got Dan to put Post-it notes with the words "I love the 1,000" throughout his house—in the kitchen, on the bathroom mirror, in the bedroom drawers, everywhere. He also jotted the phrase down on the top of each day's diary entry.

All the Post-its in the world, however, didn't make a difference in 1992. Dan finished twenty-sixth in the 1,000. That's right, twenty-sixth!

He may have fared better if he'd practiced more. As a matter of fact, Dan can't remember going to the rink even once in the three days between the 500 and the 1,000. He was still upset about the 500, where he'd finished fourth. The 500 was his best event, and he'd failed again to win the gold, or any medal.

"I was devastated," Dan said. "It wasn't a conscious thing of 'I'm not going to try.' It just hurt. It was probably a spoiled brat thing. All of a sudden, that motivation was gone."

Fortunately, he wouldn't have to wait very long to try again.

For the first time, the Olympics would be two years away instead of the traditional four. The change was done to make sure the Winter Games were no longer overshadowed by the Summer Games. Dan wouldn't have much time to reflect on what went wrong in Albertville. He'd have to soon start preparing for the 1994 Olympics in Lillehammer.

A major turning point came during the fall of 1993, at a World Cup event in the Netherlands.

"I did a workout on a Wednesday, a simulated race with a couple of hard laps," Dan said. "Afterward, I remember thinking, 'I can't wait until the one thousand this weekend.' That was the first time I ever thought that going into the weekend."

The day of the 500 in Lillehammer was finally here, and the timing could not have been more poignant: February 14, 1994, Valentine's Day, which was exactly six years since Jane's death and the first fall.

Racing better than ever—two months earlier, at the same rink, he was the first skater in history to finish the 500 in less than 36 seconds (35.92)—Dan liked his chances.

"I was pretty sure this was my day," he recalled. "Usually, when I felt like that, I won."

Through the first 100 meters, it looked like it would be his day, all right. Dan skated the stretch in 9.82 seconds, just off the 9.75 he posted when he set the record.

Then it happened. Again.

No, he didn't fall. He had fallen enough.

This time, he pushed himself too hard in the first half of the last turn, and the ice chipped away. Dan put his hand down to brace himself, and that's when he started to panic, causing him to make a second, and equally costly, mistake.

"As I tried to get back what I lost," he recalled, "I kept slipping. Then I came out of the turn and I knew I was done."

By losing those precious hundredths of a second, he'd blown another chance to win a gold in the 500. He finished eighth, at 36.68 seconds, only .35 second from first place. Even with the slip, Dan still might have won a medal, if he just hadn't panicked.

"You don't have to hammer the first half of a turn," Dan said. "The first half of it basically is for setting up the second half so you can really accelerate out of it; that's where you get your speed. I felt very good." That's when he pushed too hard "instead of waiting for it."

He was beside himself. When his coach, Peter Mueller, reminded him right afterward that he had another race in four days, Dan couldn't care less.

"I don't want to skate the 1,000," he said.

So much for that new attitude of his.

He felt like Mary Decker after she fell in 1984, that he'd let down not only himself but also the people who had stuck by him since the beginning, one heartbreak after another.

"Tell Milwaukee I'm sorry," he told a reporter from the Milwaukee newspaper.

Dan met for a few minutes with other members of the media, which went as well as it could, given the circumstances. Once that

was over, he headed to the locker room. The first thing he'd normally do there was take off his skin suit. Not this time. He sat for
about twenty minutes, alone for much of it, which he was grateful
for, his mind now doing the racing.

"I didn't shed any tears," he said. "It was more just trying to figure out what just happened and how it could have happened again."

A part of Dan would have loved to have hidden in that locker
room forever, but . . .

"Eventually, you got to leave," he said. "You've got to face people."

He also met with Dr. Loehr, who said what Dan expected him to
say: that he needed to forget about the 500 and to start focusing on
the 1,000. Dan wasn't testy, as he was with his coach. Those twenty
minutes in the locker room had done him a ton of good. He'd be
ready for the 1,000.

That didn't mean the next few days would be easy. They most
certainly were not.

Other skaters from the United States, and around the world, felt
bad for him, and every day at the rink, they let him know it. Some
offered encouraging words; others gave him a pat on the back. Dan
appreciated their support and hated it at the same time.

"You don't want pity," he said. "It gives you that reminder of
what just happened and it pokes you again."

He didn't look forward to going back to the track, but unlike
1992, there was reason for hope.

"Deep down, I knew I had a good shot in this one thousand,"
he explained, "as opposed to two years earlier when I mailed it in.
That's what kept me interested. I felt great. It was a slip, a big one,
but it was a slip. I was still skating well, better than anyone out
there."

He was relaxed as well, or as Dan put it, "I felt at one with the
ice." That's when every stroke is powerful, though not forced, the
skater using his body weight more than just his muscles to generate
speed.

"I can see it when I see somebody skate," Dan said. "They either
have it or they don't."

Of course, this being Dan, and this being the Olympics, once the
big day arrived, he didn't feel so great any longer. When he went to

warm up about ninety minutes before the race, he realized he wasn't tired enough.

You see, the time off between races was an issue he faced only at the Olympics. At every other competition, he skated the 500 and 1,000 on the same day. So he wasn't as tired here as he was used to being before the 1,000, and the fatigue kept his legs loose. To fix the problem, he got on the stationary bike for about fifteen minutes and went for a jog.

"I needed to feel a little pain," Dan said. "I made myself almost do a double warm-up."

When he got back on the ice, ten minutes before his starting time, his body wasn't the only thing that was in a good spot. So was his mind. His mind had been all over the place when he started his warm-ups, with thoughts of the race, of Jane, of how his legs felt. Now Dan felt a sense of peace. A lot of that was due to the revealing talks he had the previous three days with Dr. Loehr.

"We kind of realized that in no other competition did I ever think, 'If I win this, I will be world champion,' or World Cup champion, or whatever," he said. "But that thought entered my mind at the Olympics. Was that the difference? I don't know. That was the only different thing I could think of."

Knowing his quest was about to end also made it easier to find that peace.

"I was very aware that this was my last Olympic race," Dan said. "I didn't want to expect anymore. If I expect to win, it doesn't happen. Don't expect. Don't think. Don't do anything. Go out and skate."

The race began, and, man, did Dan ever go out and skate. Starting on the outside lane, he reached 200 meters in a rapid 16.71 seconds. He kept a good pace, turn after turn.

But, wouldn't you know it, on the second-to-last turn, at close to 700 meters, he began to slip again, his left hand falling toward the ice. Was this really how the dream of winning the gold medal would end for Dan Jansen? With another slip? Or, worse, another fall?

"It was just at the point you're starting to get fatigued, yet you're going very fast," he said. "It's hard to fight that force when your legs are getting tired."

Hard, but not impossible, and the key was he didn't panic, as he did in the 500. He was very fortunate the ice didn't break this time, and that he didn't step on one of the small blocks that marked the lanes. An inch or two more and . . .

He would have gone down and that would have been it right there.

The danger soon passed, and for the last 250 meters or so, nothing got in his way. When Dan reached the finish line, there was just one word to describe how he felt.

"Relief," he said, "because I skated to my potential. And I didn't care if someone beat me after that."

Moments later, he saw the official time: 1:12.43, his best ever in the 1,000. *Anyone's* best ever! He'd set a new Olympic, and world, record. He really loved the 1,000 now.

Others followed, but no one skated faster. Just when it seemed out of his grasp for good, Dan was finally an Olympic champion.

Before he knew it, he was standing on the top step of the podium, the anthem playing, his mind churning. He thought about his country and how proud he was to represent it. He thought about his parents and the fund-raisers they had hosted. And he thought about his sister and how he hoped she was watching.

Dan wished the anthem would go on and on. He'd waited long enough to hear it.

"It was like the shortest song I ever heard," he said. "In a blur, all of a sudden, it was done."

As it came to an end, he looked up to the heavens and gave a salute. To Jane.

"I didn't even realize I had done [the salute] until I saw my sisters [afterward]," he said. "I hadn't thought about it before."

What a way to end the day for Dan Jansen. Only the day wasn't over just yet. He went on a victory lap, and he didn't go alone. He carried his eight-month-old daughter, named . . . Jane.

Robin, his wife, passed Jane down from the stands, one person to another, into the hands of a security guard who gave her to Dan. He wasn't expecting her.

"If I hadn't looked there, I probably would have skated right past," he said.

In the weeks that followed, Dan took another victory lap. He spoke to President Clinton and the First Lady on the phone; received letters from former presidents Carter, Reagan, and Bush; went on *The David Letterman Show*; and was finally honored with that parade he'd hoped for in 1984—three, to be exact, in West Allis, Milwaukee, and Greenfield, Wisconsin.

He earned each and every one.

Y ou could say Dan is still taking a victory lap.

He gives motivational speeches—who couldn't learn a thing or two from the trials he went through?—and does commentary for NBC during the Winter Olympics. People remember him, though perhaps not always how he might wish them to.

"You're the guy who fell," some tell him, or "You're the guy whose sister died."

Which, when you think about it, is why so many people were drawn to Dan in ways they weren't to Eric Heiden.

Heiden won five gold medals. In one Olympic Games! That seemed almost superhuman.

Dan, on the other hand, lost someone very close to him, and there's nothing more human than that.

"Had I just gone out there," he said, "and won a gold medal, and Jane was healthy, it would've been a nice story, a kid from Wisconsin wins a gold medal, but people don't relate to that as much. Anyone can relate to losing a sister or a brother or a parent."

Yet as much as winning the gold has meant to Dan, it hasn't meant everything. His dad was right all those years ago when he tried to comfort a twelve-year-old in tears after not winning a national championship. There is more to life than skating in a circle.

"I understand every athlete's desire to win," he said. "It was mine and I've been competitive since I was a kid. And I don't want to sound like I look back and it doesn't mean anything, because it does. But I do think that, when it's all said and done, whether it's a year later or twenty years after, if all you got out of it was winning or losing, then you did not get anything out of it. I also think that was the reason I was able to let it go before the last 1,000 and perform the way I did. Nothing was going to make me suicidal."

At the same time, Dan acknowledged, without those who are driven, if not obsessed, to win, sports wouldn't have the urgency that makes it so compelling. Someone has to lose for someone to win.

"Yes, we make more of winning than it is," he said. "On the other side of that, the crazy thing we're talking about is probably what makes us want to be there. Why was my goal to get to the Olympics? I watched Eric Heiden do that in 1980, and I thought, 'That's amazing, I want to do that!' That's why NBC pays a billion dollars to cover the Games."

Then what about the kids today who dream of doing what he did, or of being another Apolo Ohno, who won eight Olympic medals in the sport? Or dream of being a star athlete in any sport? What does Dan say to them? What they probably need to hear, that's what.

"I don't want to demean what you do," he tells kids, "because I went through it and felt the same. It's your life when you are doing it, but it's not really your life. You can train as hard as you can train and then you are going to go out and try your best."

The message, he realizes, isn't for everyone.

"I sometimes warn people that, if they want me to come talk to them, here is what I talk about, and it may not be what you, as a coach, want someone to say," he said. "We're all competitive, but as I get older and look back, as cliché as it sounds, it was more about the journey than the end result."

Does that mean he would be as satisfied as he is these days if the end result had been different, if he hadn't won the gold in Lillehammer? If he'd *never* won the gold? No doubt about it.

"If you're content with yourself and the effort you put forth, that's all you can do," he said.

That became clear to him in Lillehammer. Though coming to that realization during the four days between the 500 and 1,000 was actually the end of a process that began six years before, in Calgary.

"I started to broaden my view of life," he explained. "It was no longer necessarily a drive to win. It was to be my best."

Even so, it took a while to get there. In 1992, as he stood on the line in Albertville, winning the race was still the foremost thing on his mind, not skating to his potential. It took everything that happened in his life—the loss of Jane, the two falls, the poor performance in the 1992 Olympics, the birth of a child—for Dan to reach this point. Without going through those experiences, and learning as much as he did, it's hard to imagine him finding peace at the very end in Lillehammer.

"I might not have even been looking for a difference," he said. "I may have just said, 'I'll try this [skating for the gold] one more time.'"

Dan was fortunate. He discovered what truly mattered to him, and why, perhaps, he had yet to win on the biggest stage, when he could still do something about it. Many athletes don't reach that kind of self-awareness until their careers are over, if they reach it at all.

They have to find peace somewhere else. In love, perhaps. Or in embracing their fate in history, even if it's on the opposite end of the one they wanted. However they find it, what matters is that they do. None of them—Craig Ehlo, Calvin Schiraldi, Aaron Krickstein, Mike Lantry, Mary Decker, and so on—deserves anything less.

Dan Jansen found his peace in the best place of all. He then went out and skated the race of his life.

EPILOGUE

Year after year, no matter the sport or setting, history does indeed repeat itself. Not only does it provide us with worthy winners we will admire for the ages, but it also keeps serving up those who suffer the most heartbreaking losses. In the first half of this decade alone, we've already witnessed one defeat that will no doubt rank among the toughest of all time.

That was in 2015 when Pete Carroll's Seattle Seahawks came within 1 yard of winning back-to-back NFL championships, but fell, 28–24, to the New England Patriots in Super Bowl XLIX. As the world knows, with just twenty-six seconds left, rather than giving the ball to running back Marshawn Lynch, who'd led the NFL in touchdowns that season, Carroll elected to have Russell Wilson throw a pass in the middle of the end zone that was intercepted. You can't come any closer and *not* win it all than the Seahawks did.

No wonder Rodney Harrison believes that Carroll's call from the 1-yard line "will stick with him for the rest of his life," that "in his lonely moments, he goes back and wrestles with this in his mind all the time."

Rodney, you remember, knows precisely what it feels like to come up just short on the grandest stage in sports, due mostly to a single play.

Well, with all due respect, Rodney, that's not how Carroll rolls. If there's a more positive human being in the game of football—anywhere—than Pete Carroll . . . forget it, there isn't. The man doesn't have lonely moments. Or if he does, he certainly doesn't share them with the rest of us.

"It wasn't any different than other things I've been through,"

Carroll suggested. "You get to the truth of it, and you use the information that you just gained to be better and then you start moving ahead. I don't want it to affect the rest of my life negatively, so I'm not going to let it."

For Carroll, this wasn't some piece of wisdom he had read in a book or picked up in a mandatory league seminar. As is the case with most lessons that remain with you forever, Carroll learned this through experience.

In the 2006 Rose Bowl, his USC Trojans were vying for their second consecutive national title when, with nineteen seconds left, they gave up the winning touchdown on a run by Texas quarterback Vince Young. The critics let Carroll have it, mostly for giving the ball to running back LenDale White instead of the Heisman Trophy winner, Reggie Bush, on a huge fourth-and-two from the Longhorns' 45 late in the game. If the Trojans had converted, they might have put it away.

Yet Carroll, who explained that Bush was never given the ball in similar short-yardage situations, came to terms with the loss. He knew he'd have to do the same with the Super Bowl.

"Only seconds had passed," he explained, "and I knew what I was up against. From that moment, I was preparing to handle it, knowing there was a responsibility to a lot of people that would be taking a cue from however I dealt with it."

In the locker room, as a matter of fact, just minutes after the game, he helped his players begin the long healing process. To his credit, though, he also made sure that everyone enjoyed the space to come to terms with what happened in his own time. Then, in a team meeting upon returning to Seattle, he went over the sequence of decisions the coaches made during the final drive so his guys would understand precisely what they were thinking instead of accepting what others might tell them in the off season.

"We tried to coach our way through it," he said.

The same week, Carroll accepted an offer to appear on NBC's *Today*. That took courage. Many coaches, or players, in a similar situation would have dropped out of sight, perhaps for months. Maybe longer. Not Pete Carroll.

"I wanted to be able to speak to everybody," he continued, "to give them a sense of how we were dealing with it, what they needed to know, instead of just going underground. Let's go to it and get at it, and see if it couldn't help people understand. It wasn't like somebody died. It was a football game, but it was the Super Bowl and everybody cares, rightfully so."

He also took it upon himself to learn more about the subject of grief, even doing a Google search of the word, to gain a sense of what his players would likely be encountering over the next few months. The idea, he said, was to help them "get to where they were able to heal, and move ahead." He never lost sight of the bigger picture.

"You're going to go up and down with the opportunities, and I don't want to be like that," he elaborated. "I want to teach people to be other than that. So they can be consistently good, on a high level, over a long period of time."

Carroll's approach wasn't much different, in essence, than the one adopted by Texas Rangers manager Ron Washington after his team had come within one strike of winning the 2011 World Series: Deal with the pain as quickly, and fully, as possible, because the longer you put it off, the more difficult it will be to cope with once you do take it head on. Calvin Schiraldi and Craig Ehlo needed decades to come to the same conclusion, and they found out the heavy price that comes when you delay your grief.

Still, in Carroll's case, even doing everything correctly in the immediate aftermath didn't mean the grief would simply disappear. It doesn't work that way. How one grieves, and heals, has never been an exact science, whether it has to do with the death of a loved one or the loss of a football game.

In the early going of the following 2015 NFL regular season, the Seahawks didn't seem to be—well, the Seahawks. They dropped four of the first six games, and didn't climb to the .500 mark (4-4) until early November.

Regardless of injuries, and the unpredictable intangibles that can steer a season in one direction or the other, you had to wonder whether the Seahawks were still affected by the loss to New England or, more to the point, the manner in which they lost. Football players are not robots. They are human beings. How could the Seattle players, from time to time, *not* think about how close they had come to winning back-to-back Super Bowls, something that had been done only eight times in NFL history?

"Absolutely," Carroll said when asked if he had noticed any lingering effects in the 2015 season. "Whether you win or whether you lose, there's a big fallout of sorts in dealing with the circumstances that follow up. So we won it [in 2014] and saw all of that, and we lost it and saw all of that."

Finally, though, the grieving process, in his view, came to an end.

"There was a time in the middle of the year when it was no longer the issue with any key individuals," Carroll insisted. "We had moved on and we got back to the kind of relationships, and communication that it takes to play at a real high level. Just like we did the year before, we really hit full speed when we were able to leave it behind."

And it really did look like they hit full speed. The Seahawks won eight of their final ten games, leading most people to label them as "the team nobody wants to face in the playoffs." Yet, once in the postseason, it took a miracle miss on a 27-yard field goal attempt by Minnesota kicker Blair Walsh at the end of their playoff opener to squeeze by the Vikings, 10–9. The win sent them to the second round where they trailed Carolina 31–0 before falling, 31–24. Their season was over, leaving us to forever wonder what true impact the Super Bowl loss had on them. If this core group of Seattle players does bounce back to capture another title in the next year or two, we'll conclude that it was no big deal, or, as Everson Walls would put it, just "another brick in the wall."

On the other hand, if they don't win it all again, and soon, we'll trace it back to the pass in the Super Bowl that was intercepted by Malcolm Butler. The pass that, in the minds of many, should never have been thrown.

At this point, of course, we don't know whether Seattle's loss, in the years ahead, will be remembered the way we remember the Red Sox' collapse against the New York Mets in the 1986 World Series, or Dan Jansen's falls in the Olympics. It's simply too early to tell. The magnitude of any setback for a team or individual in a signature event usually isn't known for years, not until the most unforgiving critic of all, history, has its say.

Take, for instance, The Catch in the 1981 NFC title game or The Shot in the 1989 NBA playoffs. Big plays at the time, sure, but they didn't become *legendary* plays until the two players at the forefront of each—Joe Montana and Michael Jordan, respectively—became legends themselves. How they performed in the decade that followed made us look back to those moments as the beginning of their greatness, as something more than just game-winning plays. Had those moments come from athletes who don't belong in the conversation of the greatest of all time, those plays might have receded into the background by now, and the two victims, Craig Ehlo and Everson Walls, wouldn't be asked about their "failures," to this day.

No doubt there are many other factors that have a huge impact on how special a single moment, game, or match, is regarded by history. Let's face it, as dramatic, and inspiring, as Jimmy Connors' victory over Aaron Krickstein was in the 1991 U.S. Open, the match, coming in the fourth round, had no reason to be historic, and it would not have been, if not for CBS showing the highlights year after year during the Open's frequent rain delays. Before long, the match gained a life of its own, enhancing the Connors brand and providing Krickstein, a celebrated junior who never attained stardom as a pro, the recognition he wouldn't have received otherwise.

Likewise, Christian Laettner's shot to beat Kentucky wasn't even in a Final Four. Yet it is immortalized because, at the time, he was the ultimate villain coming through with a heroic shot, and due to the fact we see it again and again on television every March during the NCAA basketball tournament.

There are, as we've seen, countless different lessons to be learned from the way different individuals have dealt with their setbacks, and there will be many more in the years ahead as others cope with similar heartbreaks. Because those heartbreaks are coming, that you can be sure of, as long as games are played, and the most talented athletes in the world put everything on the line.

Just look at what transpired in a single week in April 2016.

First, Villanova won the national championship on a three-pointer at the buzzer over North Carolina. In twenty years from now, will we remember anyone on either team? Will we remember it was Kris Jenkins who hit the shot? Who knows?

Six days later, we all felt awful for Jordan Spieth when he fell apart on the twelfth hole in the final round of the Masters golf tournament. Will this loss haunt Spieth for the rest of his career? That depends on how he fares down the road. If he were to never win another major title, this failure might become the moment that will define him in our minds. But if he learns from it, if, in some way, this moment spurs him to even greater heights, then this loss may come to represent something very different. For example, one of the most epic collapses in the history of golf—Arnold Palmer blowing a seven-shot lead over the final nine holes of the 1966 U.S. Open—isn't ingrained in our consciousness. Instead, when we think of Arnold Palmer, we think of his impact on the game, his appeal to the masses.

We can also be certain that, year after year, there will be new moments that remind us why we care about sports in the first place. Jean Van de Velde may have been a bit misguided, to be kind, when it came to how he played the final hole in Carnoustie, but he was absolutely right in one respect: the reason we invest so much in these games, and in athletes we have never met, is because of the emotions they trigger. They touch us, both those who succeed and, often even more, those who don't. We see that, in addition to being talented, they are human.

In these moments, those who finish on the losing side will need time to deal with the effects. It doesn't matter who they are, or where they come from, or what they accomplished before the loss. No matter what history chooses, or how each individual deals with his or her role in it, the pain of coming up short in the big moment never totally disappears. Nor, I suspect, would most participants want it to.

"I'm never going to not feel it," Carroll said. "I'm never going to let it go. That's not my way of doing it. Put it where it needs to be put so I can go ahead and do the things I want to do and be the person that I am. Those are all the same lessons our team has been introduced to for years."

Calvin Schiraldi said it best. If given the chance, he wouldn't want to turn back the clock, and retire the Mets in the tenth inning of Game 6. Sure, he would have saved the game, and ended the curse, and been a hero in Boston forever, but that also means he would not be the person he is today, and not have spent the past twenty years helping high school boys learn how to play baseball and become men.

As many of these athletes now understand, there are wonderful lessons to be learned from difficult times, lessons that can change your life for the better.

So there's no need to feel sorry for them. They don't feel sorry for themselves. They have enjoyed experiences they'll cherish forever, no matter how things might have turned out. Losing the way they did taught them to be more empathetic toward others and better able to comprehend the true differences between losses that matter and losses that don't.

One hopes that the athletes who suffer the heartbreaks of tomorrow will come to the same conclusions.

That losing is a big deal, but that losing isn't everything.

ACKNOWLEDGMENTS

They say that dreams do come true. For me, this book is living proof of that, and it's only possible because of a long, long list of dream makers.

Starting with the team at SMAC Entertainment, led by Constance Schwartz-Morini with strong assists from Tim Cullen, Adrian Amodeo, Jose Diaz, Sarah Politis, and Alissa Rothman, who combine to manage my life. The gang at WME then steer my career, with Josh Pyatt leading the way. But I know that without the guidance of Jay Mandel this project would never have gotten off the ground. Jay took an idea I presented to him on a phone call and turned it into this book. Thank you to Jay and his assistant, Lauren Shonkoff, for being there whenever this neophyte writer had questions or needed help.

Hopefully our fantastic editor at HarperCollins, Matt Harper, took some of that burden of holding my hand through this process away from others. I certainly know how beneficial he has been. New York/Los Angeles, East Coast/West Coast, no matter the time of day, I could always count on Matt and his entire team, including Lisa Sharkey, Katie Steinberg, Lynn Grady, Kendra Newton, Alieza Schvimer, Katerina Rosen, and a bunch of folks who I'm sure I'm not even aware of because they all did what they do so seamlessly.

I truly would have been lost without my partner in crime, Michael Arkush, who not only helped me turn my thoughts into words, and words into pages, but also did so with a passion beyond any I could have ever imagined.

It goes without saying that we benefited from the kindness and openness of all the athletes and coaches who opened up their hearts and let us in. But let us also say thanks to those who shared with us many cherished family photos of their "little ones" before they were "famous ones." I think Anita Jacobellis, Lindsey's mom, may have given us her entire photo collection. Judy Michaels, Lou's very kind widow, and their son, Ed, provided some pretty cool pics as well.

There are numerous folks who either helped us get in contact with the various participants, or even helped convince them that our task here was about more than just rehashing tough moments in their lives. Laura Marcus was there to help with that challenge when this book was nothing more than an idea. Countless others were important, including Rich Dalrymple, Mark Lepselter, Dave Pearson, Joshua Schwartz, Mike Selleck, Judy Daley, Pete Wellborn, Mike Klingaman, Toby Zwikel, Kath O'Connor, Tom Cunneff, Jon Miller, Bruce Madej, Susan Hazzard, Mike O'Malley, Susan Wellborn, Tricia Byrnes, Brian Paulette, Bill Johnston, Jamaal LaFrance, and some who prefer to remain anonymous.

I'd be remiss if I didn't acknowledge the guys that I am fortunate enough to spend every Sunday with during the football season: Terry Bradshaw, Howie Long, Michael Strahan, Jimmy Johnson, and Jay Glazer on the set; plus Eric Shanks, Bill Richards, and John Czarnecki lead a cast of hundreds behind the scenes. Michael Berger does yeoman's work with us on Sundays, but extended that beyond the pale in his assistance on this book. This is not just a "thank you for giving me a great life," as U2's Bono likes to say to fans; I truly mean it. Their support on *Fox NFL Sunday* has been invaluable to me, as has their friendship. Trust me, both extended into this project. Whenever I had simple questions about the process of writing this, my first book, or about players whom they witnessed, coached, or played, with or against, they were all there to help out. I know that whatever I do, I couldn't without those brothers having my back.

I know I speak for Michael Arkush when I say that our wives, Pauletta Walsh and Viollette Menefee, deserve special praise, and probably some type of award for putting up with us during this entire process. Michael and I may be cuddly, but I'm sure it wasn't as easy as you two made it look. Thank you!

It's easy to spotlight those who are in our lives at present, but let us not forget those who helped us get here. Our family (including my brother, Will, who I watched a few of these moments with) and friends. The teachers in high school and the professors at Coe College in Iowa who encouraged me to think and write back when I was too young to have anything to write about. John Campbell, who took a kid with zero television experience under his wing and taught him the ins and outs of the business. Those who took a chance on hiring me at each of the pre-FOX stops I made along the way in Cedar Rapids, Des Moines, Madison, SNN, Jacksonville, Dallas, and New York. Plus the mighty David Hill and Ed Goren, who gambled on me when I was doing what we call the "milk games" (going to about 2 percent of the country on an NFL Sunday) and put me in the FOX studio.

As they say at all the award shows, there are probably several other people I am leaving out, but I hope you all know that your help was so very appreciated. Any omissions are the result of bad memory and not meant to be bad manners.

A big thank-you to all the great announcers who appear in this book, past and present. The fantastic calls each of you made during the sporting events we loved helped transform them from just moments into memories. For that we will always be indebted to you.

Of course, the reason those great announcers had calls to make is because of the people we all got to know a lot better in this book. Our information gathering began while meeting with Al Downing at Dodger Stadium in December 2014; Al taught us what was possible if we only listened.

From there, each and every one granted us numerous (and I do mean *numerous*) interviews to provide details about their private lives and public moments that many had never revealed before. To them, the words "thank you" don't seem like enough. I hope they feel that we did their individual stories justice.

—Curt Menefee